MUSIC AND CONFLICT
TRANSFORMATION

Toda Institute Book Series on Global Peace and Policy
Series Editor: Majid Tehranian

Published and forthcoming:

Music and Conflict Transformation

Harmonies and Dissonances in Geopolitics

Edited by

Olivier Urbain

in association with
The Toda Institute for Global Peace and Policy Research

Published in 2008 by I.B.Tauris & Co Ltd
6 Salem Road, London W2 4BU
175 Fifth Avenue, New York NY 10010
www.ibtauris.com
In association with the Toda Institute for Global Peace and Policy Research

In the United States and Canada distributed by Palgrave Macmillan
a division of St Martin's Press
175 Fifth Avenue, New York NY 10010

ISBN: 978 1 84511 528 9

A full CIP record for this book is available from the British Library
A full CIP record for this book is available from the Library of Congress

Library of Congress Catalog Card: available

Typeset by Jayvee, Trivandrum, India
Printed and bound in Great Britain by
T J International Ltd,
Padstow, Cornwall

To Yoko,
My dear wife,
for being a challenging
intellectual partner,
and for all the support
behind the scenes

Contents

Notes on Contributors

Karen Abi-Ezzi, Ph.D. is Lecturer in the Department of Peace Studies at the University of Bradford, UK. Her research interests are in the area of peace processes in the Middle East, particularly in relation to the application of discourse analysis and social constructionism to enhance understanding of mediation processes. As a peace researcher, she has been collaborating with NGOs working for reconciliation in Lebanon.
k.abi-ezzi@bradford.ac.uk

June Boyce-Tillman, Ph.D. is Professor of Applied Music at the University of Winchester, UK and has been a Visiting Fellow and Scholar in residence in Indiana and Cambridge, USA. She has written widely and run workshops internationally on the association between music and education, gender, healing and spirituality, working particularly on Hildegard of Bingen.
junebt@globalnet.co.uk

Cynthia Cohen, Ph.D. is the Executive Director of the Slifka Program in Intercommunal Coexistence at Brandeis University, in the USA, and Director of Coexistence Research and International Collaborations. She has written widely on the contributions of the arts and culture to building peace, as well as on the ethical dimensions of peacebuilding practice. She maintains "Creative Resources for Coexistence and Reconciliation," a virtual resource center.
http://www.brandeis.edu/go/createcoexistence

Johan Galtung, Ph.D. is the founder and co-director of TRANSCEND, a peace and development network, as well as Rector of TRANSCEND Peace University. Widely recognized as one of the founders of Peace Studies, he has published more than 100 books and 1,000 articles on the topic. He is the author of the United Nations' first-ever manual for trainers and participants: *Conflict Transformation by Peaceful Means: The TRANSCEND Approach* (United Nations Development Programme 2000).
http://www.transcend.org

Anne-Marie Gray, D.Mus. was an Arts Lecturer in the Department of Education, University of KwaZulu – Natal, South Africa. She retired in 2006. Before lecturing at the university she was a piano and violin teacher and a Lecturer in Music and Integrated Arts at Durban College of Education. She has published books for arts education which are used in South African secondary schools. davidgraysr@mweb.co.za

Vegar Jordanger is Director of the NGO, Building Peaces in Trondheim, Norway. He currently works at the Department of Psychology at the Norwegian University of Science and Technology, where he pursues his PhD studies on terrorism and risk perception. His peace research interests include: the role of magical and mythical operators in contemporary religio-political rhetoric, identity dynamics and the role of emotions in dialogue processes, and music and art in conflict transformation. He has published on these topics in several languages. jordange@svt.ntnu.no, http://www.buildingpeaces.org

George Kent, Ph.D. is Professor in the Department of Political Science at the University of Hawai'i. He is co-convener of the Commission on International Human Rights of the International Peace Research Association. He works on human rights, international relations, peace, development, and environmental issues, with a special focus on nutrition and children. kent@hawaii.edu, http://www2.hawaii.edu/~kent/

Felicity Laurence, Ph.D. is Lecturer in the Music Department at Newcastle University, UK, children's choir specialist, and a composer. She has written about children's singing and published children's choral works (*African Madonna*, CUP 1990, Arbugi 1997, *Dreams of Mother Earth*, Arbugi 1998) whose themes address intercultural relationships. Her research explores musicking and empathising within and beyond educational contexts. felicity.laurence@ncl.ac.uk

Rik Palieri is a professional musician, composer, singer, banjo player and storyteller. As composer, his original songs have been praised by folk legends like Pete Seeger, U. Utah Phillips and Jimmy Driftwood. He has performed in almost every state in the continental USA as well as in Europe and Australia. He has appeared on TV and radio shows worldwide, as well as at numerous folk festivals, such as the Philadelphia Folk Festival, the Champlain Valley Folk Festival and the Vancouver Folk Festival. http://www.banjo.net, http://www.myspace.com/rikpalieri

Maria Elena López Vinader, M.A. is a professional music therapist, and international director of Music Therapists for Peace. She has her own radio program entitled Imagine: Peace is Possible. She is co-convenor of the Commission on Art and Peace of the International Peace Research Association and co-director of the Transcend: Art and Peace Network (T:AP). She designs workshops and courses where she integrates the healing power of music with logotherapy and peace education.
musicapaz@yahoo.com.ar

Kjell Skyllstad is Professor Emeritus of the Department of Musicology at the University of Oslo, Norway. As founder and director of Intermusic Center (www.intermusiccenter.com) he was an early pioneer and promoter of inter-cultural work in Norway. Exploring the field of music education for conflict transformation and peace, he became research director of the Norwegian Resonant Community project, and later led out in music cooperation projects with India, Sri Lanka, Thailand, Indonesia, Zimbabwe and Croatia.
kjell.muller.skyllstad@broadpark.no

Olivier Urbain, Ph.D. is a Research Fellow at the Toda Institute for Global Peace and Policy Research, Tokyo, Japan. He was previously Professor of Modern Languages and Peace Studies at Soka University, Japan. A firm believer in the power of music for conflict transformation, he is the founder and co-convenor of the Commission on Art and Peace of the International Peace Research Association.
urbain.olivier@gmail.com, http://www.toda.org

Peter van den Dungen, Ph.D. is Professor in the Department of Peace Studies at the University of Bradford, UK. His main research interests, in addition to peace history, concern the potential of peace museums as sources and expressions of a culture of peace. He is the founder (1992) and general coordinator of the International Network of Museums for Peace and editor of *Peace Museums Worldwide* (Geneva: UN Library, 1998). He has organized numerous events and lectured widely for the worldwide promotion of peace museums.
p.vandendungen@bradford.ac.uk

Baruch Whitehead, Ph.D. is Associate Professor of Music Education at Ithaca College, USA, where he is also the founder and director of the Orff-Schulwerk Certification Program, the director of After School Program for Underrepresented Students, and the founder and director of the Syracuse Gospel Choir "Unshackled." An accomplished oboist, he also organizes workshops on African music and dance.
bwhitehead@ithaca.edu

Preface

Olivier Urbain

One can wonder why the acclaimed researcher and academic Johan Galtung, one of the founders of peace studies, finds himself side by side in this volume with one of the greatest figures in protest music, Pete Seeger, the man who has offered "Where Have all the Flowers Gone" to the anti-Vietnam war movement, and who let Martin Luther King Junior discover "We Shall Overcome." However, the real question is: why has it taken so long? It is high time for the human brain and heart to join forces to explore and apply the power of music for peaceful and effective conflict transformation.

With contributors coming from all continents, a mixture of academics and professional musicians, with differing and sometimes conflicting opinions concerning political issues and the nature of music, this volume is vibrating with harmonies and dissonances. We have also striven for gender parity, with seven of the fifteen chapters written by women. Still, the book sends a clear and unified message that music does have important roles to play in conflict transformation, and that the research has only begun.

Most chapters refer to other ones in the book, providing a sense of unity and collaboration that was intentional from the start of this project. However, the numerous dissonances found in this volume also have their relevance. As I was making the final preparations of this manuscript for publication, the phrase "unity in diversity" sprang from the dozens of pages scattered on my desk.

A few examples will illustrate this point. Whereas the first chapter entitled "Music and Empathy" discusses the theoretical implications of this concept at length, the chapter "Working in the Trenches" shows how music has been put to use in reality to bring out empathy in tense situations. The same contrast between theory and practice, between academia and testimonies, applies to the difference between June Boyce-Tillman's two chapters. The first one "Music and Value in Cross-Cultural Work" lays out a highly theoretical model, and the second one "Music and Peace Making in Educational Contexts" describes how these concepts have served as inspiration for actual musical compositions and performances. There is definitely a movement from abstract to concrete throughout the four parts of the book, from the intricate theories of "Frameworks" to the more concrete applications of "Politics" to the influence of music on people's lives in "Healing and Education" to the very down-to-earth interviews- and anecdotes-based "Stories from the Field."

Sometimes seemingly incompatible ideas appear to live side by side in this volume. For instance Cynthia Cohen shows clearly that music is not a universal language, while Vegar Jordanger and Maria Elena López Vinader use the universality of music as the basis of some of their discussions.

The political positions of Yair Dalal and Gilad Atzmon on the Middle-East are on opposite ends of the spectrum. Whereas Atzmon believes the best way to stop the violence is to depict the dark side from outside Israel, Yair Dalal is convinced that to the contrary, it is much better to emphasize harmony and understanding from inside the country.

It is to be hoped that the reader will find these contrasting views on the power of music for conflict transformation stimulating, and that many more people will join us to pursue this fascinating research.

Among many others found in this volume, I would like to highlight some suggestions for further research.

Based on Felicity Laurence's representation of Stein's theory of empathy, it would be interesting to create a model of the structural relationships within musical materials and see how both frameworks can fit, with examples from musical works and events. Cynthia Cohen's list of cases where the specificity of the music has led to positive conflict transformation can be expanded. June Boyce-Tillman's model can be used to explore and debunk the dominant values of Western cultures further, and to define the roles of music based on other values. Johan Galtung's suggestion that there are numerous conditions for the uplifting and unifying power of music to be conducive to peace begs for further clarification of these conditions .

Based on Anne-Marie Gray's emphasis on the importance of music to understand history and lead to reconciliation, one could explore many other case studies besides South Africa. Baruch Whitehead's exploration of the role of a few songs in the development of civil rights in the USA could be carried out for other countries and regions. Karen Abi-Ezzi's exploration of the use of music as resistance needs to be pursued further, perhaps along the lines mentioned by George Kent: "Is insurrectionary music unpeaceful music?"

Kjell Skyllstad has shown us that current research on the uses of music in prisons and multicultural schools is very promising, and needs to be continued and expanded. The fact that he was able to receive support from official agencies should inspire many more researchers to follow suit. Vegar Jordanger invites us to explore whether "collective vulnerability" through music, which is shown to produce positive results at the micro-level, can also take place at the meso- and macro-levels. The suggestion of Maria Elena López Vinader that "we are music" could be explored further in the natural sciences, and research into the potential of music therapy to heal communities has just started.

Rik Palieri has compiled a short list of cases when music was actually used to stop violence, and this could be continued. I have shown how Yair Dalal is able to express more than one culture through music, and many other examples can be found. The interviews by June Boyce-Tillman showing that people are very sensitive to multicultural education through music offer another promising way to research the power of music for conflict transformation and peace.

With conflicts becoming more and more numerous and violent in our twenty-first century, it is to be hoped that this volume will encourage many more people to explore the potential of music for peaceful conflict transformation, no matter how harmonious or dissonant the geopolitics of our planet sound at this moment.

Foreword

Peter van den Dungen

Given the many, often seemingly intractable conflicts between groups or countries in many parts of the world, which bring nothing but death and destruction, as well as feelings of hopelessness and powerlessness, it is imperative that attempts to halt and reverse the cycle of violence draw on the widest possible range of peacemaking instruments and mechanisms. In this context, the potential contribution of the arts has traditionally been ignored or marginalized, and also today is insufficiently appreciated. Of all the arts, music is undoubtedly the art form with the potential to affect people more immediately and more deeply than any other. It can stir the emotions as nothing else, inspire people to the loftiest thoughts and sentiments, and bring them together in indissoluble bonds. These remarkable and unique attributes of music have long been recognized – not least in the forging of armies, with military bands boosting unity and morale. The potential of music for peacemaking rather than war-making has been little explored and is in need of more research. Only today are advances in neuro-psychology uncovering the biological structures and physiological processes of the brain which are at the root of these phenomena and thereby helping us to explain them.

In this well-conceived and well-structured volume, Olivier Urbain has brought together a collection of fascinating and frequently revealing essays which demonstrate the power inherent in music to contribute, in the most diverse manner, to processes of healing. This term is used here in its socio-political sense, and refers to the coming or growing together of societies which have been ridden by violent conflict. The many interesting case studies are drawn from a great variety of countries and settings, and they convincingly demonstrate the power of music – all kinds of music – to have a profound impact on the processes of peacemaking. There is already a voluminous and still expanding literature which deals with the effects of music on the healing of individuals who are suffering from physical, emotional, or mental illness. A substantial body of empirical work is testimony to the effectiveness of music therapy. Such therapy is increasingly being applied around the world in hospitals and hospices, prisons, schools, and other social institutions, with highly beneficial results.

The various ways in which music has been used for social and political healing are well illustrated in this volume which combines case studies consisting of practical applications of music therapy with chapters presenting theoretical and conceptual approaches to the subject. This combination of theory and practice makes for fascinating reading, offering a wealth of insights and opening up new and unexpected horizons for the reader. These advantages of a multi-authored volume are not compromised here by what is all too often a lack of coherence and integration in publications of this kind. The editor and his contributors have made a commendable effort to make this a team effort as frequent cross-references suggest.

Almost twenty-five years ago the Peace Museum in Chicago organized a memorable exhibition entitled "Give Peace a Chance: Music and the Struggle for Peace." This may well have been the first, and possibly so far only, exhibition of its kind. It mainly documented and celebrated the protest music of the 1960s, focusing on the American war in Vietnam, the struggle for civil rights in the USA, and the nuclear arms race, issues of life and death which all came together at that time. They inspired a rich and often wonderfully uplifting and empowering outpouring of music which deeply affected a whole generation, the legacy of which is still being felt today. This volume also deals with the role of music in mobilizing people and thereby providing a focus for protest and resistance. Indeed, important as the contribution of music (and the arts in general) is for healing fractured relationships, its possible use as an instrument to prevent violent conflict or to de-escalate a potentially catastrophic confrontation, is no less significant.

This book can be warmly recommended for anyone who is interested in the subject, and will especially appeal to all those many people who are passionate about music and about peace – two of humanity's most profound expressions which, when combined together, constitute a formidable force for good.

Dr. Peter van den Dungen
General Coordinator,
International Network of Museums for Peace
Department of Peace Studies
University of Bradford (UK)

Acknowledgements

First and foremost I would like to thank the team of the Toda Institute for Global Peace and Policy Research for encouraging me to start this book project in July 2004, and for their constant support of our team of contributors. The personal and warm encouragements of the founder of the Institute, Daisaku Ikeda, as well as its director, Majid Tehranian, and its deputy director and research director Tomosaburo Hirano, have been the driving force behind this project. I also wish to thank the Honolulu staff, Satoko Takahashi and Angel Ryono, as well as the Tokyo staff, the managing director Masaichi Ueda, as well as Yoshiko Matsumoto, Hiroshi Morita and Tetsunori Watanabe for their fantastic administrative support.

I wish to thank my wife Yoko Urbain for her tremendous support at all levels, and my parents Maurice and Yvette Urbain for their enthusiasm for this project. Sadly my parents both passed away in 2006 without being able to see the published work, but they were hopeful concerning the final result and provided strong encouragement at every turn.

Obviously this book would not have materialized without all the contributors who have poured their energies into their excellent research and writing, going all the way to Madrid in 2005, keeping in touch through all kinds of changes, and being able to persevere through many delays and unexpected events. Special thanks to Peter van den Dungen for providing a very useful review of the manuscript and for writing the foreword.

The list of people who have continued encouraging me to complete this project, in Belgium, Canada, the USA, Japan and throughout the world, would be too long, and to make sure I do not forget anyone, I wish to thank everybody who has contributed to this project, without any exception.

Also I wish to thank I.B.Tauris, especially Alex Wright for his encouragement to keep up with deadlines, as well as Dr. Richard Willis and Colin Morgan of Swales & Willis Ltd. for the supervision of the proofs, and the copy-editor, Katie Young.

Finally I wish to thank all those who have tried, and are trying, sometimes succeeding, to make this world a better place, through small and big actions in everyday life, in particular all those striving to use the power of music and the arts for peaceful and effective conflict transformation.

Olivier Urbain
Tokyo, July 3, 2007

Multimedia Material Accompanying this Volume

The authors of this book have prepared multimedia material, photos, videos, music and more, in order to enhance your reading experience. To view the material designed by Maria Luisa Antonaya, Ph.D., visit http://www.toda.org and select "projects" and/or "music."

If you have any questions concerning this multimedia material, feel free to contact Dr. Antonaya at marisa.antonaya@gmail.com

Introduction

Olivier Urbain

Music is a very effective way to communicate and inspire.
(Ani DiFranco, politically outspoken US folksinger in Campion 2005)

Music has an inexplicable way of elevating humankind to its noblest action.
(Youssou N'Dour, foremost Senegalese singer; N'Dour 2004)

The Roles of Music

With the success of their internationally acclaimed album *Living Like a Refugee* (Anti Records 2006), the band "Sierra Leone's Refugee All Stars" (RAS) proves that both statements can be combined and validated. These musicians fled their native Sierra Leone during the horrendous civil war of 1991–2002 only to find themselves under attack from the Guinean army in a refugee camp. It was in another camp deep in the countryside of Guinea that they were able to launch their band. Today they tour the world with their highly popular blend of traditional West African music, roots reggae and rhythmic traditional folk. Indeed, their music is a highly "effective way to communicate and inspire," and they have shown that despite their intense suffering, they have experienced music's "inexplicable way of elevating humankind to its noblest action." This is confirmed on their official website:

> While each of the stories in these songs is told from the band's personal experi-
> ence, it is the special gift of Sierra Leone's Refugee All Stars that the messages
> they deliver are truly universal. Born in the midst of a violent, decade-long civil
> war, through music they have found a place of refuge, a sense of purpose and a
> source of power. The band has seen the worst that this world can offer – yet,
> through their unflinching spirit and joyful music, they celebrate the best in all
> of us.

(The Rosebud Agency 2007)

At the same time, despite Youssou N'Dour's optimism, music does not always promote noble actions. Ani DiFranco's statement begs for clarification concerning the kind of content that music is supposed to convey, if it is indeed "an effective way to communicate and inspire." The list of examples below show that music sometimes contributes to peace, but sometimes not at all:

- Pete Seeger gathered huge crowds against the Vietnam War around the song "Where Have All The Flowers Gone?"
- In 1999 the Israeli conductor Daniel Barenboim (2002) and the Palestinian literary critic Edward Said organized a concert in Weimar, Germany. Half the musicians were Palestinians, the other half Israelis. The performance and rehearsals leading up to it had a lasting effect on all participants.
- During WWII the Nazis played Wagner in the concentration camps to march millions of people to their death. (Menard 2004). They also forced prisoners who were musicians to play in order to calm down the masses waiting to be slaughtered.
- Oud and violin player Yair Dalal had 40 Palestinian and 40 Israeli children perform together in Oslo in 1994.
- The US military blasted hard rock to scare people during the battle of Fallujah in 2005.
- British singer Billy Bragg exposed some of the hidden reasons for the Iraq war in the song "The Price of Oil."
- Music is used in fast food restaurants to make sure customers do not stay too long, allowing others to replace them and consume more.
- Music is used in prisons to encourage inmates to improve their lives and find a way to reintegrate into society after their release by continuing their musical activities.
- Since 1999, the playing of the Japanese National Anthem Kimigayo (Imperial Reign) has been compulsory at Japanese school ceremonies. It is the same song that spurred the Japanese Imperial troops to commit atrocities during WWII, and the teachers who resist today are often punished (McNeill 2004).
- After enthusiastically dancing for hours to the beat of traditional Hutu performers, a representative of the UN Refugee Agency UNHCR, learned with horror that the lyrics were about the need to eliminate all Tutsis (Karsenty 2003).

These examples show that music has tremendous power to move people in any direction, towards peaceful and noble goals, or violent and destructive ones. In an article announcing the broadcasting of the complete works of

Beethoven by the BBC for six days and nights in June 2005, Norman Lebrecht captured the ambiguous nature of the links between music and peace in the use of the works of one of its greatest Western classical composers:

> The "Ode to Joy" of the Ninth Symphony has served as a rallying call at communist conventions and insurance sales meetings; it is the unifying anthem of the European Union and, to diehard nationalists, the emblem of German musical supremacism. Beethoven represents peace in a French novel (titled "Jean-Christophe") by Romain Rolland and street violence in "A Clockwork Orange" by Anthony Burgess.
>
> (Lebrecht 2005)

The writers of this book are well aware of the problem: like any other human endeavor, music can be used to enhance human life or to destroy it. We have decided to explore the ways music can promote a more peaceful world, and how people can use music to move from a culture of war and violence to a culture of peace. In this book we examine the power of music to enhance peace in diverse ways, sometimes by supporting a political stance, like in the case of Ani DiFranco's lyrics, sometimes by healing and elevating people's spirits, like Youssou N'Dour's music. We are aware that these different ways in which music plays various roles for peace sometimes emphasize the bright side, sometimes the dark side, and that both are intertwined, like the yin and the yang, hence the book's subtitle: "Harmonies and Dissonances in Geopolitics."

To add scientific backing to our explorations, we take as the starting point the achievements of music therapy, a recognized professional field. There is now ample empirical evidence that music can help cure a whole range of illnesses, and that it can promote well-being at many different levels: physical, emotional, mental, social and spiritual. Music therapy is also showing results in small groups, couples, families, and even in settings such as boards of directors or small businesses. Based on the promising results of studies in the emerging area of "community music therapy" (Pavlicevic and Ansdell 2004), it is possible to imagine the development of research into the power of music to heal even larger human groupings, pointing the way towards a new field that could be called "social music therapy."

It is worth mentioning that a discipline devoted to the enhancement of health and harmony found its beginnings in the consequences of a war:

> The large influx into hospitals of WWII Veterans was significant for the development of music therapy. The medical authorities, in the USA in particular, were concerned to develop facilities for these returning veterans. Musicians, especially performers and music teachers, began to be employed regularly in hospital

teams. But the medical and scientific communities were not so easily convinced by the early anecdotal stories of patients being reached by music when they responded to little else. Challenges were made to the musicians to verify and systematize their work.

(Bunt 1994)

From these humble beginnings, originally meant to relieve the suffering of WWII veterans, the field has grown steadily until today. Music therapy is now taught in universities all over the world, it has its own professional organizations, conferences, journals, and it is part of the national health care system in a growing number of countries. The testimonies of tens of thousands of people who owe their recovery to music therapy are now part of hospital records. We can rest assured that the positive uses of music and its power to enhance health and well-being have been studied, researched and practiced so thoroughly as to leave no doubt concerning their validity.

How far can we stretch the healing powers of music to promote a more peaceful world? This is the question that motivates this book.

What is Peace?

There are numerous definitions of peace, and the authors of this book each have their own. Despite our differences we agreed on a common framework provided by the research of Johan Galtung, one of the pioneers of peace studies. Like many other peace researchers, he believes that conflicts are part and parcel of the human lot, not to be avoided, but to be transformed. He defines peace as "the capacity to transform conflicts with empathy, creativity and nonviolence" (Galtung 2000). The contributors to this book agree on the centrality of conflict transformation, and on the idea of peace as constructive conflict transformation, as announced by the title "Music and Conflict Transformation."

The chapters of this book illustrate how music can be used to enhance the three qualities mentioned above, empathy, creativity and nonviolence, along with many other human attributes such as courage, wisdom and compassion. Since conflicts appear when people have incompatible goals, creativity is needed to unlock the powers of the imagination, enabling each party to see the conflict in a different way. However, creativity can also be used to manipulate, swindle, or trick people. Without empathy, creativity cannot guarantee peaceful solutions to conflicts. Nonviolence is essential for successful conflict transformation, but it must be accompanied by creativity and empathy to be effective. Thus, we see how these three elements are interdependent, and must all be present in order for real peace – and not just the idea or desire for peace – to exist.

Johan Galtung's definition was chosen because it allows for a very high level of abstraction that encompasses most partial definitions of peace. Each writer of this book has a slightly different definition of peace, and of what needs to be emphasized in order to achieve it, but Galtung's definition embraces these diverse attempts to define peace.

In my chapter about Yair Dalal, I describe how he promotes peace through good relationships between people of diverse backgrounds with his blend of Arabic and Jewish music. The kind of peace I have in mind here is not just the absence of war. I view peace as the vibrant and dynamic state of a society in which everyone can enjoy life to the fullest, with full employment, adequate social protection, abundant food, water, pure air, and shelter, warm and joyful communication between people, participation in governance, justice, equality, freedom, mutual respect, and a fulfilling intellectual and cultural life. In other words, what comes to mind is the realization of the concept of "human security" in all its aspects. This is an image far removed from the simple negation of war. However, even in this ideal community we would not be able to avoid conflicts. What really matters is to learn how to transform conflicts constructively, in the best ways possible, making use of the best skills humanity has to offer, including Galtung's recommendations.

In her chapter, Cynthia Cohen focuses on reconciliation, which is one form of peaceful conflict transformation, and Felicity Laurence makes empathy, one of the three qualities recommended by Galtung, the centrepiece of her explorations. Rik Palieri sees peace as the good atmosphere generated by folk music, whereas Kjell Skyllstad sees it in the improvement of the lot of prisoners. Karen Abi-Ezzi considers the exposition of the fundamental causes of conflicts and resistance to unjust authorities as essential to peace. It is clear that hiding the truth and submitting to unfair treatment will not allow one to transform conflicts with empathy, creativity and non-violence, and this once more validates Galtung's definition.

Different Levels of Conflict Transformation through Music

Three examples from Japan will show the huge differences in scope that exist in the work of musicians striving for peace. In this volume we do not rank efforts for peace, and all endeavors are considered worthy of attention, at the micro-, meso- or macro-levels. Shinji Harada devotes himself to the promotion of peace in small communities around Shinto shrines and small gatherings in concert halls and spa resorts; whereas Shoukichi Kina is trying to transform the status of Okinawa into an independent, multinational entity free of US military bases and of Japanese government interferences. Somewhere in between, the Min-On Concert Association, established in 1963 by Daisaku Ikeda, invites artists, bands and orchestras to perform in Japan for the sake of cultural exchanges and the enhancement of dialogues between people of different civilizations. For instance, it was the first Japanese organization to invite the entire troupe of La Scala from Milan, Italy to Japan, in 1981.

At the micro-level, Shinji Harada, born and raised in Hiroshima, believes that the starting point of peace is simply human kindness (Harada 2006), and today he writes songs for children, praising such virtues as family harmony, or love and respect for nature. A former megastar on the pop scene in Japan in the 1980s, he continues to have a large following of loyal fans. He often participates in international peace events, but places the emphasis on small gatherings where he can offer people a sense of community and warmth. For instance, on 5 August 2006 he participated in the "Universal Peace Day" at Riverside Park in New York City, organized by the "August 6 Coalition" dedicated to the abolition of nuclear weapons. The event is described as an interfaith service at the Riverside Church, with music, dance and speakers, including a Hiroshima survivor (Universal Peace Day 2006).

Shoukichi Kina played a substantial role in the Japanese folk rock scene in the 70s and 80s. He was a pioneer in the electrifying of Okinawan folk music. His song "Hana" sold 30 million copies throughout Asia and was translated into several languages. He was elected a member of the House of Councillors in July 2004. At the macro-level, Kina has established an NGO called "All Weapons into Musical Instruments Peacemakers Network." As the title shows, its goal is to transform weapons of destruction into sound-making tools, and during an official ceremony in Japan on 7 July 2002, Kina received an old machinegun from the Defense Minister of India, and offered him an Okinawan string instrument called a "sanshin" in exchange. He also went to Iraq in February 2003 to try to stop the impending war. His actions are described here:

> The main mission of the NGO, "All Weapons into Musical Instruments" shall be to request weapons from the Iraqi Government as well as other countries and dismantle them to construct peace monuments. Okinawa experienced the ravages of the WWII to a very large extent. Even after 58 years of this war, 75 per cent of the US Army Base presence in Japan is located in this small island.

This resulted in losing indigenous culture, increased crime rate, accidents and other social evils. This NGO, founded by the Okinawan musician, Shoukichi Kina, was established to counter these negative developments as well as to stop wars and to promote peace throughout the world. To this end, Shoukuchi Kina and his band, Champloose have held peace concerts at the UN Headquarters and other parts of the world. Similarly, the main objective of the proposed concert to be held in Baghdad shall be to avoid a US attack on Iraq and to request the two governments and their people for creative action towards peace by mutual dialogue.

(Peacemakers Network 2007)

Finally at the meso-level, the Min-On Concert Association has been promoting dialogues of civilizations and cultural exchanges through music for more than 40 years. Joining hands with cultural groups in 82 countries around the world, Min-On's mission statement reads:

We are committed to deepening mutual understanding and friendship between countries with international musical culture exchange projects that go beyond differences in nationality, race and language.

(Min-On 2007)

Origin and Organization of this Book

In 2004 the Toda Institute for Global Peace and Policy Research called for proposals for projects showing the power of the arts to promote peace. We are very thankful that our project proposal was chosen. Our original team of 13 gathered in Madrid, Spain for a few days at the end of May 2005, after agreeing on a first framework for the book. Until then, our main theme was to be the ways in which music promotes empathy. However, as a result of our many discussions in Madrid, we realized that our book was really about peace in general, and not only about empathy. Nonviolence, creativity, and many other ingredients necessary for the development of peace were going to be integral parts of our work. Despite many differences and disagreements, everyone stayed on board, and we rewrote the table of contents together until we agreed on the organization of the volume. Two more people joined us during the Fall of 2005.

The first section, *Frameworks*, opens our exploration of the links between music and peace-enhancing human qualities.

In chapter 1, *Music and Empathy*, Felicity Laurence examines the concept of empathy and how it relates to music. In chapter 2, *Music: A Universal Language?*, Cynthia Cohen offers a set of questions one might consider when planning interventions designed to promote reconciliation. How do we choose the music? In the chapter *Music and Value in Cross-Cultural Work*, June Boyce-Tillman offers several models useful when considering the links between music and peace in different cultural contexts. The closing chapter of this section is Johan Galtung's *Peace, Music and the Arts: In Search of Interconnections*, which explores the uplifting and uniting power of music, and how it can be used for the sake of peace.

The second section, *Politics*, gives examples of political uses of music. The first two chapters deal with the relationships between black and white people on two different continents. In chapter 5, Anne-Marie Gray shows how vocal music of polarized South African societies can contribute to ensuring the future of a shared past as well as contributing towards reconciliation, unforced nation building and positive transformation. In chapter 6, Baruch Whitehead shows how music has helped the USA move from a highly racial and prejudiced society to the somewhat better one we know today through the civil rights movement of 1955–69.

In chapter 7, Karen Abi-Ezzi presents the work of an Israeli-born reed player who is an outspoken critic of the violent policies tearing the Middle East apart. Finally in chapter 8, George Kent shows how music can be used to promote the reverse of empathy: hatred, prejudice and violence.

The third section is entitled *Healing and Education*. Kjell Skyllstad explores the healing power of music in prisons in chapter 9. In chapter 10, Vegar Jordanger shares a convincing experiment in conflict transformation in the Caucasus. In chapter 11, Maria Elena López Vinader describes the work of Music Therapists for Peace. Finally, in chapter 12, Kjell Skyllstad explores the power of music to transform conflict in general, and in interethnic conflicts in particular.

The fourth section, *Stories from the Field*, contains numerous personal experiences of professional musicians as well as anecdotes and interviews. In chapter 13, Rik Palieri shows the strength of folk music to convey a political message, and reports on his exclusive interview of folk legend Pete Seeger. In chapter 14, I discuss Yair Dalal's experience on the ground in the Middle East, based on interviews and conversations. In chapter 15, June Boyce-Tillman shows how she has applied the theories laid out in chapter 3.

This book offers readers a taste of the power of music for conflict transformation, and presents avenues for the further exploration of the potential of music for the enhancement of human life and society, taking into account the harmonies and dissonances that characterize geopolitics today.

References

Barenboim, D. and Said, E.W. (2002) *Parallels and Paradoxes: Explorations in Music and Society*, London: Bloomsbury Publishing.

Bunt, L. (1994) *Music Therapy: An Art Beyond Words*, London: Routledge.

Campion, J. (2005) "Ani DiFranco interview" (unedited transcript), Backstage at Mid-Hudson Civic Center, Poughkeepsie, NY, 4/21/02, in *Aquarian Weekly*, http://www.jamescampion.com/ad-dialogue.html

Galtung, J. (2000) Conversation with the author.

Harada, S. (2006) Interview with the author in Tokyo.

Karsenty, N. (2003) Conversation with the author.

Lebrecht, N. (2005) "Virtual Beethoven: BBC to air composer's complete works, with the symphonies available for free download," *The Evening Standard* [London] 6 May 2005,. http://www.andante.com/article/article.cfm?id=25487

McNeill, D. (2004) "Rising Japanese right calls the tune: hoisting the Hinomaru," *ZNet,* http://www.zmag.org/content/print_article.cfm?itemID=5038&sectionID=17

Menard, T. (2004) "The Aryan myth: Richard Wagner," *The IB Holocaust Project*, http://cghs.dade.k12.fl.us/holocaust/wagner.htm

Min-On (2007) "Cultural exchange and performing arts," http://www.min-on.org/

N'Dour, Y. (2004) "Transformative power," in music as a force for peace, July 2004, special issue of *SGI Quarterly*, http://www.sgi.org/english/Features/quarterly/0407/feature3.htm

Pavlicevic, M. and Ansdell G. (2004) *Community Music Therapy*, London: Jessica Kingsley Publishers.

Peacemakers Network (2007) http://peacemakers.ohah.net/

The Rosebud Agency (2007) *Living Like a Refugee* [CD] by The Refugee All Stars (biography), http://www.rosebudus.com/refugeeallstars/Biography.html

Universal Peace Day (2006) http://www.august6.org/node/87

PART I

Frameworks

Chapter 1: Music and Empathy

Felicity Laurence

In this opening chapter, I hope to locate the concept of empathy within the overall structure of this volume. I will briefly derive an initial position for the concept within the area of music and "musicking," and reiterate its importance within discourses of peacebuilding, peace education and reconciliation. I will then proceed to a closer look at what must be understood as a relatively new concept, with a somewhat tangled derivation, and whose meaning, in fact, is far from clear cut. I will, albeit briefly, focus upon certain key "explorers" in the field, together with several selected aspects of empathy which they have identified, each contributing a specific relevance to the wider ongoing concerns of this book. I will suggest some possible conceptual linkages between the fields of empathy and of music, which may in turn offer some illumination of music's role in promoting empathy. I will conclude with a suggested working definition of empathy.

Locating Empathy

The direct pursuit of peace, in terms of effecting reconciliation between groups in conflict and of inculcating peaceful values and nonviolent behaviour, is but one use, and, I would suggest, perhaps the rarest, to which music has been put. It may be argued that of music's purposes, many and probably most, serve the ongoing ends of power relationships one way or another; an exception, as Olivier Urbain points out, may be the benign use of music in healing, which is documented across the globe and throughout human history. Nevertheless, there is now a small but burgeoning area of exploration into the peacebuilding potential of music, and many of the subsequent chapters in this volume document instances where music does indeed appear to have played a role, whether direct or indirect, in achieving peaceful relationships between people. We may discern a number of emergent themes in the accounts presented here: music is often seen to unite us, and also to promote our self-awareness and self-esteem, mutual tolerance, sense of spirituality, intercultural understanding, ability to cooperate, healing – to name but a few. Above all, there is a recurrent conjecture that music can enable people, somehow, to "get inside" each other's minds, feel each other's suffering and recognize each other's shared humanity – that is, in common understanding, to have *empathy* for each other. The concept of empathy seems to have acquired here a general if implicit significance, although in some accounts it features more explicitly, as in Maria Elena López Vinader's discussion of music therapy.

I suggest that music, along with all its other functions and effects, indeed offers a specific potential to enable, catalyze and strengthen empathic response, ability and relationship, and that it is this *potential* capacity which lies at the core of music's function within peacebuilding. For the mechanisms of how this potential is realized, and the empathic effects are achieved, we may consider the matrix of interrelationships between inherent structures within the music object, the ways in which music is used and valued in different cultures, and the structures, patterns and processes of peacebuilding and reconciliation. Cynthia Cohen explores this territory in her examination of congruence between aesthetic forms within the arts and the "forms" of interaction between people as a basis for reconciliation (Cohen 1997); she and June Boyce-Tillman, respectively, pursue specific aspects of this area in ensuing discussions.

Shifting our focus from the music object, and from the abstract notion of something called "empathy," to look instead at what humans are actually *doing* when they "music" and when they empathize, offers another set of perspectives with which to approach an understanding of how musick*ing* may enable empathizing. The former activity is caught simply enough in its verbal form, "empathiz*ing*"; for the latter, things are more complex in this language. Christopher Small has coined the term "musicking" with an elaborate and innovative account of what this means:

> To music is to take part, in any capacity, in a musical performance, whether by performing, by listening, by rehearsing or practising, by providing material for performance (what is called composing), or by dancing.
>
> (Small 1998: 9)

Small suggests that the meaning of "musicking" is revealed in the *relationships* brought about in its course. These include relationships between people, within the musical patterns, between these patterns and the people making them, and so on. He contends that during a musical performance, *ideal* relationships, *as thus conceived by all those taking part* (my italics) in whatever capacity, are produced:

The act of musicking establishes in the place where it is happening a set of relationships, and it is in those relationships that the meaning of the act lies. They are to be found not only between those organized sounds which are conventionally thought of as being the stuff of musical meaning but also between the people who are taking part, in whatever capacity, in the performance; and they model, or stand as metaphor for, ideal relationships as the participants in the performance imagine them to be: relationships between person and person, between individual and society, between humanity and the natural world and even perhaps the supernatural world.

(Small 1998: 13)

And, he explains, when we "music," we "explore, affirm and celebrate" these relationships (ibid.).

Small's positioning of relationships at the kernel of his concept offers a direct conceptual link to the concept of empathy. The nature of this connection has been analyzed in detail elsewhere (Laurence 2005), but may be glimpsed as the nature of empathy and empathizing are further explored below.

Empathy has been identified as one of several key elements of peace (see Introduction). Others go further, for example in the suggestion that "empathy may be the *single most important quality* [which] must be nurtured in order to give peace a fighting chance" (Ray 2003, my italics).

In Ray's demand that empathy "must" be nurtured in people's development, lies also the implicit recognition that it *can* be thus nurtured. Inasmuch as we are concerning ourselves here with how people might be *learning* to empathize, in our specifically musical context, it is of pivotal importance that empathy is amenable to development and therefore to being educated. Empathy is not a character trait, or skill, which we simply either "have" or "lack."

Thus, we have empathy as an integral element of peace, with empathic ability both at the core of peacebuilding and also educable, and music and musicking a possible means of achieving empathic education and empathic relationships. However, we reach at this point something of a snag, for the concept of empathy turns out in fact to connote different things for different people. While the metaphorical "stepping into another's shoes," accompanied by a humane and caring prosocial intent, perhaps sketches the most general perception of what constitutes an empathic response, we do not have to look very far to encounter other explanations and a more complex view. As we contemplate empathy now, it may be surprising to learn that, far from being a straightforward area which might offer some hope for our beleaguered human species, it is instead a veritable maelstrom of currents of meaning. The fact is that empathy has been a muddled concept from the very beginning.

Origins and Dilemmas

The idea of an essential binding force between humans which allowed for the direct agency of the individual in behavioural and moral choice was explored during the Enlightenment period by Adam Smith. He suggested that we can and do subject our own behaviour to internal control because of sympathy, which he saw as the emotional connection between people through which they are able to share feelings (Smith 1759/1976). He describes a universal "fellow-feeling" which allows us to feel the emotional state of another, and also to respond compassionately to another's plight, and whose mechanism is our imaginative power rather than direct perception via the senses. His predecessor David Hume (1739/1968) had already addressed the concept of sympathy as the communication of one person's internal states, "inclinations and sentiments" (Sharma 1993: 2) to another and explored its role in the moral imperative to care for one another. Reflections of the works of these two seminal moral philosophers ripple throughout the subsequent philosophical and literary oeuvres of their time, as exemplified in William Blake's verse:

Can I see another's woe,
And not be in sorrow too.
Can I see another's grief,
And not seek for kind relief.
    (Blake 1789–1794/1970)

Sympathy was thus a long-established concept in Western thought when, in 1873, Robert Vischer introduced the term *Einfühlung* ("feeling into") into the unrelated field of German aesthetic theory, to describe the mechanism of understanding the aesthetic object (Wispé 1987). Empathy's "feeling into" was soon extended to explain peoples' understanding of each others' consciousness. There then began a parallel trajectory of the two terms "sympathy" and "empathy" during which the latter moved towards and became intertwined with the former. A first translation of *Einfühlung* as "sympathy" was not taken up, *Einfühlung* eventually being translated as "empathy" in 1909, but provides nevertheless evidence of the conflation of meaning which subsequently became a chronic problem.

As the concept has developed and been postulated as the source of moral development in Hoffman's theory (Hoffman 2000), and as Rogers' central principle of psychotherapeutic healing (Rogers 1976), it has acquired a multiplicity of definitions. Some are scarcely related to others, although the initial concern with the connection of one consciousness with another remains a universal core element. In a recent doctoral thesis, Schertz (2004) is scathing of the conceptual morass, pouring scorn upon attempts to reconcile such explanations as "empathy as perspective taking" with "empathy as affective response." Virtually everyone addressing the concept bemoans the ongoing ambiguity, and/or proffers their own definition.

The Contribution of Edith Stein

Nearly a hundred years ago, another doctoral student was complaining about this lack of a clear philosophical base for what was at the time a "hot" concept attracting wide interest in philosophical and psychological fields. Edith Stein probed very deeply into the nature of the empathic experience, developing a complex set of insights, concerns and dilemmas which appear constantly, albeit usually in far less sophisticated form (and usually unattributed), throughout the subsequent literature. I offer now the briefest tracing of her argument, which shares with Smith his attention to imaginative processes rather than direct perception.

Stein argues empathy as a process involving an initial cognitive act of intellectual comprehension of another's feeling and inner state, with ensuing reflection leading to one's own feeling in response to the other's experienced feeling. To explain this, she offers the notion of "primordial" experience, meaning actual and direct personal experience deriving from one's own "perception, memory or other kind of comprehension" (Stein 1917/1989: 4). Crucially, Stein distinguishes this from any form of direct experience of *another's* feeling. The empathic feeling we have *in response to* another's response, feeling or plight is our own original (primordial) experience; but the perceived feeling of the other is *not* our own feeling, however strongly we may respond to it, identify with it or have experienced similar feelings to it. Thus, while we can comprehend others' experiences, they do not become our own nor do they have the same quality of reality for us, but they *do* give rise to a parallel and related feeling which *is* "primordial." This distinction forms one of several structural and distinctive elements of Stein's theory. Another key element is her positioning of the empathic act, rather than, for example, sensory perception, at the core of how we know about the feelings and inner states of others.

Stein emphasizes empathy as a *process* occurring over time in a number of stages rather than a discrete event or single action. She allows for this process to be affected both positively and negatively by various factors throughout its ongoing stages, and even for the possibility of its being blocked to the point of incompletion, which she designates as *negative* empathy. This differs from what might now be construed as negative empathy, where empathic understanding of the other is employed as a tool of exploitation and manipulation. In perhaps the most blatant example of this, in any military situation there will be attempts to get inside and, in Stein's term, "grasp" the mind of the enemy forces, for the ultimate purposes of at best, thwarting their plans and at worst, killing them. Such empathizing lacks sympathy, which Stein isolated as a possible element of the empathic process, the part that has to do with sharing, or "taking on" a feeling after initial "grasping" or comprehending in the first act within the empathic process. She suggests in fact that it is sympathy which is the direct (primordial) experience resulting from the initial empathic act during which the other's experience is first perceived. This, and other facets described, appears in Figure 1.1, which I hope may help the reader to explore her analysis.

I extract at this point the two specific aspects of, respectively, emotional contagion and similarity, each of arguably special interest in the current context of this collection of essays.

Emotional Contagion

The absolute and constant retention of awareness of self, as separate from another's consciousness and experiences, was for Stein a further core tenet of empathy; however, she did allow the existence of a "feeling of oneness." This arises where a number of people experiencing the same event might be responding with the same, or extremely similar feelings: but it results from a cognitive and reflected awareness of the likeness of each other's responses, and does not involve any dissolution of interpersonal boundaries. This "feeling of oneness," conceptually distinct from the "fellow-feeling" which constitutes sympathy, can nevertheless lead to a sense of a "higher we," and ultimately, to an enrichment of community.

This is very different to a situation where a mass of people is engulfed by an emotional "bath," thereby losing individual awareness and agency. Stein suggests that when feelings are expressed as a direct result of our witnessing the expression of another's feelings, there is a phenomenon not of comprehension but of *expression*, involving a non-cognitive transference of feeling which is not empathy at all, but contagion. In fact, Stein argues, in contagion our attention is no longer on the other's experience at all, but on our *own* emotional state and response. In her description of mass contagion (Stein 1922/2000), she explains how mass differs from community. The latter is characterized by its

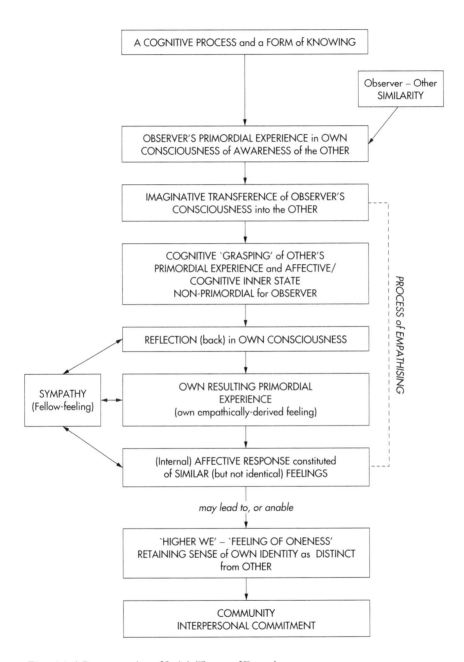

Figure 1.1 A Representation of Stein's Theory of Empathy

members' mutual commitment, where individuals attend to one another, are concerned to comprehend one another, and develop a "unity of understanding." The mass lacks all of these qualities; feelings, ideas and even beliefs are taken on and absorbed without reason or reflection, and although there may *appear* to be shared understanding, understanding is not the goal and is hardly possible in a context of abrogation of self.

We speak these days of mass hysteria and look to those reels of Hitler mesmerizing his audiences to see the nature of this apparently mindless sweeping-through of emotion. It appears that within such a crowd, the sense of individual self tends to vanish or be yielded up in favour of a sense of being at one, which seems to exert an irresistible pull. In that one's self is gone or diminished, however, this sense may be argued to be delusional, related neither to Stein's "feeling of oneness" nor Smith's "fellow-feeling," both of which require intact self and mutual regard, and both of which allow communal sharing of response, as discussed above. Contagion is not empathy, and may in fact be *antipathetic* towards the empathic process of understanding other consciousness.

I would offer here for reflection the idea that music's perceived power to unite may in many instances rely upon its ability to set up such an emotional "bath." It seems possible that when accounting for feelings of unity arising during shared musical experience, we may be confusing the impression of actually understanding and even feeling sympathetic towards one's fellow "musickers" with what is in fact the experience of an emotional "wave." In doing so, we are arguably conflating this "contagious" experience with the distinct and separate phenomenon of empathy. Emotional contagion is not *inherently* negative, and may indeed lead to, or accompany, empathic response. However, people engaged in musicking may seek specifically to engender, and then celebrate emotional contagion in order to *reduce* individual sovereignty, and dissolve interpersonal boundaries. Even in an apparently benign concert performance, for example, we may be able to discern such manipulative behaviour on the part of the performers and the corresponding mass response of their audience. Looking again at Hitler's rallies, we can see his specific, Machiavellian use of music. Here is the illusion of voice (united rather than individual), but in reality, its drowning by rant and Wagner, and replacement with identity-destructive emotional contagion. The people experienced an ecstatic bonding, which led to the supreme sense of likeness which facilitated the subsequent murderous alienation of those "others," now constructed as foreign to the point of being subhuman.

As we proceed through the ensuing accounts, it may be interesting to ponder possible instances where the musicking's emotional charge might in fact be overwhelming the participants, rather than inculcating the far more complex and nuanced elements of the empathic process postulated by Stein, and its many other theorists.

Similarity

Stein suggested that empathizing with people "of our type" helps us to understand ourselves as well as the other. "What is 'sleeping' in us is developed" (Stein 1989: 116), while through empathy "with differently composed personal structures" who are nevertheless enough like ourselves, "we become clear on what we are not, what we are more or less than others" (ibid.: 116). We can even acquire new values through our empathizing, and "we become conscious of our own deficiency or disvalue" (ibid.: 116). However, she concluded that empathy doesn't really work unless the empathizer and "empathized-with" are *sufficiently* similar. This implies that empathic comprehension of anyone who is *too* unlike ourselves is not philosophically (nor therefore otherwise) possible. If Stein was right in this assertion and also in her claim that empathy must ultimately underlie all knowledge of the outer world, then that knowledge becomes a function of the extent of our likeminded acquaintance, and anyone not sharing enough of our values and perspectives can by definition teach us nothing nor, ultimately, be understood.

Stein has in fact arrived at the most profound dilemma: however well we understand the empathic act, its mechanisms and how best to develop it, it cannot be heralded as "the way to humanity" (Kalliopuska 1992) if it exists and operates only between those who resemble one another. For where it strengthens "intra-group" connection there is the spectre not only of an inevitable and concomitant lessening in empathy with those outside the group, but of the increasingly active construction of the latter's foreignness. The more we discover our intra-group commonality, the less like us those outside our group seem. The irony of this extrapolation is cruelly sharp in view of her own ultimate fate: gassed in Auschwitz as an *Untermensch* – less than fully human, unempathizable and ultimately disposable.

The issue of similarity recurs constantly in subsequent theoretical analyses, given variously as a unifying theme across theories (Katz 1963), an antecedent factor in the empathic process (Davis 1994), and as a core construct (Hoffman 2000). Empirical research indicates clear correlations between, on the one hand, empathic responses and behaviour, and on the other, perceptions of similarity (Hornstein 1978, Eisenberg 1982, Barnett 1987, Batson *et al.* 1987,

Eisenberg and Strayer 1987, Davis 1994, Colvin *et al.* 1997, Hoffman 2000). We see then that Stein's concern has been vindicated.

However, rather than accepting such a gloomy limitation, I would prefer to pursue empathy as a way both of *overcoming* perceptions of dissimilarity, and of *accepting* others' difference. It may occur to my reader that inasmuch as music and musicking experience may well have the capacity to strengthen feelings of similarity, through shared experience and participation, a crucial contribution to empathic relationships may be accomplished. This may extend beyond the effects of emotional contagion only if there is an appropriate framework of conscious, stated and thoughtful intent, and arguably, a keen awareness of the kind of relationships which prevail, or are being established and (to invoke Small's claim) explored.

Empathy and Relationship

At this point, I turn, or rather, return, to the topic of relationships, given above as key in Christopher Small's musicking. Many theorists are specific about empathy's place and value in human relationships; for example, in the view of human community as a derived function of empathizing (Stein), or of empathy as *leading to* relationships (Katz), and in Rex Oram's placing of the "empathic encounter ... at the heart of sympathetic human interaction ..." (Oram 1984: 492; note the bringing together here of the two terms "empathic" and "sympathetic"). Kohut envisages empathy as a "fundamental mode of human relatedness" (Bennett 2001), while Halasz sees empathy as a "binding" force between people, and empathic relationships as possessing a particular potency because of their "preverbal essence" (Sharma 1993). Surely, again, we have points of resonance with music, in its perceived "binding" qualities, and indeed, in its own non-verbal essence. Small posits music as a "paralanguage," in the realm of the gestural communication which we use along with verbal language, and which allows levels of communication unavailable to rational, linear, spoken language.

But what exactly *is* an empathic relationship? We can look here to the work of Mothe, who, echoing Stein's earlier emphasis upon the active and processual nature of empathy, and also in a direct "prequel" of Small's own later argument concerning music, draws an explicit distinction between the noun *empathy* and the verb *empathize*. Mothe decries the Western tendency to endow concrete reality to abstract concepts and in so doing, to neglect the human behaviour involved (Mothe 1987). Challenging the notion of a "thing" called empathy which we "have" (and, according to those whom Mothe describes as "tough-minded, empiricist psychologists," can measure), Mothe argues instead for an ongoing process of empathizing, in which we both act empathically and enter into empathic relations. Calling on Fromm's concepts of "having" and "being," he reports Fromm's noting of the existing Western preoccupation with nouns, which are in turn interlinked with a "having" mode of existence, where having things is valued above the way we behave towards others. This in turn is connected with relationships of power and corresponding disempowerment, and Mothe suggests that our society currently exhibits a predominantly "having" mode, in which power is the main "thing" which people like to have.

In this context, Mothe argues that empathizing becomes the expression of the oppositional "being" mode, wherein the empathic relationship, in direct contrast to the power relationship, is non-manipulative, cooperative, engenders interpersonal harmony and personal knowing of the other, enhances the other, and fosters acceptance and tolerance of difference. Furthermore, whereas a power relationship tends to *limit* another's possibilities and behaviour, the empathic relationship *enhances* these. To empathize well, he suggests, we need to engage in a "joint project," and above all, *actively* to *strive* for an empathic knowing of the other. This last point is for Mothe the ultimate key to empathizing; it is a welcome emphasis, extending our view beyond the confines of empathic ability, state, or trait, and into a wider arena encompassing motivation and intentionality.

Mothe's work seems to me to offer extraordinarily rich resonances for our quest to explain music and musicking's potential contribution to a more empathic, and ultimately more peaceful world. I claimed above, almost in passing, that music's main use everywhere and throughout history has arguably concerned power relationships, whether by establishing them, maintaining them, or perhaps resisting them. The music object itself (the sounds and patterns constituting the music) are argued by many to encode cultural and societal patterns, and these are invariably hierarchical, however "hidden" this may be. When we look at the actual musicking, then we may see power being expressed, yielded, and also abused, as described above in Hitler's use of Wagner to manipulate his followers. As Small points out in great detail (Small 1998), the accepted epitome of Western musical culture, the symphony orchestra, is entirely based upon a rigid hierarchical structure. Creating empathic relationships is hardly the purpose in such contexts; music is doing other work.

But . . . what if we take another kind of musicking? A musicking based, for example, upon cooperation, democratic participation, mutual, respectful listening, and care for each other's differing musical values. In such a case, our musicking might constitute Mothe's "joint project," and in its enactment, we might achieve some movement towards his non-hierarchical, other-enhancing empathic relationship. In this way, we can argue that the *way* in which we "music," our *intention* therein, and the extent and quality of voice and agency we allow each other, are all key in whether or not we can take advantage of any inherent property within the music itself, its patterns and dynamics, to move us and affect our responses and behaviour.

I am able to give only the slightest glimpse of an enormous and captivating field in this chapter. I conclude here with a working definition of empathy which reflects many of the ideas sketched above. I hope this, and my various musings upon the nature of the "empathy-music matrix," may contribute towards an understanding of the experiences and concerns described in the following pages.

In empathizing, we, while retaining fully the sense of our own distinct consciousness, enter actively and imaginatively into others' inner states to understand how they experience their world and how they are feeling, reaching out to what we perceive as similar while accepting difference, and experiencing upon reflection our own resulting feelings, appropriate to our own situation as empathic observer, which may be virtually the same feelings or different but sympathetic to theirs, within a context in which we care to respect and acknowledge their human dignity and our shared humanity.

Various, and educable, cognitive and affective capacities are needed, whose level of advancement affects the quality of our empathizing. Antecedent factors also affect how, with whom, when and how well we empathize, while expressions of "fellow-feeling," including a feeling of oneness, and prosocial behaviour towards those with whom we empathize, may follow.

References

Barnett, M. (1987) "Empathy and related responses in children," in N. Eisenberg and J. Strayer (eds) *Empathy and its Development*, Cambridge: Cambridge University Press.

Batson, C.D., Fultz, J., and Schoenrade, P. (1987) "Adults' emotional reactions to the distress of others," in N. Eisenberg and J. Strayer (eds) *Empathy and its Development*, Cambridge: Cambridge University Press.

Bennett, M. (2001) *The Empathic Healer: An Endangered Species?* San Diego, CA: Academic Press.

Blake, W. (1789–1794/1970) *Songs of Innocence and Experience: Shewing the Two Contrary States of the Human Soul*, ed. G. Keynes, London: Oxford University Press.

Cohen, C.E. (1997) *A Poetics of Reconciliation: The Aesthetic Mediation of Conflict*, Unpublished PhD, Durham, University of New Hampshire.

Colvin, C.R., Vogt, D., and Ickes, W. (1997) "Why do friends understand each other better than strangers do?" in W. Ickes (ed.) *Empathic Accuracy*, New York: Guilford Press.

Davis, M. (1994) *Empathy: A Social Psychological Approach*, Madison, WI: Brown and Benchmark.

Eisenberg, N. (ed.) (1982) *The Development of Prosocial Behavior*, New York: Academic Press.

Eisenberg, N. and Strayer, J. (1987) *Empathy and its Development*, Cambridge: Cambridge University Press.

Hoffman, M.L. (2000) *Empathy and Moral Development*, Cambridge: Cambridge University Press.

Hornstein, H.A. (1978) "Promotive tension and prosocial behavior: a Lewinian analysis," in L. Wispé (ed.) (1978) *Altruism, Sympathy, and Helping: Psychological and Sociological Principles*, New York: Academic Press.

Hume, D (1739/1968) *A Treatise of Human Nature*, ed. H.A. Selby-Bigge, Oxford: Clarendon Press.

Kalliopuska, M. (1992) *Empathy: The Way to Humanity*, Edinburgh: Pentland.

Katz, R.L. (1963) *Empathy: Its Nature and Uses*, New York: Free Press of Glencoe.

Laurence, F.R. (2005) *Music and Empathy: A Study of the Possible Development, through Certain Ways of Musicking, of Children's Empathic Abilities within a Primary School Context*, Unpublished PhD, University of Birmingham.

Mothe, M. de la (1987) "Empathy revisited," Unpublished PhD, Open University.

Oram, R. (1984) "Empathy and curriculum studies: conceptual analysis and practical application," Unpublished PhD, University of Birmingham.

Ray, A. (2003) "Cultivating empathy in children and youth," *Changemakers Journal*, http://www.changemeakers.net/journal/03october/ray.cfm

Rogers, C. (1976) *On Becoming a Person: A Therapist's View of Psychotherapy*, London: Constable.

Schertz, M.V. (2004) "Empathic pedagogy," Unpublished EdD, Montclair State University.

Sharma, R.M. (1993) *Understanding the Concept of Empathy and its Foundations in Psychoanalysis*, Lewiston, NY: Edwin Mellen Press.

Small, C. (1998) *Musicking: The Meanings of Performing and Listening*, Hanover, NH: Wesleyan University Press.

Smith, A. (1759/1976) *The Theory of Moral Sentiments*, Oxford: Clarendon Press.

Stein, E. (1917/1989) *On the Problem of Empathy*, Washington, DC: ICS Publications.

Stein, E. (1922/2000) *Philosophy of Psychology and the Humanities*, ed. M. Sawicki, Washington, DC: ICS Publications.

Wispé, L. (1987) "History of the concept of empathy," in Eisenberg, N. and Strayer, J. (1987) *Empathy and its Development*, Cambridge: Cambridge University Press.

Chapter 2: Music: A Universal Language?

Cynthia Cohen

"Music, A Universal Language" reads the title of Unesco's cultural newsletter (UNESCO). "Music, the Universal Language, Brings Together Members of US and Iraqi Orchestras" announces the headline of a newsletter from the Columbia School of Journalism (Columbia 2004). The lyrics of New York City-based hardcore punk group H_2O sing out the same idea:

> What is the universal language?
> Could it be hate if it's not love?
> Could it be money, sex or power?
> I say it's music and none of the above

Is music truly a universal language? Is that what makes musical engagement a powerful peacebuilding resource? Many artists and peacebuilders claim that music is well suited to the work of reconciling adversaries because it can facilitate communication, understanding, and empathy across differences of all kinds. As the chapters in this book illustrate, music-making can be transformative; musical encounters of many kinds can be crafted to be important resources for healing, for efforts at non-violent social change, and for building bridges.

Music's power derives, in part, from its ability to create and strengthen feelings of affinity and group cohesion. Surely, these feelings can be cultivated in the service of peace, but we should remain aware that this power can be used for evil as well as for good. It is not only nationalists and warriors who marshal music's resources with harmful results. Many artist-peace builders might also misuse this potential of music, for instance, by constructing or augmenting feelings of affinity among adversaries without engaging them also in grappling with differences and confronting questions of past and present injustice. Creating feelings of affinity without doing the hard work necessary to challenge dynamics of oppression can add insult to injury for members of oppressed communities, and do little more than allay the guilt of those who are from more privileged groups. Furthermore, when we emphasize music's universality, we might mislead ourselves into thinking that musical elements can be borrowed from here or there, without paying sufficient attention to distinct cultural meanings, such as the sacred dimensions of performance.

In this chapter I suggest that, for several different reasons, we as musician-peacebuilders should use caution when asserting that music is a universal language. Although there are some aspects of musicality that are human universals, recent developments in the field of musicology suggest that different musical traditions are actually more dissimilar than similar. People raised in very different musical cultures can appreciate some aspects of each other's music-making, but often only with serious study, and only to a degree. Moreover, examples drawn from practitioners working in different conflict regions show that, in many instances, it is not music's universal appeal that gives it much of its power as a peacebuilding resource, but rather recognition of the distinctive meanings that emerge from its place in historical events and cultural traditions. This is especially true in relation to the difficult emotional and educational tasks associated with reconciliation. Finally, notions about the universality of music can lead peacebuilding practitioners to lift "musics" out of their contexts, borrowing elements in ways that distort their meanings or violate their sacredness.

I conclude this chapter with a discussion of some of the ethical issues that arise when we bring musical elements from one culture to another. Especially in the face of globalization, we should be aware of the differences in access to resources and power enjoyed by musicians of different cultures. We should ask ourselves questions about the beneficiaries of musical exchanges. Under what conditions might individual artists, tradition-bearers, and the communities that gave rise to musical forms, benefit from cross-border musical collaborations? When are most of the monetary and professional awards reaped by production companies and artists from the developed world?

As musician-peace builders, we seek to heal individuals and to overcome barriers that divide peoples. We bring the affirmative, non-violent power of music to struggles for social justice, and the nuanced complexity of musical symbols to efforts at reconciliation. This chapter ends with a set of questions we can consider in order to enhance the efficacy and minimize the ethical risks inherent in our work.

The Universality and Particularities of Music

The aptitude and capacity for music apparently *is* a universal human phenomenon. All children are born into the world with the ability to learn to perceive and replicate rhythms, pitch, and other musical features such as tempo and phrasing of sounds. However, to a large degree, it is culture that determines how these capacities are shaped, and how individuals' perceptual proclivities and expressive abilities develop. So great is the variety and the disparateness of musical experiences and forms that many musicologists now argue that the plural word "musics" more accurately captures the range of experiences than the singular music:

> Musics only make sense as musics if we can resonate with the histories, values, conventions, institutions, and technologies that enfold them; musics can only be approached through culturally situated acts of interpretation. Such interpreted acts . . . unveil a multiplicity of musical ontologies, some or most of which may be mutually irreconcilable . . .
>
> (Cross 2003: 19)

Once we begin to explore the meanings of musical expression not as inherent in texts, i.e. in terms of composers' expressions, but rather in terms of the experiences of the composers, performers, and perceivers as they interact with each other and with texts, it becomes obvious that what participants bring to the musical encounter – the sensibilities, relationships, attitudes, historical resonances, etc. – contributes a large measure of its meaning. Some of these sensibilities and attitudes might be contingent on immediate circumstances and personal histories. However, audience members' sensibilities are also informed by the values and emotional predispositions they share with others in their cultures. As Ruth Finnegan points out in her excellent essay, "Music, Experience and the Anthropology of Emotion," in the Balkans: "Serbian epic-singing is heard with pride by Serbs but terror by their Croat neighbors . . . while in Ireland listeners of different backgrounds experience the sounds of Orange flute and drums in contrasting ways, bound into long historical-mythic associations" (Finnegan 2003: 189).

The question of the comprehensibility of music across cultural divides must be considered separately, then, in two very different circumstances: 1) when the listeners have been socialized into and/or educated about the particular musical tradition, and 2) when listeners lack such similar socialization and/or education. The philosopher Martha Nussbaum describes the limitations of cross-cultural musical understanding in this way:

> Music may be universal in the sense that people widely separated by language and culture can learn to love the same music. It is not universal in the sense that this response is automatic or without effort. The expressive content of Japanese or Indian music is utterly baffling, at first, to Western ears; so too is that of a

Mahler symphony to someone who has never heard any other symphony . . . .
Music (at any rate formally composed music) is more akin to poetry than to daily
gesture and movement: its emotional power is inseparable from a compressed
and formally intricate use of the media of expression, in such a way that only the
most superficial understanding, if any, is available to those ignorant of the poetic
(musical) tradition in question.

(Nussbaum 2003: 263, 270)

Nussbaum is certainly correct in pointing to the limitations of people situated
within one elite musical tradition fully comprehending the emotional meanings
and nuances conveyed by performances in other traditions. As peace builders,
we should be aware of an even larger gap: between the compositions of individuals that characterize musical expression in modern societies, and the expressive forms of societies based on oral cultures. Such collectivities include, for
instance, tribal and indigenous groups struggling to maintain cultural integrity in
the face of colonial impositions and globalization. In many such cultures, the
expression of the group is paramount, shaping individual emotional response to
a degree that can be difficult (perhaps impossible) for persons socialized into
the cognitive-emotional structures of literate societies to appreciate.

The socio-biologist Ellen Dissanayake describes how works of art and rituals in pre-modern societies inscribe the bodies of participants with kinesthetic
patterns that can be understood to create embodied dimensions of the very
unity they celebrate. "In pre-modern societies, where arts and ceremony are
joined," she writes, "aesthetic empathic means are invariably used to express
the group's perceptions of the world" and, therefore, to create feelings of unity
and belonging among group members (Dissanayake 1992: 140–93). An example can be found in African dancing and drumming, "inseparable modalities,"
through which African people:

express and experience the most complex, the deepest aspects of African philosophy. The drum translates to us the rhythm of the universe and the dance
transports us to a phenomenal dimension in which we become a part of the connecting thread that binds all being, thereby making the universe whole . . . The
power of the African drum is inescapable. In unison the drums become compelling, forceful. This is no academic, cerebral exercise; neither is it peripheral or
detached. It is rather visceral and involved . . . African symbol is spiritual truth,
not its representation.

(Richards 1993: 68)

So in every culture, the rhythms and textures of the cultural forms experienced
by children inscribe themselves onto each person's "perceptual apparatus"

(Benjamin 1978: 222) contributing to lifelong aesthetic sensibilities and tastes. Of course, education can make the forms of other cultures accessible, comprehensible, and even pleasurable. Nevertheless, it is reasonable to ask whether and to what extent it is possible for cultural outsiders to experience the same depth and quality of resonances as those whose very ways of perceiving the world were shaped within a particular aesthetic tradition.

With these questions and reservations about music's universality in mind, I would like to consider some examples in which musical processes *have* been used to facilitate peacebuilding processes. My examples illustrate how music has contributed to specific instances of reconciliation, or the rebuilding of relationships in the aftermath of mass violence. First, a brief exploration about the nature of reconciliation, focusing on the kinds of learning (about self and other) that it entails.

Conceptualizing Reconciliation and its Processes

What is reconciliation? Imagine a continuum that displays interpersonal and inter-communal relationships according to the degree to which the parties to a conflict acknowledge and act upon an understanding of their interdependence. At one end, we might find complete disregard for the other and thorough denial that one's well-being and integrity are dependent upon the other's well-being and integrity; as in inter-communal relationships of war, apartheid, and slavery and interpersonal relationships of deceit, manipulation, and violence. At the other end of the spectrum, we find not a conflict-free utopia, but rather cooperative inter-communal relationships, where decisions are made through democratic or consensual processes, and where conflicts are addressed proactively through agreed-upon procedures and structures. On an interpersonal level, this end of the spectrum is home to functional families, friendships, and fellowships – relationships in which the well-being of each member is understood to depend upon the well-being of all. It is not devoid of conflict – conflict being an inevitable part of life and necessary for growth and development – but a realm of relationships where conflicts are engaged productively.

Reconciliation can be understood in relation to this continuum as a set of deep processes designed to transform relationships of hatred and mistrust into relationships of trust and trustworthiness. It also can reflect a shift in attention from blaming the other to taking responsibility for the attitudes and actions of one's self and one's own community.

The precise activities that comprise reconciliation work, and the order in which they are undertaken, must be decided in each particular context. They must take into account the nature of the preceding alienation or violence, the trajectory and stage of the conflict, the individuals and cultures to be brought into relationship, the leadership resources available, and the larger systems within which the conflict and peacebuilding processes are embedded. Nevertheless, it is safe to assume that processes of coexistence and reconciliation almost always involve former adversaries in culturally-inflected versions of at least some of the following tasks, although not necessarily undertaken in this order:

- Appreciating each other's humanity and respecting each other's culture
- Telling our own and listening to each other's stories, and developing more complex narratives and nuanced understandings of identity
- Acknowledging harms, telling truths, and mourning losses
- Empathizing with each other's suffering
- Acknowledging and redressing injustices
- Expressing remorse, repenting, apologizing, letting go of bitterness, forgiving
- Imagining and substantiating a new future, including agreements about how future conflicts will be engaged constructively (Cohen 2005).

All of these processes involve learning about one's own community and the other. They involve learning new skills and expanding the meaning of concepts, often "unlearning" what was formerly believed to be true. In this sense, reconciliation can be conceptualized in terms of education. Taken together, these processes represent a daunting array of tasks and challenges, especially considering that the learning they represent must be undertaken in ways that reach deeply into the person and broadly throughout society.

Furthermore, in many instances, widespread ethnic violence and long-standing oppressions can leave people and communities with insufficient capacities to undertake this work. People are likely to be disoriented and confused, often having lost loved ones, the places that sheltered them, and the webs of relationships that gave meaning, texture, and ethical anchoring to their lives. Peoples' abilities to listen and to express themselves so others can understand are often impaired. Along with bombed-out villages and desecrated shrines, capacities to discern when trust is warranted, to respond to problems creatively, and to imagine a different future have often been destroyed. Those who have perpetrated abuses or are implicated in other's suffering (even through omissions) may be straitjacketed by inexpressible shame, fear, and self-loathing.

Music and peace projects can be crafted, then, to overcome the after-effects of violence, both by facilitating necessary learning and by restoring the capacities and nourishing the sensibilities required for reconciliation.

Contributions of Music to Reconciliatory Efforts

It is possible to imagine music contributing to each of the seven conciliatory processes listed above. Several of the chapters in this volume, for instance, describe projects in which people experience the "musics" of a different culture or even an adversary society, and learn to value and respect the other's culture in part through appreciating its musical expression. Such projects would illustrate the first item on the list above. I will describe projects in which music contributed to two other conciliatory tasks: appreciating the narratives of the other and mourning losses.

Music and understanding the narrative of the other

In a project I directed in the early 1980s in Cambridge, Massachusetts, music played a powerful role in assisting members of alienated communities to understand each other's narratives. In response to a racially motivated murder in a local high school, the municipal arts council sponsored a series of oral history projects that facilitated the sharing of stories among younger and older people from the city's major racial and ethnic groups. In particular, we sought participation from members of the African American and Portuguese American communities, two of the groups implicated in the high school violence. In one such project, the Cambridge Women's Quilts Project, women and girls depicted scenes from their lives in colorful quilt patches. As the quilt was being constructed, we enlisted the talents of singer-songwriter Betsy Rose to work with the project's younger participants to compose a song about the quilts. They based their song on the melody of a familiar Portuguese folk ballad. Betsy worked with the young people to write verses retelling their own stories and the stories of the older project participants. The active reframing of stories required people to listen carefully to the meanings of the stories and the feelings behind them. When the group sang the completed ballad, we could re-enact and re-experience the close relationships that had been developed through many months of sewing together and talking.

The form of the ballad echoed the form of the quilt, with each story celebrated through both a patch in the quilt and a verse of the ballad. The juxtapositions of the different stories invited people to discover relationships among their experiences and to acknowledge both similarities and differences. As we performed the ballad at various events where the quilts were displayed, the project reached larger audiences in neighborhoods throughout the city.

Like all art symbols, the ballad communicated on many different levels at once. The form was familiar to many, with its repeating chorus that was easily learned, and rhyming narrative verses filled with detail. The content of the verses, however, provided images of everyday life, some common to all (such as mothers fashioning their daughters' hair and children swimming) and some resonating with the particular cultures of the city (Italian families making wine, Jewish families lighting Sabbath candles, Jamaican children reminiscing about gardens back home, African American girls jumping rope, etc.).

For members of the Portuguese community, not only the form, but the melody was familiar. The incorporation of a traditional melody was designed as an acknowledgement of this particular subculture. It also served to provide the support of the familiar as members of the Portuguese community were being invited and challenged to open their hearts to what was likely to be new and, at first, threatening: the stories of their neighbors, people who previously had been associated with feelings of foreignness, difference, and fear.

Music's contribution to this peacebuilding project derived in part from its commonly understood elements: the form of the ballad, the repeating chorus, and the verses filled with details. Part of the peacebuilding potential of this music-making process was precisely the ballad's melody for one segment of the community, who could find support in the familiar resonances as they were being asked to embrace their interconnectedness with others whom they had come to distrust, even to hate.

Music and mourning losses in Phnom Penh, Cambodia

Halfway around the globe from Boston, another project incorporated music to evoke not the familiarity of everyday life, but memories of an overwhelmingly confusing and horrifying period in the recent past. In the Cambodian capital of Phnom Penh, Ly Daravuth included recordings of Khmer Rouge songs in a nuanced and complex installation work entitled "The Messengers," which was part of a larger exhibition entitled "Legacy of Absence." Through the exhibition, the artists of Cambodia had been invited to address the legacy of the genocide. It is a particularly anguished legacy, since many of those who survived the Khmer Rouge, although surely victims themselves, also participated for some period of time as perpetrators.

Ly Daravuth's "The Messengers" includes images of children, at first appearing as victims of the Khmer Rouge. At the end, though, the viewer comes to realize that the faces are actually not only young cadres recruited in the Khmer Rouge army, but also images of contemporary children, distressed to appear as though they emerge from the same era as the young cadres. The work was designed "to interrogate [the] process of interpretation as much as the content of what is presented" (Ly and Muan 2002).

Interestingly, in a context where there has been very little public or private reckoning with the era of the genocide, local visitors to the exhibition repeatedly asked the curators, Ly Daravuth and Ingrid Muan, if they could make CDs of the Khmer Rouge songs for them to take home. Muan and Ly comment:

> Some of these furtive requests seemed tinged with nostalgia for that time. Open, non-dogmatic, filled with various interpretations and standpoints of the Khmer Rouge era, the very ambiguity of the exhibition and its refusal to judge these multiple views seemed to allow these visitors to begin to care to recast themselves, as, perhaps, former Khmer Rouge. For who were the Khmer Rouge if everyone in Cambodia today publicly claims to have been their victim? . . . We hope that the images [and the sounds] in the exhibition . . . open a space for reflection that will perhaps be one small step in coming to terms with the terrible events of Cambodia's recent past. What it means for Cambodia to mourn can only be determined when what has happened is taken on as the individual responsibility of everyone.
>
> (ibid.)

Choosing to focus on painful history with a quality of attention that allows for mourning is difficult under any circumstances. When memories of the past are infused with cross-currents of fear, rage, and shame, it becomes almost impossible for people to bring themselves to that history. Here is a case when a kind of music, with its particular and conflicted resonances for the people who survived the years when those revolutionary songs were performed and heard, offered just enough of a prompt to support, as Ly and Muan suggest, what might be "one small step in coming to terms" with painful wounds that Cambodian society has not yet begun to heal (AsianWeek 2001).

The particularity of music

While music can facilitate communication across many differences, these two examples illustrate how the particular resonances of certain musics among members of certain communities give music much of its power as a resource for peace. It is the familiarity of particular songs that offers a degree of support for the Portuguese Americans to listen to the stories of the neighbors they had come to fear and for Cambodian genocide survivors to begin to face and come to terms with their anguished history.

Dilemmas of Musical Cross-Cultural Encounters

Musicians in many regions of the world often find themselves performing for mixed audiences, drawn from diverse communities and cultures. Even in regions of conflict, they often bring elements of divergent cultures into their compositions, as if demonstrating to their communities the generative potential of cross-boundary and cross-cultural cooperation. Musical sharing across borders seems to be organic and virtually inevitable, a celebration of human creativity, adaptability, and diversity.

When peacebuilders and musicians purposefully extract musical elements from one culture to facilitate activities in another, or intentionally bring the "musics" of enemy communities into single compositions, there are several issues that should be considered in order to avoid possible harms. I have witnessed drumming workshops, for instance, where people from one community were quite offended to see sacred elements from their own rituals incorporated into a session led by an outsider to their community, with no acknowledgement of the sacred dimension or explanation of the meaning of the actions. Such appropriations can interfere with the development of trusting and respectful relationships.

Lena Slachmuijlder, a musician and peacebuilding practitioner who has worked in South Africa and Burundi, raises such questions in a very compelling working paper entitled *The Rhythm of Reconciliation: A reflection on drumming as a contribution to reconciliation processes in Burundi and South Africa*. In it, she emphasizes the power of drumming as a resource for reconciliation, sharing interviews with Hutu and Tutsi drummers who repeatedly prioritized their identity as drummers above their ethnic affiliations, and repeatedly saved each other's lives during periods of violence. Drummers from Burundi, West Africa, and the United States have helped Hutu and Tutsi boys build respect and trust, bringing them together through drumming lessons, workshops, and performances. Although herself a leader of such processes and an advocate of drumming as a resource for reconciliation, Lena has identified several ethical questions that emerge in such projects (2004):

> Collaborating with master drummers through the years, who intimately know and understand the powerful importance of the drum in their cultures and traditions, has raised cultural and ethical dilemmas about using traditional drums in a

deliberate way in the service of reconciliation. In Burundi, drumming is no longer reserved for specific clans or exclusively presented to the king. Every weekend in Burundi's capital Bujumbura, young couples invite traditional drumming groups to grace their weddings, much to the delight of an increasing number of career drummers. Traditionalists scoff at this notion that ordinary people should be able to have such simple access to such a powerful and sacred Burundian cultural icon.

The use of the djembe and other traditional West African drums for team-building in South Africa poses similar dilemmas. Like most traditional drums in Africa, djembe have a historical and traditional role related to communication by or for the kingdom, communication with the ancestors, and/or ceremonial uniting of the community. I have witnessed the near outrage and disgust felt by master drummers from West Africa, newly arrived in South Africa, upon realizing the banal usage of the djembe in South Africa. Taken out of its context, it has lost all of its sacredness, and is no longer reserved for certain players or occasions.

This raises questions: how far should we go in bringing the drum out of its historically sacred role toward modern usages? Is not negation of its ancestral, spiritual powers a negation of the very potential of those related forces to contribute to the reconciliation processes? Without a cultural recognition of the drum, can the drum still be used effectively as a tool of healing, bringing people together, and repairing relationships?

In June 2004, when the United Nations Mission in Burundi took over officially from the African Union, Burundian drummers played at the handover ceremony. Many Burundians were particularly horrified at the implication of playing the Burundi drums for foreigners, as one would for a king in days past. The analogy was too strong; it resonated with the negative reminiscence of colonialism, and the Burundi drummers' presence signified the submission of Burundian culture to an outside force.

As musician peacebuilders, we must be alert to the meanings of the musical traditions of the communities in which we are working. Are certain musical forms embedded within sacred domains and others secular? Does a music's power derive from its connection to other ritual elements or its integration into everyday life?

To avoid potential harms that always accompany peacebuilding efforts, we should also consider the dynamics of power that inscribe the relationships between peoples who seek to coexist and to reconcile. As mentioned above, contact among musicians and musical cultures is ubiquitous, and can result in enormous creativity, vitality, and innovation. In fact, musicians often seem to lead the way, helping other members of society to imagine the generative potential of bringing their own cultural expressions into closer engagement with those of former enemies. Still, when "musics" are shared across relationships marked by extreme inequities, it is unusual for the benefits of those collaborations to devolve equally onto all of the participants and each of the communities. While the musical exchange itself could be characterized by mutual respect and equality, the political and social inequities can insinuate themselves into the process, with cultural appropriations contributing to heightened feelings of resentment and betrayal. Well-intentioned exchanges can unwittingly reflect and exacerbate patterns of cultural appropriation, unequal distribution of resources, and the homogenizing forces of globalization.

Questions for Musician Peacebuilders to Consider

In her groundbreaking work on the evaluation of peacebuilding practice, Mary Anderson suggests that, at a minimum, we should seek to "do no harm." Beyond that, she asks practitioners and doners to consider questions of effectiveness (Anderson 2004: 4). Here are some questions we as musician-peace builders can use as starting points to reflect on both the effectiveness and the ethical dimensions of our work.

About efficacy

- Is it possible to extend the positive effects of musical encounters into political and social life? If so, how?
- What are the possibilities and limitations of focusing resources on children rather than adults?
- Can arts projects be linked with other peacebuilding efforts so that emotional, cognitive, and relational gains can be connected to political, economic, and ongoing cultural projects?

About ethics

- What are the dynamics of power present among those involved in the project and among the various cultures and communities involved?
- How can these be acknowledged and addressed in a respectful way?
- What are the risks involved in transplanting a cultural form from one culture into another setting? What is gained and what is lost?
- Who benefits (politically, economically) from cultural forms when they are lifted out of context?

- How can we minimize the risk of reinforcing an inequitable status quo by creating short-term "good feelings" with no contribution to substantive or lasting change?

Conclusion

In this chapter, I have argued that we can make our work most effective when we take into account not just the universal dimensions of musical experience, but its culturally specific manifestations as well. For reasons of both efficacy and ethics, I have argued that music's contribution to peacebuilding is rarely captured in the phrase "music is a universal language." This phrase minimizes the very real differences between different "musics," and the extent to which the socialization and education of the listener contribute to the meanings that will be derived in a musical encounter. It obscures the peacebuilding potential inherent in the particularities of "musics" and different communities. Understanding these particularities can help in crafting musical encounters that nourish the capacities required for reconciliation, such as vitality, receptivity, and imagination. They can also be crafted to meet the daunting educational challenges inherent in conciliatory work.

Glossing over music's particularities can lead us into ethically troubling situations when, for instance, we allow to dissipate the emotional affinities that musical experiences can facilitate, without exploring avenues for larger societal impact. An over-emphasis on the universal dimensions of musical experience also can obscure the very real power asymmetries that inscribe themselves onto musical encounters across differences. Unless engaged constructively, these power differences can perpetuate the underlying dynamics of the conflicts that musical interventions may actually be intended to transform.

Music is a powerful medium for expression, communication, healing, and transformation. As peace builders, we can access this potential when we embrace not only musics' universal appeal, but their particularities as well.

References

Anderson, M. (2004) Collaborative Learning Projects, *Reflecting on Peace Practice Project*, http://www.cdainc.com/rpp/docs/ReflectingOnPeacePracticeHandbook.pdf

AsianWeek (August 3–August 9, 2001) *Khmer Rap: Cambodian American Youth's Words Awaken Stifled Generation in Cambodia*, http://www.asianweek.com/2001_08_03/feature_khmerrap.html

Benjamin, W. (1978) "The work of art in an age of mechanical reproduction," in *Illuminations*, ed. H. Arendt, New York: Schocken.

Cohen, C. (2005) "Creative Approaches to Reconciliation," in M. Fitzduff and C. Stout (eds) *The Psychology of Resolving Global Conflicts: From War to Peace*, Westport, CT: Greenwood Publishing Group, Inc.

Columbia University (2004) *Deadline in Depth*, http://www.jrn.columbia.edu/ studentwork/deadline/2004/symphony.asp

Cross, I. (2003) "Music and biocultural evolution," in M. Clayton, T. Herbert, and R. Middleton (eds) *The Cultural Study of Music: A Critical Introduction*, Oxford: Routledge.

Dissanayake, E. (1992) *Homo Aestheticus: Where Art Come From and Why*, New York: The Free Press, pp. 140–93.

Finnegan R. (2003) "Music, experience and the anthropology of emotion," in M. Clayton, T. Herbert, and R. Middleton (eds) *The Cultural Study of Music: A Critical Introduction*, Oxford: Routledge.

Ly, D. and Muan, I. (2002) *The Legacy of Absence* (exhibition catalogue), Phnom Penh: Reyum Publications.

Nussbaum M. (2003) *Upheavals of Thought: The Intelligence of Emotions*, Cambridge: Cambridge University Press.

Richards, D.M. (1993) "The African aesthetic and national consciousness," in K. Welsh-Asante (ed.) *The African Aesthetic: Keeper of Traditions*, Westport, CT: Greenwood Press.

Slachmuijlder, L. (2004) Brandeis University International Center for Ethics, Justice and Public Life, *The Rhythm of Reconciliation: A reflection on drumming as a contribution to reconciliation processes in Burundi and South Africa*, http://www.brandeis.edu/ ethics/fellowships/bif/bif_2003/working_papers/Slachmuijlder.pdf

United Nations Educational, Scientific, and Cultural Organization (n.d.) *Culture Newsletter*, http://www.unesco.org/culture/news1/newsen.htm

Chapter 3: Music and Value in Cross-Cultural Work

June Boyce-Tillman

A five-fold model of the musical experience – Materials, Expression, Construction, Values and Spirituality – is introduced in this section to show how values are expressed in a musical event.

Introduction

This chapter is concerned with the way in which we embody particular value systems in music making activities as Cynthia Cohen has indicated so clearly in her chapter. Because much of the "musics" that make up our Western concerts are "masterpieces" from Western culture's past, the values that we are presenting may also be values that we have had to abandon in the wider society, like those of colonialism. Intercultural "borrowings" have happened throughout the history of western music like Mozart's use of so-called "Turkish" percussion; but the way this has been done, like Mozart taking a set of instruments from an "exotic, other" culture and placing it in a Western context, is not unlike how imperial powers have plundered the property of the countries they have invaded. My question is how can the way we bring cultures together musically reflect ethical ways of cultural interaction? How can we use music to promote empathy, creativity and nonviolence? How can it be used in active peacemaking? Can we see the exploration of ways of examining music as resistance to dominant Western value systems? Is this a way of challenging the individualistic, materialistic, consumerist, earth-ravaging Western culture? Or, looking at George Kent's chapter, are we, in any particular project, cementing the divisions within our society? To examine these questions, I shall use frames in order to look at music through various lenses that interact.

Theoretical Framework: The Five Lenses for Musical Experience

I have written elsewhere (Boyce-Tillman 2001) about how in a piece of music five domains interact. These are:

- Materials
- Expression
- Construction
- Values
- Spirituality

All music consists of organisations of concrete Materials drawn both from the human body and the environment. What is used in a particular piece or tradition depends on availability of materials in certain geographical locations and the technical abilities of those involved. The choice of instruments and vocal colours and ranges will also dictate musical pitches and rhythms – the keys and scales that can be used, and associated motifs and melodic and rhythmic patterns. Different traditions also value quite distinct vocal and instrumental

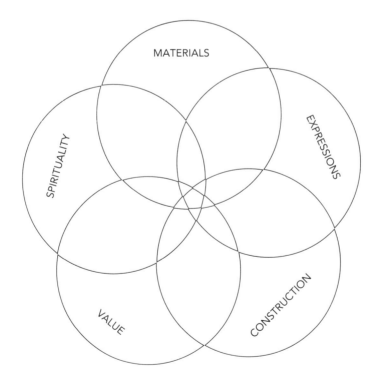

Figure 3.1 The Five Lenses for Musical Experience

colours. However, although in the West we can and have regarded these sounds as "pure" tone colours, other cultures with different value systems do not see the Materials of sound in the same way and they are inseparable from their meaning. For example, the mbira or finger piano in Zimbabwe is closely associated with the ancestors and this has prevented its use in Christian contexts.

In this area also, the relationship between the body of the performer/composer and the environment is established. The Materials from which instruments are made provide an intimate link between human beings and the natural world. In traditional societies, the process of making an instrument involved a reverence towards, for example, the tree that gave its wood for the making of the drum, and the player would regard him or herself as continually in relationship to that tree every time the instrument was played. Our industrialised society with its production lines for musical instruments dislocates the connection between the natural world and the materials of sound. The role of instrument maker is dislocated from the roles of composer and performer, but in the classroom this link can be re-established.

The area I have called Expression is concerned with the evocation of mood, emotion (individual or corporate), images, memories, story and atmosphere on the part of all those involved in the musical performance. This concerns mood and atmosphere. If there are words present then these often govern this area and control the range of emotions that will be experienced (in contrast to the more "veiled" quality of purely instrumental music).

This area is where the subjectivity of composer/performer and listener intersect. The intrinsic meaning of the music reflecting the subjectivity of composer and performer is often completely changed by its intersection with the subjective experience of the listener. The listener may well bring extrinsic meaning to the music – meaning that has been locked onto that particular piece or style or musical tradition because of its association with certain events in their own lives. Popular music, in particular, often conjures up a range of associations (Green 1988, 1997) including the emotion engendered by cultural conditioning. For a Catholic brought up in Northern Ireland, for example, the sound of the pipes and drums associated with the Protestant marching bands may well make any music using them unacceptable. This is the area where empathy, imagination and identity creation interact.

In the area of Construction, effectiveness often depends on the right management of repetition and contrast within a particular idiom. The way in which contrast is handled within a tradition – how much or how little can be tolerated – is often carefully regulated by the elders of the various traditions, be they the composers or theoreticians of the Western classical tradition or the master drummers of West African Yoruba traditions. For example, the degree of repetition in the pop tradition is often much greater and more overt than in avant-garde Western classical music. This is one reason why the audience for the two traditions is so vastly different.

Construction issues are well-documented in the pieces that make up the classical canon (Goehr 1992), indeed some might say over-documented. The principles and terminologies developed in the Western classical tradition have often been applied to other cultures, without sufficient regard for how thinkers within those traditions have regarded their own processes of musical Construction. For example, the more circular structures of oral improvised traditions (Vander 1986) often sit uneasily with the use of the terminology associated with the more linear notated traditions. How musical form is perceived in orate (Ong 1982) musical cultures differs markedly from its perception in literate musical cultures.

The area of Values is related to the context of the music making experience and how the value systems of the surrounding tradition are reflected in the music. All musical experiences are culturally related. It has been an area that has traditionally been ignored by Western classical theorists, unlike ethnomusicologists and popular music theoreticians (Shepherd and Wicke 1997: 138–9) who have favoured a de-contextualised approach to music.

Musical performances contain both implicit and explicit value systems. Some are within the sounds of the music itself and some are to do with the context of the music making. Extrinsic values are present in the context of the performance. There is a difference between a school nativity play and a High Mass in Westminster Cathedral. The available finance will be culturally determined. Opera, for example, is an expensive form reflecting the age of a rich aristocracy in Europe.

Intrinsic and extrinsic values interface in the examples in the book. In the chapter on Yair Dalal's work, his use of musicians from various backgrounds has an effect on the construction of the music. Felicity Laurence examines the expressive characteristics of empathy in detail, giving a guide to musicians embracing this as a value. Rik Palieri shows how the words of the songs provide clear value systems for the less clear value systems of instrumental traditions. Kjell Skyllstad shows the power of intention in the use of music in prisons and what this might mean for the ways music is constructed. Karen Abi-Ezzi shows how values of justice impinge not only on the nature of the music but also on the life of the performer who expresses the value systems.

Intrinsic values are present in the creation process. A truly democratic process will involve everyone in all decisions. The level of democracy that has

operated in the process will be reflected in the values of the final product. Notions of intrinsic values are a subject of debate in musicological circles (McClary 1991, 2001) but as soon as a text or story is present, Value systems will be declared within the piece, like the challenges in Billy Bragg's song "The Price of Oil," and the healing of Youssou N'Dour. All musical pieces stand in relation to the culture in which they are created, even if that relationship, like the protest songs of the sixties, is one of challenge. In a conversation with the director of various choirs I discovered a person who included in some programmes only musical pieces that she would consider as challenging cultural constructions of women (Ring Frank 2003).

Social anthropologists like Gooch (1972) have shown how value systems are culturally specific. For example, the values of Western culture favour products over processes, challenge over nurture. Drawing on the work of Michel Foucault (Foucault/Gordon 1980), I have elsewhere (Boyce-Tillman 2005) explored the notion that certain value systems become subjugated within Western culture. I have attempted to express this in a diagram:

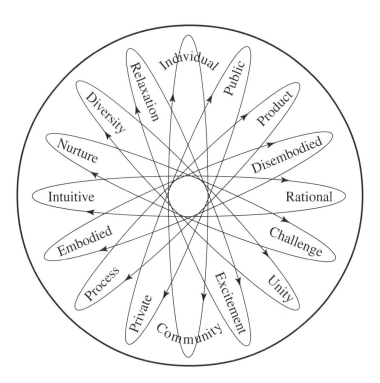

Figure 3.2 Value Systems

In this diagram we see that the right-hand side represents the dominant values of Western culture:

- The individual
- The public
- The product
- The disembodied
- The rational
- The challenging
- The united
- The exciting

The Western classical and popular traditions reflect these values. Correspondingly, the left-hand side is often devalued by either receiving no financial reward, or being regarded as "not as good" or ridiculed. When it comes to the bringing together of various systems we often find that other traditions embrace different value systems, and problems of bringing together systems that have previously been seen as being diametrically opposed, become apparent. We shall explore this more in the case studies below.

If we study examples quoted in Olivier Urbain's Introduction we will see how we can examine the area of musical values. The use of Wagner by Nazis (like the use of "The Ride of the Valkyries" for one advance of the helicopters in the film *Apocalypse Now*) has affected the way many people hear his music now. This is (in my opinion) an example of how extrinsic value systems are created. Yair Dalal's concert on 14 September 1994 celebrating the 1993 Oslo Accords, shows the expressive and transformative power of situations where values have been part of concert planning. The power of intention in value systems is well illustrated by the use of music in fast food restaurants and therapeutically in prisons. The nationalistic value systems of national anthems, especially those associated with imperialist cultures, throw up identity questions in a globalised world. Similarly, Beethoven's "Ode to Joy" contains many mixed identity messages for contemporary audiences and its use as a European national anthem has compounded the problem. The advent of the discipline of music therapy in the twentieth century illustrates very clearly the rise of a different value system challenging the prevailing philosophy of Romanticism of art for art's sake. These examples show that awareness of the dimension of value systems can contribute to an examination of which "musics" will lead to positive effects and which to negative ones.

The fact that the value systems are in flux/flow was reflected in some of the tensions we experienced in the gestation of this book. Some problems we encountered were around explicit and implicit value systems in music and how peace (nurture) and justice (challenge) interface in musical projects. The issue of words and their power when associated with music, whether sung or in terms of written material associated with the text (Blake 1997), illustrates the power of words enhanced by music. The third dilemma shows how the tensions within the value systems work. The tension between challenge and nurture and the flow between them raises issues of the tension between the examination of the causes of conflict and the need for the nurturing power of hope.

In music written for a particular religious tradition, we have music written in which religion and spirituality enmesh and we have already seen how the values of the surrounding culture are reflected in its music (Sullivan 1997: 9–10). But the musical experience in itself can be regarded as a spiritual/liminal experience in its own right (Boyce-Tillman 2004). I am defining Spirituality in this model as the ability to transport the audience to a different time/space dimension – to move them from everyday reality to "another world." Academic postmodernism with its mistrust of metanarratives has completed the marginalisation of this area, already started by post-Enlightenment suspicion of anything concerned with magic or belief. But the perceived effectiveness of a musical experience is often closely related to this area. Insofar as a musical experience takes us out of "everyday consciousness" with its concerns for food, clothing and practical issues and moves us into another dimension, we regard the musical experience as successful, whether we are a composer, performer or listener. Indeed, some would see music as the last remaining ubiquitous spiritual experience in a secularized Western culture (Boyce-Tillman 2001).

I have used the term "spiritual experience" within which I have subsumed the following:

- flow coming in from psychologists of creativity like Csikszentmihalyi (Csikszentmihalyi, M. and Csikszentmihalyi, I.S. 1988)
- ecstasy often associated with the idea of "the holy" coming from the religious/spiritual literature
- trance coming from anthropological, New Age and psychotherapeutic literature
- mysticism, coming from religious traditions, especially Christianity
- liminality (Turner 1969, 1974).

This last term taken from ritual is a space away from the ordinary where transformation can take place reflecting Galtung's definition of peace as "the capacity to transform conflicts with empathy, creativity and nonviolence" (Galtung 2000). The five lens model shows how to create a liminal space in which positive transformation – the active face of peace – can happen. Through understanding the importance of intrinsic and extrinsic values in music and the way they interface with the other areas of musical experience, we have pointers on how music can contribute to conflict transformation. Empathy, creativity and nonviolence can be examined through the lenses. Empathy is an important part of the expressive lens; creativity enables new constructions and new materials to be put together, as outlined in my later chapter, to embrace the value systems of conflict transformation. Nonviolence can influence all the areas, especially of expression. When these three values interplay in the five areas the negative possibilities of the values – the manipulation of creativity, the negative associations of empathy and the passive acceptance of injustice – can be avoided.

Case Studies

For the purposes of this book I shall examine the values underpinning peace making initiatives in music, for they present a variety of problems for decisions in the area of Values which have implications for all the areas of the musical experience. The experiments started in the twentieth century and worked at every level. Instruments had already been regularly imported from other cultures and continued with Debussy's entrancement with Javanese gamelan music. Expression from other cultures was often used, such as 'exotic' stories and poetry by Western composers like Gustav Holst's opera *Savitri*. Structural fusions at the level of Construction were less often attempted and little attention was given to Value systems because, as we saw above, these were not regarded as relevant to music. Spiritually they often drew on a notion of a universal philosophy expressed in music. The best known example from the middle of the century is the Beatles' "Within You Without You" on the album *Sgt. Pepper's Lonely Hearts Club Band*, a song which reflects the West's interest in Hinduism.

Case study one: the meeting of Christianity with indigenous traditions

The notion of establishing a better relationship with indigenous traditions was explored by Christian traditions from the mid-twentieth century onwards. Christianity embarked on a deliberate cross-cultural approach in its work, in what was once called the "Mission Field." It started to become aware of how along with its belief system it had exported Western culture. The first efforts to right this aspect of colonialism were in the area of music and resulted in such popular works as *Missa Criolla* and *Missa Luba*. These attempted to use the vernacular of the indigenous traditions within Christian worship.

It was a deliberate attempt at peace making with the indigenous culture. If we analyse the way it was done, in terms of Materials, these pieces use those of the indigenous tradition. Expressively, it represents a merger of the expressive character of the indigenous style and the Christian Mass. The forms are taken from the indigenous culture. These pieces had sufficient value in the West to support a tour by the group and a successful long-playing record but because of the texts they reflect the Value systems of Christianity. At the level of the Spiritual claims were made that these fusions were "religious" not just Christian. Such claims were based on the cross-cultural intentions of each originator.

Case study two: the use of recorded material in Western composition

This case study is an extension of the Christian fusions identified above. *African Sanctus* was the work of the composer/explorer David Fanshawe, who was given the Winston Churchill Scholarship in 1972 to collect the tapes that form the African elements in the piece. It too had the intention of merging Western with African traditions:

> *African Sanctus* attempts to fuse different peoples and their music into a tightly knit unit of energy and praise. It reflects the changing moods of music today and I hope moves with the times, for we are all living and sharing life together on a very small planet . . . I hope *African Sanctus* will stimulate and inform both listener and performer and that the total sound will reflect the music and people of Africa. What others have said in words, I have tried to say in music.
>
> (Fanshawe 1963, Sleeve notes)

At the level of Materials the work uses tapes of African singers and players alongside rock and classical instruments from the West. The Expression mixes the characters of the various African traditions, the Christian Mass with that of opera and commercial music. The forms reflect the interplay of the African tapes with the Western forms of David Fanshawe's own tradition. They are fitted into Western shapes and structures. The recipient of the royalties was David Fanshawe. Although it is clear from his book (Fanshawe 1975) that the African performers gave permission for their pieces to be used and that he treated them with respect and friendship, there is no record of any of the royalties being given to them. (This is in marked contrast to systems being developed by ethnomusicologists.) Indeed, Western notions of ownership of music are in direct conflict with the collective ownership that characterizes such notions in the societies from which he collected the material. There is a notion of Spirituality in the composer's intentions which relate to praise of the "One God." This is very much within the frame of monotheistic religions which would have shaped Fanshawe's own thinking. The work clearly fits into a long-standing Western colonial tradition.

But the use of tape for such "borrowings" is a new phenomenon and differ-ent from the integration into one's personal style of elements of other cultures. For many audiences and performers, however, Fanshawe's work has repre-sented a valid fusing of various traditions in the interests of world peace. Whether, however, at the level of Value it represents a valuing of both traditions equally, is highly debatable and this presents considerable ethical problems. The capacity to collect the material on tape sets it apart from both "Missa Luba" which required a live tour for the performers, or the Beatles' song where the elements were fused musically into the structure.

Case study three: Paul Simon and Graceland

In the area of popular "musics" the fusions have sometimes been linked with a deliberate concern for justice. Paul Simon in his recording of *Graceland* in the more folk/popular tradition had the explicit intention of justice within the context of apartheid in South Africa. Again African performers are used along-side the resources of Western popular music. The texts are newly constructed and they have more of the character of Western commercial traditions which within themselves have elements of the African traditions that passed via jazz into Western popular music. The fusion is therefore not so complex as in Western classical works whose roots are more from the classical Graeco-Roman traditions. Paul Simon describes how working with the African musicians affected the structure of his songs:

> In the process of working, I discovered ways of turning the form around, from constantly listening to the way African guitarists and the bass players were alter-ing what they were playing from verse to verse. *Graceland* is like that, because choruses didn't have to always be the same. They could repeat, they could use material from a verse, they could introduce some new lyric idea and retain ele-ments from one chorus to the next.

> (Simon 1994: 11)

Some of the royalties were channeled back to the South African Musicians Alliance so the level of Value was shared. The recording certainly helped the valuing in the West of lesser-known traditions of South Africa.

Case study four: the meeting of orality and literacy

In the figure showing subjugated value systems we saw how Western societies value products above process (often using unethical processes in the interest of cheaper products). Indigenous traditions are often orate (with no notation systems). This led to different structural systems. The discovery of the evolving nature of the musical structure of traditional "musics" has been an important contribution that traditional "musics" have made to Western classical and popular music. Judith Vander, working on the songs of the Shoshone Indians, saw the songs as characterised by inexact repetition (Vander 1986).

Terry Riley, father of minimalism, described his meeting with more improvisatory musical structures, which he found through his contact with eastern "musics": "In the last ten years I have given up the traditional role of the composer in favour of self-interpretative improvisation" (Riley 1978: 144).

His work "Morning River" for Francis Silkstone's multicultural ensemble "Sounds Bazaar" illustrates this clearly (Riley 1999). At the level of Materials it often uses voices of various kinds (including vocalisations), and instruments such as cello, keyboard and surbahar. The form unfolds freely and meditatively, reflecting the intention of much of Riley's work. Small motifs unfold slowly in a notated form that resembles improvisation. It uses scales from other traditions, particularly on the surbahar. The piece was commissioned by "Sounds Bazaar" to which the Norwich Festival contributed. Notions of a "universal spirituality" underpin much of Riley's thinking and the texts are deliberately about questions of meaning rather than the giving of definitive answers.

This case study shows a genuine attempt at fusing value systems, which is very different from the inclusion of indigenous instruments from orate traditions (played by Western musicians) within notated pieces where they have to be accommodated to the structures of Western music.

Case study five: the development of WOMAD

One high profile example of intercultural work in music is Peter Gabriel's development of the Real World Records label and the WOMAD (World of Music, Arts and Dance) organization specifically to bring together musicians from all over the world. Started in 1980, it had its first festival in 1982 with this intention: "We aim to excite, to inform, and to create awareness of the worth and potential of a multicultural society" (Gabriel 2000).

By bringing together so many different musicians, exciting fusion pieces occur. These are released on the Real World Records label and issues of value are carefully addressed. The work of Peter Gabriel and WOMAD represents a real attempt at methods of fusion that reflect ethical value systems. This is achieved by doing it with live representatives of the various cultures and remunerating them for their work.

Conclusion

This chapter has set out a model of five lenses for examining the musical experience. It has shown how these areas interact powerfully with one another so that if there is a change within the area of Values, all the other areas, such as the Materials used and the meaning that is given to them, the structural principles of the music and notions of Spirituality will be affected. It has used this lens as a way of examining ethical issues in various cross cultural contexts. More of these will be looked at in my later chapter.

References

Blake, A. (1997) *The Land without Music: Music Culture and Society in Twentieth-Century Britain*, Manchester: Manchester University Press.

Boyce-Tillman, J. (2005) "Subjugated ways of knowing," in C. Clarke (2005) *Ways of Knowing*, London: Imprint Academic.

Boyce-Tillman, J. (2004) "Music as spiritual experience," keynote address for conference of the Alister Hardy Society and The Modern Church Person's Union.

Boyce-Tillman, J (2001) "Sounding the sacred: music as sacred site," in Ralls-MacLeod, Karen and Harvey (ed.) *Indigenous Religious Musics*, Farnborough: Scolar.

Boyce-Tillman, J. (2000) *Constructing Musical Healing: The Wounds that Sing*, London: Jessica Kingsley.

Boyce-Tillman, J. (1996) "A framework for intercultural dialogue in music," in Malcolm Floyd (ed.) (1996) *World Musics in Education*, Farnborough: Scolar.

Csikszentmihalyi, M. and Csikszentmihalyi, I.S. (1988) *Optimal Experience. Psychological Studies of Flow in Consciousness*, Cambridge: Cambridge University Press.

Fanshawe, D. (1975) *African Sanctus*, London: Collins.

Fanshawe, D. (1963) *African Sanctus* (CD sleeve notes 6558 001), Philips label.

Foucault, M. (1980) *Power/Knowledge: Selected Interviews and Other Writings 1972–77*, Hemel Hempstead: Harvester Wheatsheaf.

Gabriel, P. (2000) http://realworld.on.net

Galtung, J. (2000) Telephone conversation with Olivier Urbain.

Goehr, L. (1992) *The Imaginary Museum of Musical Works: An Essay in the Philosophy of Music*, Oxford: Clarendon Press.

Gooch, S. (1972), *Total Man: Notes Towards an Evolutionary Theory of Personality*, London: Allen Lane, Penguin Press.

Green, L. (1997) *Music, Gender, Education*, Cambridge: Cambridge University Press.

Green, L. (1988) *Music on Deaf Ears: Musical Meaning, Ideology and Education*, Manchester and New York: Manchester University Press.

Langer, S. (1982) *Feeling and Form: A Theory of Art*, London: Routledge and Kegan Paul.

McClary, S. (1991, 2001) *Feminine Endings: Music, Gender and Sexuality*, Minneapolis: University of Minnesota Press.

Ong, W. (1982) *Orality and Literacy: The Technologizing of the Word*, London and New York: Methuen.

Rahn, J. (1994) "What is valuable in art, and can music still achieve it?" in John Rahn (ed.) *Perspectives in Musical Aesthetics*, New York: Norton.

Riley, T. (1999) "Morning River," Unpublished Score.

Ring Frank, J. (2003) Unpublished conversation with author, Boston, Massachusetts, USA.

Shepherd, J. and Wicke, P. (1997) *Music and Cultural Theory*, Cambridge: Polity Press.

Simon, P. (1994) quoted in T. White, *Lasers in the Jungle: the Conception and Maturity of a Musical Masterpiece* (CD 9 46430–2), Warner Brothers.

Sullivan, L.E. (1997) *Enchanting Powers: Music in the World's Religions*, Harvard: Harvard University Press.

Turner, V. (1982) *From Ritual to Theatre: The Human Seriousness of Play*, New York: Performing Arts Journal Publications.

Turner, V. (1969, 1974) *The Ritual Process: Structure and Anti-Structure*, Baltimore: Penguin Books.

Vander, J. (1986) *Ghost Dance Songs and Religion of a Wind River Shoshone Woman*, Monograph Series in Ethnomusicology, Number 4, Los Angeles: University of California.

Chapter 4: Peace, Music and the Arts: In Search of Interconnections

Johan Galtung

Some time ago a Norwegian art gallery, Galleri Lista Fyr in Lindesnes, at the southern tip of Norway, put on an art exhibition. The name was FOLK-05 local global ("folk" means people), and the aim was to "communicate and understand people through visual arts." More than 20 artists from seven countries participated with various efforts to bring art to the people.

I was asked to write the preface to the catalogue. A strong believer in correspondence between form and content I decided to try my hand at a poem; it somehow flowed naturally as I started writing. Here it is, in Norwegian and English (you may find the Norwegian version more convincing. . .):

ART AND PEACE

Let us be lifted by the arts
like the artists have lifted them
upwards, outwards, beyond the ordinary
beyond the run of the mill;
making us see far
beyond borders and cleavages
in our untidy human landscape
into other eyes that
also have been lifted
beyond the ordinary
to be united
in peace.

KUNST OG FRED

La oss loeftes av kunsten
som kunstnerne har loeftet den
oppover, utover det vanlige
utover hverdagen
slik at vi kan skue langt
utover grenser og kloefter
i vart uryddige menneskelandskap
inn i andre oeyne som
ogsa er blitt loeftet
utover det vanlige
for a forenes
i fred.

There are three ideas here. So let me start deconstructing my own micro-art, using techniques of intellectual commentary.

Firstly there is the thesis that art can lift us up, beyond the ordinary. Art may make us forget the ordinary, catapulting us for some time to a virtual, more spiritual level where we meet a pure, more detached reality, a form in space (visual art, sculpture) and/or time (music, literature), detached from empirical reality. This thesis sounds plausible.

Secondly there is the idea that this uplifting may unite us. There is some plausibility to this too. We are uprooted by good, touching, engaging art from our here and now, with all its pain and pleasure, into the world of the artist who fills us with some of his or her form and content, thereby unifying us, making us one in the art. Like in Christ or Allah, which is why some religions insist that art should be religious, wanting it to reinforce unity in Christ rather than a secular art establishing alternative foci for unity crystallization – or no art at all. Art is power.

Thirdly the thesis that such unity will be conducive to peace. Of course, the micro-artist in me stands for what he wrote. And of course the macro-social scientist in me, in casu peace researcher, would like to contextualize in all kinds of ways. So, here we go, relativizing the three theses to various contexts.

Uplifting Music

There is no doubt that art is uprooting, but uplifting is another matter. In a very specific context like music therapy, uplifting might be an explicit goal, as Maria Elena López Vinader shows in her chapter. There is military music which is pompous and good for marching and killing, e.g. US soldiers' chanting "trained to kill, and kill we will." When I was a young boy, German soldiers marched past our windows in occupied Norway singing an incredibly heart-warming tune, with lyrics by Horst Wessel, a Nazi hero. Since I could not understand the words at all, I felt that these soldiers could not be that bad. Sometimes the fact that the lyrics are incomprehensible can be used as a tool for resistance, as Anne-Marie Gray shows in her chapter.

Art uproots us into a virtual reality. Words that come to many people's minds when they try to describe how they feel, are "floating," "oceanic," "eternal," "endless," "I wish this feeling could last forever" – some type of *kairos*. Time in the standard sense of *khronos* is suspended, and space is irrelevant because the viewer/listener/reader is encapsulated in the art, the virtual space provided by the artists. Other words for "lifted" is touched, moved – taken into that virtual space because something has touched our soul and moved it on. This is probably how Yair Dalal can touch people from all parts of the Middle East with his music, as described in the chapter about his work.

And then this may not happen at all. We sit through a concert, walk through an art gallery, read a book – yet nothing touches our soul, nothing moves us. Is there something wrong with us? With the artist? Or the art product? Or, possibly a better angle, with the relation? Not the right art for me-here-now? To say honestly "it did not touch me" seems as much a human right as the right to have access to that moving, uprooting, uplifting experience.

Crucial for what we are exploring here is whether this type of uprooting into another existence does take place. But even so there are some rather important questions that need to be addressed.

Firstly art is not alone in having this effect. The religious experience is similar. So is any creative experience like that of the artist and the scientist, and that of the more ordinary, daily kind, like bringing cosmos out of the chaos of an untidy household, fixing the agenda problems of the day, in other words furnishing time adequately, cooking a well composed meal and consuming that meal. And, of course those famous conveyor belts into virtual reality, alcohol and drugs, which do not require any effort or talent. What is wrong about them, apart from addiction? Precisely that, they do not uplift and sustain us through our own efforts, but may pull us down and crush us.

Secondly the uplifting may be of a very short duration. We have compared it above to intoxication, so it may be better this way. There are passages in Mozart's Piano Concerto No. 20 and Bach's *St Matthew Passion* that drive me out of my mind. For sure I should not be driving in that altered state. However, there is no law against it. In his chapter, Vegar Jordanger shows us how short-term "collective vulnerability" can be triggered by music and used effectively in conflict transformation sessions.

We could interpret uplifting differently, not as an instant rapture but as a gradual step-by-step process that makes us party to the sublime, yet within sight of the ordinary, the run of the mill. Like gradually becoming more educated, as June Boyce-Tillman shows in her chapter on music and value. So much for uplifting.

Music and Unity

Let us then expose the unity hypothesis to the same treatment. Yes, we all know it, sharing great art in a concert, the theater and the art gallery creates a sense of belonging to some unity. We share the body language of others partaking in the same experience and note reactions similar to our own. We sense communality.

But so do people listening to a raving demagogue, ranting at high decibel levels his necrophilic content into ugly forms; whether on top of democracy or dictatorship. The structure of that unity may be vertical, "we are all united in . . .," meaning in his "union." But there is also a horizontal unity like the one produced, however unconsciously and subtly, by talking the same language, producing a greater self beyond little me alone. Very different from listening to a foreign tongue, with accompanying Other – production: how different they are, these "bar-bar-ians."

There is something "vertical," establishing an automatic hierarchy, in any art produced by an individual artist infused with and inspired by some talent we ordinary mortals do not possess. If his name is "Anonymous," like the composer of a very catchy tune, it may help a little but not much. If it is "popular art," emerging from nowhere and no place in particular, we may sense "horizontality," a sense of belonging to a community of equals, as a very useful illusion.

Does it really matter? Difficult to say. Art is not only form and structure, but also content and culture. The sticking point is that unity-creation by art may also serve as a training in verticality, giving in, submitting, even succumbing to the signal from above. That signal may be peace, but may also be the opposite, as George Kent shows in his chapter.

The "Fyr" in the Norwegian gallery in the introduction means lighthouse. This is a fine metaphor for guidance in highly "untidy" seascapes, waters, away from reefs and shallows, into the tranquil waters of safe anchorage. But, as is well known, many a ship was stranded by the lures of a fake lighthouse, mounted by pirates who then practiced their craft, well trained in killing and pillage.

Music and Peace

Of course, war – collective violence organized by zero, one, two or more governments – is also based on unity, mainly of the vertical kind when governments are involved. But the horizontal unity of a guerrilla-resistance insurgency movement isn't peaceful either, and they may, like a peace movement marching, for hours, days, and weeks, be moved by music, poetry, literature, and a love of nature and culture. Is an intermediate phase of resistance necessary on the way from violence to peace? Karen Abi-Ezzi explores this question in her chapter.

Being immersed in the same language does not guarantee peace either, and the same applies to culture in general in all its ramifications. It depends on which culture. If conflict solution and non-violence are major cultural elements, then maybe yes, if not then maybe rather no (the word resolution is avoided on purpose because it sounds too final for these kinds of long-term processes). Love and sex and marriage are certainly forms of unity. And yet, national unity, like in the case of the war that tore apart former Yugoslavia, may prove even stronger, driving wedges between men and women, parents and children, because their identities as Bosniaks, Serbs or Croats had become central. Christmas carols unite families, and national anthems unite nations, maybe for peace within. But do they unify for peace beyond conflict borders? Cynthia Cohen explores this paradox in her chapter.

Being myself a producer of words assembled into essays and books, I may be inclined to believe in verbal messages as a necessary condition to go beyond borders. There has to be a text somewhere with a clear message, maybe even of the "who should do what, when, where, how and why" variety, for peace to follow. A text, not a sub-, super-, deep text or context, just a text. There may be a context of music or art. But it strikes me that Gandhi, Martin Luther King Jr. and Mandela–de Klerk–Tutu communicated with words, well crafted, but still words. They did not sing them, even if a context of music and/or religious symbolism were present.

However, standing up for the word does not mean any rejection of music. I would only like to know more about what music does to us if/when it generates peace. So let me give you an example:

Imagine four very dedicated musicians, A, B, C and D, all with very strong egos. Two play African instruments, say the djembe and the barimbau, and two play European instruments, say, the piano and alto sax. They are invited to perform for an hour at a conference dedicated to peace.

What happens then is not very promising: they all insist on performing alone, shining alone. You can only get me performing alone, in the context of nobody else. Four possible outcomes of sheer prevalence, with any one of them ruling the ground alone.

Imagine the organizers stand firm and reject any solo performance. We may then have four musicians sulking, their egos wounded, each individually or collectively announcing their non-availability for that occasion.

But some organizer may come up with the lower form of conflict transformation, the compromise. We give you fifteen minutes each, you cannot have the whole hour for yourself, but wouldn't 15 minutes still be better than no minutes at all?

The reader has already created the far better solution in his or her mind: the quartet! All four get one hour to shine, but not as monopoly, alone, literally speaking in concert, thereby creating more than the sum of soloisms, that alpha on top of both A and B and C and D. And the result is an astounding extra alpha, even intercultural, in the composition. Kjell Skyllstad describes this phenomenon in his chapter on conflict transformation.

What have we got here? The process of conflict transformation by positive transcendence, neither prevalence, nor withdrawal from the whole performance, nor a stingy compromise unsatisfactory to all, but something new, beyond, transcending the conflict between them.

This is beyond words alone. This is peace through art by way of isomorphism and structural identity. The art lies in being peace rather than just expressing and verbalizing peace. Make an orchestra, and have musicians from many points in "our untidy human landscape" create together, Iraqis, Americans/Britons/Australians, Palestinians and Israelis and so on. Together they can produce a creative structure, not the destruction made by their governments.

So, where are we now? Uplifted, yes; united, yes. But the potential for peace is not necessarily in the music or in any accompanying text, but in the structure of the performance. Of course that structure of peace as something both cooperative and creative becomes even more compelling when empirically contrasted with the three alternatives of prevalence, withdrawal and compromise. But maybe we sense them in their poverty even if they are not there? In the quartet or the symphony there is that jump into a new reality which is more than the sum of the parts. And the argument would be that the kind of conflict solution that is peacebuilding, as opposed to merely conflict settlement, has exactly that quality. And there is the hypothesis that we sense this without having to be told.

But creativity is also in any piece of art. The artist is always creating a new reality. When s/he is only repeating his/her old reality, s/he is, in a sense, a decorator with words, tunes or color. Creativity is to art what innovation is to the engineer. Of course we can build on what has already been created or invented. However, somewhere, past, present or future there has to be that jump.

For peace to come about, we must add empathy and nonviolence. Those two crucial human qualities are the central themes of Felicity Laurence and Rik Palieri's chapters, respectively. For the composer or performing musician, empathy with the instrument, the performer and the audience, is of key significance. And, when we go beyond solo performance, empathy with the other performers, tuning souls and spirits to each other is like tuning their instruments before starting. Like for peace, the more demanding the greater the spiritual span between them.

How about nonviolence? A word comes to our musical attention: soothing, the kind of music we might like to accompany acupuncture, surgery, dentistry. Gregorian chant or Oriental music, undulating, no beginning, no climax, no end. Lullabies are often made that way.

This may put agitated minds to rest for some time. But, isn't it peace in the sense of pacifying? Maybe, yes. And maybe that kind of music is only a part of the message. Maybe a more complete message is found in the A-B-A of a classical sonata, quiet-storm-quiet; or in the four movements of a classical symphony, ending with a harmonious solution in the fourth movement, to the tensions suggested in the first movement, the quiet of the andante of the second, and the storm of the third. *Durch Leiden zur Licht*, "through suffering to light," was Beethoven's motto. Isn't that exactly what struggle, not fighting, for peace is about?

So again we arrive at isomorphism, this time with structure over time, as the answer to the search for interconnections.

And at that point we may even be close to the conclusion that there is more peace in music than in that much-heralded carrier of the word called literature. Aristotle launched us on a most unfortunate track with his famous distinction between tragedy and comedy. Also known for his *tertium non datur*, "there is no third possibility," we have been led to believe that these are the only forms of literary expression. Either an unhappy or bad ending, or something comical or laughable. We sense our media in that, how they distort reality by pressing it into these two forms only: violence journalism, something negative, sad, bad, or pure entertainment.

But what is the alternative? Wouldn't that be a happy, "Hollywood" ending? Not at all. Learn from Beethoven again, and maybe particularly from some of his quartets. Striving, and struggling exactly to obtain that reality where harmony is nevertheless possible, in a musical sense of ending on the tonic, a good metaphor for efforts towards peace that end conflict processes with a positive transcendence. There is a sense of release, which may also produce the needed recovery and rebuilding for the next problem or even conflict. Music that does not provide this sense is hardly peace-productive music.

But back to literature. Authors like Han Yin and Bernard Malamud have written moving novels where the actors live through enormous problems and conflicts in highly untidy landscapes and yet work it out in the end, giving them and also the reader a deep sense of elevation and strength. They transcend their problems. Not tragedy, not comedy either. "Transcendy?" So badly needed in the media, where we need a good balance between positive news, some light in all the darkness, while still not avoiding to report suffering.

Upifting, yes. Uniting, yes. But the step to peace does not come by itself. It has to be thought, felt and worked out. And that will always be tremendously helpful in our struggle for peace.

The brilliant Japanese scientist and peace activist Professor Ikuro Anzai is also a haiku master. In the 33rd haiku collection dedicated to the A-bomb Day Memorial in 1999 we read:

> Where a man sat
> a dark stain now
> and it will never go away

> (Translation by Francis Gallagher, Scotland)

The dreadful description of the effects of weapons that kill by evaporating live human beings comes to us in the quiet, harmonious form of the haiku. We could imagine equally quiet, harmonious music as subtext or context, and some soft colored background strokes with a soft brush. But the words are precise and effective, and, carefully chosen among all the words we could put into that context, their brevity actually contradicts the immensity of the horror of the context.

And maybe that is the point? Maybe that in harmony there also has to be some dissonance? Peace no doubt includes equity and mutual care. But there also has to be an element of disharmony in the harmony, of contradiction in the transformation of conflict. Peace is life, and as the Chinese saying goes: "the only contradiction-free human being is a dead human being." Something needs to be left unresolved. Good art is like good peace: always challenging.

Art and peace are both located in the tension between emotions and intellect. Another false dichotomy. Any good, deep intellectual construction gives a deep emotional satisfaction, and in the most emotionally touching piece of art there is architecture in the hidden plan, of the novel, the symphony, the painting, the sculpture. Life unites what concepts and dualisms keep apart. And art, like peace, has to overcome such false dichotomies by speaking both to the heart and to the brain, to the compassion of the heart and constructions of the brain.

Maybe that is where art and peace really find each other and interconnect most deeply: they both address both human faculties.

PART II

Politics

Chapter 5: Music as a Tool of Reconciliation in South Africa

Anne-Marie Gray

Introduction

After the ban imposed on the African National Congress (ANC) was lifted in 1990 an Interim Constitution was set in place to guide South Africa to its first democratic elections. During discussions it became clear that the country's past had to be dealt with in order to negotiate a common future.

In 1995 the Truth and Reconciliation Commission (TRC) was established. Amongst other things this was a forum for allowing perpetrator and victim to face each other and create understanding. Despite the important role played by the TRC there have been many calls to address the past for true reconciliation. This was stressed by Alex Boraine, co-chairperson of the TRC: "Dealing with the past is not dwelling in the past – it is part of the promise of the future." This chapter argues for the use of music for understanding South African history and highlighting group identity, which could lead to reconciliation. The words of Antjie Krog, the well-known white Afrikaans South African poet, express the role music can play in this process:

> And I wade into song – in a language that is not mine, in a tongue I do not know.
> It is fragrant inside the song, and among the keynotes of song and suffering there are soft silences where we who belong, all of us, can come to rest.
>
> (Krog 2002: 217)

Polarized Societies in South Africa

Before democracy, twentieth century polarized societies consisted of the predominantly black society on the one hand and whites on the other. In order to bring about reconciliation it was necessary that these societies understand each other's identity through experiences they had to face. Historical facts alone can not supply the necessary insight into group identity as dates fix peoples' lives in cycles of victories and defeats while overlooking the details of suffering, emotions, setbacks and successes of ordinary people. Added to this impediment is the fact that South African history books before 1994 were very selective, where every effort was made to turn history into propaganda for the white ruling party.

This chapter thus argues that music can function as a bridge between the past and reconciliation. It allows for the understanding of a society in terms of its own interpretations of reality, in a way that historical facts alone do not allow. This is mainly due to the fact that affect and meaning through music are derived from the social, historical and cultural contexts in which the music is situated.

With regard to the identity and experiential world of black South Africans, music is one of the most important tools for creating an authentic picture of the past. This is mainly due to the fact that music rather than politics provided a voice for black South Africans until the 1990s because there were no other channels open to protest. Steve Biko, the black activist who died in detention, spoke about the fact that any suffering experienced was made more real by song and rhythm and "is responsible for the restoration of our faith in ourselves and offers a hope in the direction we are taking from here" (Biko 1978: 60). The well-known black singer, Miriam Makeba, stated: "In our struggle, songs are not simply entertainment for us. They are the way we communicate. The press, radio and TV are all censored by the Government. We cannot believe what they say. So we make up songs to tell us about events" (Makeba 1988: Record cover). These songs were also a barometer of the mood of black South Africans and if they are to be used as a tool for reconciliation, it is the styles of the songs that should be illuminated so that white South Africans can comprehend the identity and emotions of the people singing them.

A familiarity with the roots of all South African societies is, however, needed for contributing towards reconciliation. It is therefore necessary that a tool be found which will allow black South Africans to also gain an insight into the experiential world of white South Africans before 1994. This chapter advocates for music to be used as the tool needed to conceptualize the experience of white as well as black South Africans. Through music black South Africans can learn about the identity of their perceived oppressor because it is a medium of expression which is very much part of the black culture. While black South Africans used music to mirror socio-political conditions and the contours of black thought before 1994, the music of white South Africans is as important for reconciliation because through it much historical knowledge, insight and perspective can be gained.

Although music played a different role for these polarized societies it still tells the story of a shared past. This was demonstrated at a concert called the "South Africa Love Workshop," which attempted to bridge seemingly gaping differences between white and black South Africans. Sibongile Khumalo, a well-known Zulu contralto performer, was asked to sing "My Sarie Marais," an Afrikaans folk song that originated during the Anglo-Boer War. Despite the fact that she has an ardent commitment to black South African identity Khumalo sang the song and "there was a very excited reaction from the audience who clapped and sang along and who clearly found this song and others to be an unexpectedly powerful cathartic experience for the participants and audience" (Vinassa 1993: 50). According to Khumalo:

> Once I was familiar with the origin of the song, I became aware of the similarities of the black experience to the emotions expressed by the songwriter of "My Sarie Marais," about his oppression at the hands of the English. He was fighting for his motherland. History has been so distorted that these things come as a revelation.
>
> (ibid.)

In order to demonstrate the role of music, some excerpts of songs will be given. The music of black South Africans will highlight modifications in style due to changing socio-political conditions. The central focus of their music from 1900 until 1994 will be seen to reflect oppression by white South Africans. With regard to white South Africans, music will be selected which highlights important historical facts in order to respond to the need to assess insight and understanding into the psyche of white South Africans for the purpose of using music as a tool for reconciliation.

Music of Black South Africans

In South Africa since the beginning of the twentieth century there were four main styles of liberation songs. There was *iMusic*, which were hymn-like songs; *iRagtime*, which were syncopated songs based on ragtime; songs with indigenous music elements and finally, the *Toyi-toyi* and liberation chant which from the 1980s replaced the singing of liberation songs and were used when demonstrations became more militant. The words *iMusic* and *iRagtime* are written in *isiZulu*, the Zulu language. Indigenous cultures in South Africa often add the *i* to an English word to make it authentic in their own culture.

iMusic

It was at the Ohlange Institute, a private college outside Durban, that *iMusic* protest music was mostly composed and sung. The institution was founded in 1901 by Dr John Dube, who became the first President of the South African National Native Congress (SANNC) in 1912. It was the first African-run and African-funded school, mainly for the children of the educated Zulu landowners (*amakholwe*), who had almost all been exposed to Christian mission education. This education greatly influenced their thinking and explains why up until 1914, the prevailing category of music that symbolized the identification with Christian values, was *iMusic*. It was the least politically overt musical style as it was essentially grounded in European and American church music.

In 1912 the SANNC was founded. It was the first nationwide umbrella black South African political organization and was the forerunner of the African National Congress (ANC). It consisted mainly of black elite who were products of English-medium mission schools. With Dube as President of the SANNC and principal of Ohlange, all staff and students were kept informed about conditions facing black South Africans and the school became a fertile environment for the composition of protest songs. From 1912 Reuban Caluza, a pupil and later a teacher at the Ohlange Institute, composed many songs to highlight the frustrations felt by black South Africans as they were faced with more and more restrictive measures. Caluza's songs kept blacks throughout the country informed through regular countrywide choir tours by the Ohlange Institute Choir. Tours by black performance groups in South Africa were unheard of and it can be assumed that because Caluza's protest songs in the *iMusic* style sounded like hymns sung in the Christian Church embodying the praise of God, white government officials who did not understand Zulu were unaware that they were protest songs and allowed the tours. White South Africans only heard these songs after 1990 when recordings of songs which had previously been banned became available.

To show how music was used during this period, excerpts of the lyrics of two of the songs will be given. The imposition of the Natives Land Act of 1913 was the first problem that the SANNC had to deal with. This Act laid down the basic guidelines for land division in South Africa, and the blacks were left with about approximately 13 percent of the country's total area. Caluza's direct response to the Land Act was "Umteto we Land Act," which was adopted as the official anthem of the SANNC. Excerpts from the song which had Zulu lyrics, read as follows:

We are mad over the Land Act
A terrible law that allows sojourners
To deny us our land
Crying that we the people
Should pay to get our land back
We cry for the children of our fathers
Who roam around the world without a home
Even in the land of our forefathers.

Another Zulu song "Bashuka Ndabazini?"("What is Congress Saying?"), speaks about Dube going to negotiate with the British to try and improve conditions for the blacks. The song lists grievances and refers to the fact that all blacks had to carry a type of identity book (*dompass*) which white South Africans were exempted from. Caluza ends the song with the words:

We are not even allowed a representative in Parliament
We want a black man to negotiate on our own behalf
What are we going to do as Africans?
Let us stick together like cement
We wish you well Mafukuzela (Dube)
Please ask about the demanding laws for us.

(Translations by Callinicos 1987: 112)

The hymn "Nkosi Sikele iAfrica" ("God bless Africa"), composed in Xhosa by Enoch Sontonga, was also in *iMusic* style. It replaced the Land Act anthem of the SANNC in 1919. It had the additional symbolic meaning of the struggle for democracy in South Africa and was often sung with a clenched fist with the thumb pointing over the shoulder. It thus moved away from being sung as a prayer to being a liberation song with more militant connotations. Whites, not understanding Xhosa, were often afraid when they heard the song, and many blacks were arrested during apartheid for singing it. Today this hymn forms part of the South African National Anthem. The Ohlange Choir played an important role in popularizing the hymn.

It soon became clear that Caluza, who remained the main composer of liberation songs until the 1920s, felt that *iMusic* lacked the qualities that were needed to satisfactorily express the growing resistance to declining black autonomy and deteriorating class privileges. He began composing in *iRagtime*, an example of Afro-American music, which he felt was more compatible with Zulu speech patterns as well as having ethnic components which rural black as well as those with mission education could identify with.

iRagtime

By the beginning of the twentieth century Afro-American ideas of self-advancement had become powerful alternatives to colonial ideology and major forces in the intellectual climate of the black society. Black South Africans first gained experience of Afro-American culture and ragtime through the visits of Orpheus McAdoo and his Jubilee Singers between 1891 and 1898. They performed blackface minstrelsy, which consisted of an exploitation of the slaves' style of dancing and music by white men who blackened their faces with burnt cork. Despite the fact that the performances were by whites, the music was the first representation in South Africa of black living conditions in the United States. The admiration for Afro-American values was especially high at Ohlange Institute. This was the result of concrete historical contact and similar experiences of racial discrimination between South African blacks and Afro-Americans. It is thus not surprising that Caluza's liberation and protest music shifted from the *iMusic* category to *iRagtime*.

iRagtime lyrics in Zulu continued to mirror socio-political conditions and the contours of black thought. The song "Idipu e Tekwini" ("Dipping in Durban") focuses on one of the most dehumanizing treatments that blacks seeking work in Durban had to face. They had to undergo "deverminisation" in "dipping tanks," allegedly for the sake of public hygiene. Excerpts from the lyrics articulate their discontent:

> What are you people in Durban saying about dipping?
> What is chasing people away from Durban?
> You fellow countrymen, long live the black nation.
> Talk on our behalf Mafukuzela! (John Dube).
>
> (*Caluza's Double Quartet 1930*, Compact disc cover)

Excerpts from another song "Si xotshwa emsebenzini" ("We are being expelled from work") tell about the Industrial Conciliation Act of 1924 which threatened the positions held by black professionals:

> A serious problem is facing the black nation.
> Whites are expelling us from work.
> They only employ whites
> We have been working for them for many years, without any problems.
> But now blacks are excluded from work.
>
> (Erlmann 1991: 133)

As the situation for blacks became progressively worse the black elite came to the realization that they would have to forge links with the wider African society. This resulted in a resurgence of ethnic pride, in opposition to what was perceived as white racism.

Songs with indigenous musical elements

From 1940 the ANC began injecting new life into the organization by making concerted efforts to get more support from the masses (Davenport 1987: 345). This resurgence of ethnic pride saw the entrenchment of authentic African musical elements in the liberation songs, indicating a rejection of white domination. Some of the elements found in this oral mode of singing are repetition, call and response (antiphonal) and cyclical and rhythmic patterns which invite the body to move. Indigenous music is mostly orally passed on from generation to generation with words changing to suit the situation. This oral tradition facilitated the intensification of the struggle as it allowed for political groups to assemble on an *ad hoc* basis to complain, recount and educate their members through song while using extant melodies with words to suit the situation.

There seemed to be a growing conviction that overt political confrontation was the only way in which blacks could hope to reform the South African social and political order. From the 1950s to 1994 the liberation struggle intensified and the songs encouraged this intensification by becoming more militant. This militant viewpoint was clearly supported by a new generation of ANC members who constituted a major pressure group within the ANC itself, the Congress Youth League (CYL). Among the leaders were Walter Sisulu, Oliver Tambo, Nelson Mandela and Robert Sobukwe. Many songs were sung about these leaders and their subsequent imprisonment on Robben Island. Often the names of other leaders were inserted for different verses.

After 1950 it became easier to trace the history of apartheid through the songs which became shorter and more numerous. The composers of the songs are mostly unknown as they were spontaneously articulated in response to a situation. The name of Vuyisile Mini, secretary of the Dock Workers Union of Port Elizabeth, is mentioned although it is not clear which songs he composed. Considered an activist, he was executed in 1964 and thrown into a pauper's grave amidst an avalanche of worldwide protest. A song definitely attributed to Mini was "Izakunyathel'I Africa", composed in prison in 1956 while awaiting trial on charges of high treason (Hooper 1965: Record cover). It was aimed at Hendrik Verwoerd, Minister of Native Affairs in the early 1950s and already

the brain behind the government's Grand Apartheid Policy. Excerpts from the
translation read as follows:

> Africa is going to trample on you, Verwoerd.
> Verwoerd! Shoot . . .
> You are going to get hurt.
> Verwoerd, watch out.
>
> (Hooper 1965: Record)

In 1963 the police arrested prominent members of *MK*, the military wing of
the ANC. The police claimed they had evidence that this organization was
implementing a large-scale military operation codenamed *Mayibuye* (restoring,
giving back). Nelson Mandela conducted his own defense, in which he pointed
out that the ANC needed to take more drastic action because fifty years of non-
violent resistance had merely resulted in more oppressive laws and fewer rights
for blacks (Motlhabi 1985: 68). Five of the ten accused, including Mandela,
were sentenced to life imprisonment and eventually sent to Robben Island.
The song "Tshotsholoza Mandela" mirrors political developments during this
time and also sums up the mood of black South Africans at Mandela's arrest.

> In went the leaders all over the country.
> Bundled into jails without a just cause.
> Verwoerd cautioned his people in Pretoria
> And said things were hot
> The reason?
> Mandela.
>
> (Hooper 1965: Record)

Songs sung from the 1950s can be equated to what George Kent speaks of as
insurrectionary music in his chapter. He describes this music as music which
challenges, through its contrast, the music of those who dominate (in the South
African situation, the white government). As the liberation struggle intensified
the *toyi-toyi* and liberation chant or slogan became popular.

Toyi-toyi and Liberation Chant

The *toyi-toyi* is a type of march where the knees are lifted very high and was
explained by Dali Tambo, the son of Oliver Tambo, in the following way:

> Today it is very politicised but it is very deeply cultural . . . [T]he motion, the
> energy that is expanded brings people together, it brings that feeling of society . . .
> it brings out the courage in the people taking part in the *toyi-toyi* . . . it is a cultural

form of expression and somehow intimidates the policemen . . . it is used as a weapon against apartheid.

(ANC Choir [s.a.] Video).

Chanted slogans have always been used in South Africa to give inspiration to those involved in resistance against the state. The chant is a spoken declamation where pitch movement is conditioned by the words. The chant became very popular during the 1980s and often replaced the singing of the old liberation songs. It was generally used in conjunction with the *toyi-toyi*.

All the songs of black South Africans echoed a collective cry of discontent from 1900 to 1994. Through the lyrics of the songs, South Africans are able to trace the historical context that generated the song and the modification in the styles of the songs provide outsiders with an opportunity to understand the contours of black thought before 1994.

Music of White South Africans

In order to gain some insider perspectives into the identity of white South Africans, the focus will fall on vocal music sung by white South Africans during events from 1900 until 1994. The lyrics of these songs can be considered to be important historical documents and are a useful tool for creating understanding of the situations faced by white South Africans and alert black South Africans to the fact that not all whites supported apartheid. Due to their significance as a tool for reconciliation, these songs should be documented as part of South African heritage. The following events have been selected to highlight the role of music:

- the Anglo-Boer War (1899–1902)
- early Afrikaner trade unionism
- white South Africans questioning racial discrimination through song
- alternative Afrikaner performers and composers.

Vocal music of the Anglo-Boer War (1899–1902)

Through the lyrics of the songs sung during this War, black and white South Africans today can learn, amongst other things, about the scorched earth policy, the suffering of the Boer women and children in British concentration camps, as well as the feelings of grief and longing of the approximately 30,000 Boer men and boys who were sent away from their homeland as prisoners of war. These songs are not only important historical documents, but they allow for insight into the Boer psyche. The songs are thus valuable tools which could lead to an understanding of why white South Africans, amongst other things, instituted unreasonable restrictions and division of land at the beginning of the twentieth century. They had just spent four years of fighting for their father-land against the British and they were not prepared to give it up to black South Africans. The songs sung during this war were mostly sung in Afrikaans-Nederlands, the language which links modern day Afrikaans to the root Nederlands (Dutch), while the songs selected in the next two sections have songs sung in Afrikaans. This is significant as the Afrikaner was generally considered to be the oppressor by black South Africans.

Vocal music sung during early Afrikaner trade unionism

This period of South African history is very important for reconciliation because the angry confrontations between Afrikaner trade unionism and the state were echoed in clashes between black labor, capitalism and the South African Government during apartheid. Most South Africans today are unaware of the fact that Afrikaners also marched in their thousands singing protest songs. This is generally considered to be a black worker phenomenon and it could come as a revelation to black South Africans that white Afrikaners also protested against the white government. Of special significance is the fact that during this period many black South Africans supported white demon-strators by singing protest songs with them.

The songs sung during this period of South African history are no longer heard but because the white workers identified with workers throughout the world by singing well-known songs of revolutionary and democratic move-ments in Europe, the music is available in music scores. It is important that these details be preserved for posterity to create a correct picture of the past and to understand how a society developed. As there are no television docu-mentaries about white Afrikaner trade unionism between 1911 and 1932 these songs could also be used to create an understanding of the past which is impor-tant for shaping the future. A few important examples will be highlighted.

On 4 July 1913 a strike was organized by predominantly Afrikaans white work-ers, and a demonstration was held in Johannesburg. Masses of workers marched onto the square and a German workers band played the "Marseillaise," the song of the French Revolution. After the meeting had started the police pronounced the prohibition of the demonstration and in the subsequent clash between workers and police many protestors were killed. A red flag was draped over the dead and the people's song, "The Red Flag," was sung (Callinicos 1987: 98).

Communists around the world adopted this song as the banner of the working classes and it also became the official anthem of socialists and communists in early South Africa. Not many present day South Africans, black or white, would think of the Afrikaner as identifying with communists.

The Garment Workers Union, consisting of mainly Afrikaner women, was the strongest workers union to emerge from this period. The proletarianism of Afrikaner women began, as with the Afrikaner people as a whole, as a consequence of the economic devastation which was a result of the scorched earth policy of the rural areas during the Anglo-Boer War. At the forefront of this Union were young Afrikaner women whose families were no longer able to support them. In 1922 there was a strike by members of this Union, as well as white coal miners from the Mine Workers Union, for better working conditions. After the strike many trade unionists were arrested and according to H.R. Pike some police and blacks sang "The Red Flag" and the "Internationale" (official anthem of the Soviet Union) with the strikers, indicating that they sympathized with them (ibid. 1987: 126). Many of these demonstrators were imprisoned. In 1924 they were granted amnesty and about twenty thousand people, mostly whites, assembled inside and outside the Johannesburg Town Hall to welcome the released workers. Many liberation songs were sung and the released workers explained how some of their comrades from the Mine Workers Union had gone to the gallows singing "The Red Flag," which they said should serve as an inspiration to all the workers (Sachs 1957: 4). Present-day black and white South Africans should find this information very interesting as black South Africans also sang liberation songs on their way to the gallows during apartheid.

Between 1928 and 1932 the Garment Workers Union had over a hundred work stoppages, bringing the clothing industry to a standstill. The solidarity of the members of this Union resulted in many marches and the singing of songs that poked fun at the factory owners, to traditional English and Afrikaans tunes (Witz 1984: 222–33). The knowledge and insight gained during white trade unionism is important because it shows many parallels between situations faced by whites and blacks in South African history.

White South Africans question racial discrimination through song

The fact that many white South Africans sympathized with blacks during apartheid is also important for reconciliation. As the white government censored the press, little was said about white South Africans who were critical of government ideology. The lyrics of songs by whites who criticized apartheid are a powerful tool for alerting black South Africans to the fact that not all whites, especially Afrikaners, were against them.

In 1989 the students of Stellenbosch University, a traditional Afrikaner institution, were clearly representative of the racial re-appraisal of Afrikanerdom amongst the Afrikaner youth. They had been conditioned to support the white government ideology at all costs and it was an unusual occurrence for the Afrikaner to present contrary views. The song "Studente sal nooit verloor" ("Students will never be defeated") was written for a protest march in 1989 against racially segregated residences and was followed by a ban on protest meetings of any form on the campus.

The mood of resistance among white students continued and "the uforia [sic] was something unknown on Afrikaner campuses [sic], as young students appeared with red arm bands between hundreds of marching workers in orange overalls" (Burgess 1994: 45). Traditional old Afrikaans folk songs were sung with new words and a secret tour was organized to visit the banned members of the African National Congress in Lusaka. In 1989 the students left for Lusaka despite widespread criticism. It is significant that these students did not come from backgrounds where they had suffered discrimination and yet they took part in the struggle in an indirect way. They became the conscience of many students on the campus.

Alternative Afrikaner performers and composers

"Alternative Afrikaners," was a name these performers gave themselves. It was a reflection of their style of music which was contrary to the conservative folk music usually sung by Afrikaners. This music became an avenue through which the Afrikaner could employ other musical genres, such as rock 'n' roll, to express criticism of the apartheid government. According to Brendon Smit, possible reasons for the rediscovery of rock 'n' roll by the teenage fans of Afrikaans Alternative music, was the emergence of an Afrikaner youth-orientated awareness and social identity which paralleled the teenage rock 'n' roll phenomenon of the United States of America in the 1950s: "Racial segregation in a conservative social structure was a common theme in the USA of the 1950s and SA in the 1960s" (Smit 1992: 65). The white government considered rock 'n' roll a dangerous threat to the Afrikaans culture, and more significantly it was seen as a symbol of British culture and the anti-thesis of Afrikaner values: "It certainly does lend itself, by means of its youthful rebellious connotations, adequately to Afrikaner youth protest" (Smit 1992: 67).

The musicians who sang Afrikaans Alternative music got together in 1987 where they gave concerts called *Boere-Blues*. The lyrics were so important that they were often half-sung, half-declamatory so they could be clearly heard without allowing the tune to dominate. This new consciousness among young Afrikaners produced songs that used distasteful satire that was clearly meant to shock. This was clearly demonstrated by a production *Piekniek by Dingaan* at the Grahamstown National Arts Festival. It received top honors and conveyed repressed anger and recollected fury. "Young Afrikaners have taken off their *kappies* and *veldskoene* to dance a new dance to a neo-African beat. This group of young Afrikaners is clearly not happy with the greed, political tyranny and military violence that is being ascribed to the Afrikaner and they mock at the Afrikaans jet-set with their materialistic obsessions" (*The Weekly Mail*, July 1988: 27). *Kappies* and *Veldskoene* refer to the dress of Afrikaner forefathers.

Another article on the Grahamstown National Arts Festival points out that practically all the Afrikaans productions at the festival that year surprised with their critical look at South African society. The author of the article stated that it appeared to be Afrikaners who were questioning the government of the day and that it was interesting to note that an attack had been launched upon policies from within the Afrikaner establishment (Insig 1988: 5). Another article dealing with this festival stated that "here laid bare for all to witness was the anger, the bitterness and the shame of Verwoerd's grown children – deprived of their human dignity, they are anarchistic as hell" (*The Weekly Mail*, July 1988: 27).

The rock 'n' roll rebellion translated into Afrikaans with remarkable success. By 1990 these musicians had arranged the first South African rock festival, "Houtstok" (Woodstock), which was attended by 20,000 people. The national "Voëlvry" tour was attended by 85, 000 people. These performers were banned at traditional Afrikaans universities. At Stellenbosch University, however, thousands of students mobilized to protest the banning of the performance on their campus by musicians of the "Voëlvry" tour.

David Kramer was another white Afrikaans South African who had his compositions banned for showing empathy with those involved in the apartheid struggle. He said his works were "composed because, there is a new question for me – to try and connect to a cultural history, to try and repair some of the damage that has been inflicted by apartheid. I have a great need to understand that side of my history – a side that was in a way denied to me" (*Vrye Weekblad* 1992: 18). For the purpose of nation-building present-day black South Africans should be made aware of the fact that Afrikaans singers supported and sympathized with them during apartheid.

Conclusion

There is a debate raging among Afrikaners in South Africa today about their identity in Africa and their place in the new South African society. Most of the contributors appear sincere to find a new truth but many are angry because they are still asked to apologize for being white and Afrikaans. On the other side of the scale, years of atrocities and abuses against blacks can rekindle anger and resentment.

A golden thread through the debate is a poor understanding of history. According to Max du Preez: "A poor understanding of what happened before us always leads to a poor understanding of our realities today" (2005: 12). This chapter argues for the use of the music of previously polarized societies in South Africa for reconciliation. This music is unique to South Africa and is part and parcel of the country's history and as such can play a vital role in assisting in societal integration. As Cynthia Cohen states in her chapter: "music is well-suited to the work of building peace, because it can facilitate communication, understanding and empathy across differences of all kinds."

References

ANC Choir [s.a.] London: British TV [Video].

Biko, S. (1978) *I Write What I Like*, London: Penguin.

Burgess, A. (1994) "Kampusrevolusie: Gister Se Rebelle Vandag," *Die Suid-Afrikaan*, Maart/April 48: 44–9.

Callinicos, L. (1987) *Working Life, 1886–1940*, Vol. I, Johannesburg: Ravan.

Caluza, R.T. (1931) "African Music," *Southern Workman*, 60: 152–5.

Davenport, T.R.H. (1987) *South Africa: A Modern History*, Johannesburg: Macmillan.

Du Preez, M. (2005) "We must understand our past," *Daily News*.

Erlmann, V. (1991) *African Stars: Studies in Black South African Performance,* Chicago: University of Chicago Press.

Hooper, M. (1965) *This Land is Mine*, Folkways Records Album No. FH 5588: 1–8 [Record cover].

Insig (1988) "Verwoerd Se Kinders Sing 'n Ander Taal," April: 8.

Jabavu, D.D.T. (1987) "Nkosi Sikelel iAfrika," in M. Mutloatse (ed.) *Umhlaba Wethu. A Historical Indictment*, Johannesburg: Skotaville, 153–61.

Krog, A. (2002) *Country of my Skull*, Johannesburg: Random House.

Miriam, M. (1988) *Sangoma*, Warner Records, WBC 1639 [CD].

Motlhabi, M. (1985) *Black Resistance to Apartheid*, Johannesburg: Skotaville.

Sachs, E.S. (1957) *Garment Workers in Action*, Johannesburg: Eagle Press.

"Sing Freedom!" (1993) Transcribed, collected and edited by M. Hamilton, London: Novello.

Singing the Changes in South Africa ([s.a.].[s.l.]) 4 TV Electric Pictures/ Contemporary Films Feature film [Video].

"Songs of the Struggle" (1987) *New Nation*, 2–8 July 1987: 10.

Vinassa, A. (1993) "Soul before stardom," *Femina*, September: 48–52

Vrye Weekblad (1992) "n Rebel Word Ryper," 6–12 March: 5.

Witz, L. (1984) "Servant of the workers: Solly Sachs and the Garment Workers Union, 1928–1952," MA thesis, University of the Witwatersrand, Johannesburg.

Chapter 6: We Shall Overcome: The Roles of Music in the US Civil Rights Movement

Baruch Whitehead

Introduction

Peace researcher Johan Galtung defines peace as "the capacity to transform conflicts with empathy, creativity and nonviolence" (Galtung 2000). Galtung's emphasis on empathy is an important one, for without empathy we have no framework in which to understand others. I believe that music, in its own right, defines one's culture. I teach world music at Ithaca College in upstate New York and the students always amaze me by accurately predicting what part of the world the music that I play for them is from. Although they do not necessarily have the skills to understand why the music is the way it is, there is a sense of accomplishment when we analyze the music in a culturally sensitive way, and in context. The understanding of the culture is what brings the students to the table of humanity, where we can peacefully exist. As the students learn the historical significance of the songs we can stand in solidarity with our brothers and sisters around the world who struggle for social justice and peaceful resolutions. I believe that peace has to be more than the absence of war or conflict. Peace, to me, has to encompass the totality of human nature, experiences and emotions. Music is one way in which we, as humans, can connect. Music can be a catalyst to peaceful harmony on earth, although not all music is used for peaceful purposes, as George Kent shows in his chapter. When used properly music can be the framework for constructive conflict transformation, which will result in a peaceful state. However, before conflicts can be transformed, the groups in conflict must accept and respect each other as equals in order to avoid exploitation and oppression. White Americans must accept African Americans as their equals and African Americans must not abandon their black consciousness to appease White America. We must look at the problems that exist and separate us in order to create a peaceful dialogue.

History will record the great flood of 2005 in which Hurricane Katrina devastated the city of New Orleans and exposed the racism and despairing conditions of people of color living in the United States. Until all citizens of the United States and beyond have enough strength to respect each other, peace cannot and will not exist. Lessons learned or not learned from the civil rights struggle need to be examined and put into a constructive framework. No longer do we live in the days of slavery, Jim Crow Laws, segregated schools and a host of other unjust laws. However, we have another journey to once and for all confront our demons of racial conflicts in the United States before peaceful transformation can occur.

The Civil Rights Movement (1955–69) in the United States was a tumultuous time that pricked the conscience of many Americans. Filled with racial tension and basic human rights violations, America was torn apart at the very fabric of her existence. Before comprehending the racial strife in America, it is important to examine the history of the Africans who were forced to live there.

The Music of the Slaves

From the mid-1500s to mid-1800s, European invaders found much profit in the African slave trade. Africans were traded like cattle and, for tax purposes, considered to be three-fifths of a person. The oppressors often came to the shore of Africa in the name of religion under the auspicious reasoning of doing "God's Will"; they paved the way for slave-traders to pillage and rape villages. The Africans couldn't overcome their superior weaponry and in the end were forced to become slaves, or die while trying to escape.

The majority of slaves came from West Africa. The "slave castle" in Cape Coast serves as a continuous reminder of the brutality of the slave trade. Europeans offered Africans high-commodity items to act as a conduit to the slave trade. Africans helped to enslave their brothers and sisters in order to receive these items. Oddly enough, slave-traders would not seek to enslave the local villagers but would travel long distances to bring slaves to the castle. Many of the captives had to walk many miles to reach a place where, shackled to trees, stripped naked, beaten and harassed, they were made to wash in the flowing water of the river In a ritual known as the "last bath." Following the last bath, they were again shackled and made to walk, in some cases, over twenty miles to the slave castle. Many died en route from starvation and beatings. The oppressors received the captives at the castle and forced them into a warehouse that was meant for cargo. Cape Coast Castle could hold up to 1000 male captives and 500 female captives at any one time. The typical stay was between four and six weeks, in dungeon-like rooms. The male dungeon measured approximately 60ft by 30ft with one small window for ventilation. Captives were shackled together and had to eat where they slept, urinated, and defecated. Trenches were dug around the outer walls of the dungeon to receive waste and bodily fluids. The female captives were also shackled, separated from the males, and had a smaller dungeon. They were often displayed in the courtyard below the governor's quarter so that he could decide which female captives he would rape.

Captives who proved to be a problem were placed in a cell to die slowly through starvation. Those meeting this fate were often strong males who dared to fight back; their oppressors kept them in a weakened position through starvation and beatings.

When the slave ships arrived, captives were ushered through a tunnel to reach a gate marked "Point of No Return." They would then be lead down the stairs and on to waiting boats that took them to the slave ships. Once aboard the ships, they were packed into the hull, often with 1500 slaves shackled together like caged animals. The slave ship was worse than the dungeons because there was no room to move, and food and water were given sparingly. The voyage is what historians called the Middle Passage. Thousands of Africans lost their lives through starvation, beatings, or by throwing themselves into the ocean. Approximately ten million Africans were taken from their homeland during the slave trade. The majority of African slaves came from the West African countries of Cameroon, Congo, Ghana, Guinea, Ivory Coast, Nigeria, Senegal, and Togo. The close proximity of these countries to the Atlantic Ocean provided easy access for the slave ships.

Once in America, the slaves were sold and forced to endure years of torture, abuse, rape and assimilation. In 1863, during the American Civil War, President Abraham Lincoln signed the Emancipation Proclamation, which freed the slaves. Several years before, Britain had chosen to no longer participate in the slave trade, paving the way for Lincoln's actions.

Slaves brought their music with them; one must understand that music in Africa requires a holistic approach that incorporates singing, dancing, and playing instruments. Music brought the slaves joy and happiness. Slave-masters would often ban drumming because they thought it was used as a form of communication. This was precipitated by the Stono Rebellion of 1739 in Charleston, South Carolina, where slaves used drums as a signal to other slaves to join in the fight for freedom and to kill white men. The rebellion was quickly stamped out by local militias and, as a result, a number of slaves were beaten and hanged (Cooper 2001).

Slaves were forced to assimilate through language and music, although some were permitted to have their own religious services, which they called "camp meetings." The slaves would go into the woods away from the slave masters to sing and shout. These sessions were very spirited and served as social and religious gatherings. Slaves also gathered on many Sundays for a day of music making and worship. One of the most popular venues in the Deep South was located in New Orleans, Louisiana, and was called Congo Square. Cooper describes the scene in his book, *Slave Spirituals and the Jubilee Singers*, "Men and women danced in large circles, slowly increasing the tempo until they fell exhausted to the ground" (Cooper 2001: 17–18).

The music of the slaves were often songs that described their condition and aided them in performing their everyday duties. These songs were called "field" or "work" songs and were characterized by a strong rhythmic pulse with different tempos. Songs were composed for nearly every task and were malleable, easily changing tempo or text depending on the current situation. This practice of altering the text became widely used in the music of the civil rights years.

There are three amendments to the United States Constitution that are important to the development of the lives of African Americans: the thirteenth, fourteenth, and fifteenth. These amendments freed the slaves, made them citizens of the United States, and gave them the right to vote, respectively. Once the slaves were freed, many didn't know what to do. With no money or available resources, some decided to stay on Southern plantations while others moved north in search of a better life.

It was many generations before the African Americans gained equal treatment under the law. Music was an essential part of the struggle for freedom. Slaves continued to use music for encouragement and worship. However, during the civil rights years, traditional religious songs were transformed into freedom songs. The familiar songs were given new texts that represented the struggles of the movement. In the book by Guy and Candie Carawan, *Sing for Freedom*, Rev. C.T. Vivian is quoted as saying:

> I don't see anyone having struggle separate from music. I would like to think that a movement without music would crumble. Music picks up people's spirits. Anytime you can get something that lifts your spirits and also speaks to the reality of your life, even the reality of oppression, and the same time is talking about how you can really overcome: that's terribly important stuff.
>
> (Smithsonian 1997: 10)

The black church was the gathering place for the Civil Rights Movement because music was an important part of the struggle. Many freedom songs were rooted in traditional African American hymn-style singing. It is interesting to note that in the majority of authentic African music, the use of harmony is rarely found. Most often there is a single-line melody or melodic idea. Through assimilation, African Americans adopted the European style of singing in four-part harmony. Although the slaves adopted this European style, they added much syncopation and often improvised their own melodies and harmony.

Coretta Scott King, wife of the slain civil rights leader Dr. Martin Luther King Jr., perhaps the greatest recognizable leader of the Civil Rights Movement, stated in the book *Voices of Freedom:*

> What happened throughout the mass meetings is that there were songs interspersed. They had an order of service, and so sometimes they would do what you call the long meter. Someone would come and sing, without an instrument at all. Then they would have someone who played the piano or organ, and they would start just like they start at the church services. And they would sing the songs and the hymns of the church. "What a fellowship, What a Joy divine, Leaning on the everlasting arm." They'd sing spirituals like "Lord I want to be a Christian in my Heart," "Oh Freedom Over Me, Before I Be A Slave I'll be buried in my Grave and go home to my Lord and be free." They would end, of course, after Martin's message, with a song and a prayer, a benediction and prayer. And everyone would go home feeling good and inspired and ready to go back the next morning to a long day of hard work. But I think they could take it a little better, really even the work that had been difficult became easier. It was something about the experience that gave all of us so much hope and inspiration, and the more we got into it, the more we had the feeling that something could be done about the situation, that we could change it.
>
> (Hampton and Fayer 1990: 30)

Highlander Folk School: "We Shall Overcome"

Perhaps the genesis of music in the Civil Rights Movement occurred at Highlander Folk School in Mounteagle, Tennessee. The school was founded in 1930s by Zilphia and Myles Horton, white activists in the struggle for African American rights. They provided an integrated setting, about twenty years prior to the Civil Rights Movement, where blacks and whites worked together for a common cause. The Highlander Folk School was a gathering place for many of the early leaders of the movement, including Rosa Parks who passed away recently at the age of 92. Communities came together from throughout the South to share information, strategies, and to encourage one another. It was one of the first non-segregated venues that brought blacks and whites together.

Singing Southern gospel songs became a focal point of these meetings. In the summer of 1960, one of the earliest conferences of song leaders was established when activists from Alabama and Tennessee joined with Northern protest singers and songwriters. This began the cross-fertilization of freedom songs throughout the United States (PBS 1990).

The Highlander Folk School was one of the earliest venues that incorporated the unofficial civil rights anthem "We Shall Overcome." This popular freedom song was actually first sung by slaves and adapted for the Civil Rights Movement. The evolution of this song to its current existence is a product of African Americans and European Americans working together, stealing and trading ideas. In its original form, the lyrics were "I will overcome someday" and the song was performed in the traditional shout style, with hand-clapping and movement.

Civil Rights Version	*Original Version*
We shall overcome	I will overcome
We shall overcome	I will overcome
We shall overcome some day	I will overcome some day
Oh, deep in my heart	Oh, deep in my heart
I do believe	I do believe
We shall overcome someday	I will overcome someday

In 1945 in Charleston, South Carolina, striking tobacco workers sang an adapted version of the song. This marked the first time "We Shall Overcome" was used in a social protest situation. Singing this song gave the strikers a sense of assurance that they would overcome and reach their goals. In 1946, strikers brought songs to the Highlander Folk School, which was a training center for labor organizers.

Zilphia Horton was responsible for disseminating commonly known songs and introducing new texts that reflected the struggle of the Civil Rights Movement. She traveled through the South bringing songs from different regions to share with protesters. She collaborated with Pete Seeger, also a white civil rights activist, who introduced many of these songs to Northern audiences. Seeger adapted and added verses to the song and began to perform it. He mentions this in an inclusive interview included in Rik Palieri's chapter in this volume. One of the verses he added was "we walk hand in hand." In fact, the tradition of holding hands and singing actually began during the labor movement.

Students from the Highlander Folk School carried "We Shall Overcome" throughout the country. It appeared again in Rome, Georgia, where textile workers were protesting in the 1940s.

Dr. Martin Luther King Jr. learned the song at the 25th Anniversary celebration of the Highland Folk School after hearing it performed by Pete Seeger. The year 1955 marked the death of Zilphia Horton, but her philosophy of "using music as a means to unite people in struggle lived on" (PBS 1990). After the urging of Pete Seeger, Guy Carawan, a "California hillbilly" and another white activist, filled the position of music director at the Highland Folk School. Carawan studied black music, and was the first to spread the songs under the new genre of "Freedom Songs." According to Pete Seeger, "he (Carawan) went through all the Southern states risking his life . . . to spread song." In his own words, Carawan said:

> I really feel privileged to have come here to Highlander and just been lucky enough to be here in this period of history when so many things were happening so fast. In 1959, that way of singing "We Shall Overcome" was literally unknown around the South. Zilphia had died and I had come here to fulfill some of her role to get singing going and "We Shall Overcome" was one of the main songs that I was able to teach here in workshops to people who didn't know it.

> (PBS 1990)

Carawan spent many years teaching "We Shall Overcome" to people all over the South, preparing for the Civil Rights Movement. April 1960 marked the first South-wide gathering of people involved in the sit-in movement. Singers from Nashville learned "We Shall Overcome" and took the song home with them. It became a theme song of the city within a week. One reason for the song's popularity was the ease with which verses relevant to the movement could be added, whether for sit-ins, marches, or other protest activities. In the Nashville movement, the "principle of nonviolence had a lot to do with the interpretation of what was happening" (PBS 1990).

Mary Travers, a white civil rights activist from the folk group "Peter, Paul and Mary" stated that "When people sang it ("We Shall Overcome"), you felt like folk music was doing its job. If you look at it historically, music has always been the accompaniment of social change" (PBS 1990).

With hits like "Blowin' in the Wind," Bob Dylan and other folk artists challenged Americans to think about their actions through the poignant lyrics of the song. These were movement songs that spoke to the very essence of what was going on throughout America and these songs galvanized both blacks and whites for the cause of civil rights in America.

Even in the face of death, "We Shall Overcome" provided activists with a reminder of what they had to do and that they couldn't stop, even in their grief. The main reason was that the movement was important to all of humanity.

Freedom Songs

Nashville was one of the first cities to hold campaigns against segregation. Pre-existing songs were given new texts that reflected the changing issues of the times and development of the movement. In Raleigh, North Carolina, Southern students organized the Student Non Violent Coordinating Committee (SNCC). These students collaborated to plan and coordinate campaigns for the struggles by singing songs of the Civil Rights Movement, as well as older freedom songs that they taught to their communities.

In 1961, Freedom Riders from the South traveled to Mississippi to protest the segregation Jim Crow Laws of the South. Many of these students were placed in jail for an extended period of time. Here, they learned and sang freedom songs from around the country. The students adapted old songs and wrote new songs to describe their situation in jail.

In Atlanta, Georgia in 1964 "Sing for Freedom" was organized and sponsored by the Highlander Folk School, the Southern Christian Leadership Conference (SCLC), and the SNCC. Here, activists from the North and South came together to sing freedom songs and participate in workshops. In 1965 in Edwards, Mississippi, another conference was organized that focused on freedom songs and African American history.

Perhaps one of the most influential singing groups during the civil rights period was the "Freedom Singers." Members were Rutha Mae Harris, Charles Neblett, Cordell Reagon and Bernice Johnson Reagon (founder of the famous singing group "Sweet Honey in the Rock"). The group started in 1962 when Pete Seeger heard them and suggested that they travel around the country singing to raise money and awareness for SNCC. His wife booked them on a tour of colleges on the North and West Coasts where they were able to reach 100,000 or more people in integrated audiences. They believed that music was a stabilizing force in the movement, something that they could all participate in. They were not only talented singers but activists as well.

Other events, like the March on Washington, brought national and international attention to the plight of African Americans in the United States via mass media. Harry Belafonte was instrumental in pulling together white and black entertainers, such as Sammy Davis Jr., Marlon Brando, Charleston Heston, and James Baldwin, to draw attention from a wider audience. The march also gave millions of people the opportunity to hear the national anthem of the Civil Rights Movement, "We Shall Overcome," and to see blacks and whites unite for the cause of freedom. Another white civil rights activist, Joan Baez, sang "We Shall Overcome" during the march. She believed that music could be used as a vehicle for nonviolent protest. Dr. King delivered his famous "I Have A Dream" speech to thousands of marchers at the Lincoln Memorial in Washington, DC, and music was an important part of this momentous event. Mahalia Jackson, the world famous gospel singer, performed "How I Got Over."

Peter Yarrow (of Peter, Paul, and Mary) made the following observation during the March on Washington:

> I had the feeling, in those first marches that we were part of, that the songs were a different kind of rhetoric. There were a lot of people in America that were fence-sitters, that were just not about to think about the possibility of change and alteration, and were dead against it. When they heard the music, something human was touched and it was undeniable.

(PBS 1990)

President John F. Kennedy's assassination in 1963 dealt a huge blow to the cause of civil rights in the United States. Many African Americans believed that Kennedy shared some of their goals in the struggle, particularly his support of a Voting Rights Act. The Voting Rights Act would abolish the racial policy of having people qualify to vote. Lyndon B. Johnson, Kennedy's vice-president, worked to get many of his policies through congress after his assassination.

During the mid-1960s approximately twenty-five families had lost loved ones because they dared to crave freedom. Local laws still barred blacks from voting and change seemed impossible. Activists organized a series of marches in Selma, Alabama that put pressure on the federal government to address voters' rights issues. In the summer of 1964 the Mississippi Freedom Summer was launched. Volunteers from all over the United States flooded Mississippi to help African Americans register to vote and recruit for the newly founded Mississippi Freedom Democratic Party, chaired by Fannie Lou Hamer. She would later deliver her famous speech at the Democratic National Convention where white democrats refused to recognize her new party, a grass-roots African American political organization. Her words of questioning democracy and freedom in this country were televised throughout the country.

Mississippi was the home to staunch racist policies and corrupt government leadership. It was a hotbed of confrontation in the Deep South. William Simmons, an eyewitness to many of the horrific events in Mississippi, made the following observation in the book *Voices of Freedom*:

> The first wave of student volunteers left for Mississippi from Oxford, Ohio, on June 20. Andrew Goodman, a white twenty-year old from Queens College in New York City, rode with two experienced civil rights workers from CORE,

twenty-one-year old James Chaney, a black native of Meridian, Mississippi and white twenty-four-year-old Michael Schwerner from Brooklyn, New York. On June 21, their first assignment took them to a small town near Philadelphia, Mississippi, and the site of a church that had been burned. As a safety precaution when on the road, the three young men had trained to maintain regular telephone contact with the COFO Organization.

(Hampton and Fayer 1990: 188)

Peter Orris states in the same book:

Those of us that had gone to Washington returned to Oxford, Ohio, in the middle of the second week of the training session. We had driven thirty hours straight, and we arrived in Oxford late one evening to find the college in a state of extreme remorse. In front of the dormitory area, there was a large circle of volunteers and SNCC organizers. They were in the dark and they were singing freedom songs. They had linked arms. We asked what had happened, and they described the situation to us. Three civil rights workers Andrew Goodman, James Chaney and Michael Schwerner had disappeared. Our reaction was horror. The sorrow that went through the camp was profound.

(Hampton and Fayer 1990: 189)

Indeed the civil rights workers had been murdered and these murders received national and international attention because whites and blacks were being killed in the fight for civil rights. The freedom songs gave many people the strength to carry on. Songs like "Keep Your Eyes on the Prize" were sung with new lyrics throughout the Civil Rights Movement.

Violence in Selma pressured President Johnson on August 6, 1965, to sign the Voting Right Act, which was the most important response by the federal government to the Civil Rights Movement. President Johnson, in his historical speech on this legislation, invoked the words to "We Shall Overcome":

What happened in Selma is part of a far-larger movement which reaches into every state of America. Because it's not just Negroes, but really, it's all of us who must overcome the crippling legacy of bigotry and injustice . . . and we shall overcome.

(Boyd *et al.* 2004: 235)

Dr. King still faced many obstacles despite the Voting Rights Act. He worked for numerous campaigns for the underprivileged, including the Poor People's Campaign. This campaign worked with poor whites from Appalachia, Caesar Chavez and the Hispanics from California, people from big cities of the north and some of our Asian minorities. The Civil Rights Movement was devastated by the assassination of Martin Luther King. Andrew Young, one of King's companions on the night before he was murdered stated:

> Dr. King sang "We Shall Overcome" the night before he was assassinated. Even though he was somewhat discouraged, he drew strength from the crowd's enthusiasm. The preaching and singing revived him when medicine and doctors had been unable to do so.

(PBS 1990)

Black Panthers: Say it Loud, I'm Black and I'm Proud

Malcolm X, black Muslim minister and member of the Nation of Islam commented on the March on Washington:

> I can't understand why Negroes should become so excited about a demonstration run by whites in front of a statue of a president who has been dead for a hundred years and who didn't like us when he was alive.

(brothermalcolm.net 2007)

Malcolm expressed a growing sentiment among some blacks that non-violence wouldn't produce peaceful resolutions in America. This sentiment led to the organization of the Black Panther Party movement of the late sixties. Music became an important outlet for the expression of "black power." Songs like "Say it Loud I'm Black and I'm Proud" were sung by thousands of disgruntled black youths. Other songs like "Getto Kitty" and "Sweet Sweetback's Baadass" expressed a growing intolerance for peaceful nonviolent protest.

Malcolm X was shot on 21 February 1965 at 3:10 P.M., at the Audubon Ballroom in New York City, by a black male later identified as Talmadge Hayer. Rumors suggested the Nation of Islam leader Elijah Muhammad was involved in the murder of Malcolm X because he separated himself from the Nation of Islam under Muhammad's leadership. Their rift was well-publicized. Muhammad denied any involvement in the murder.

Three years later in 1968 Martin Luther King was assassinated. After the assassination of Dr. King, things changed rapidly for the movement. King's death gave further rise to the militant arm of the movement, with the Black Panther Party taking the lead. This Black Consciousness group called for black determination, and preservation. In 1967 Carl Stokes became the first black mayor of a major metropolitan city, Cleveland, Ohio. Approximately 35 percent of Cleveland's population at that time was African American.

Stokes was able to pull together a coalition of black and white voters for his election.

Off of the heels of Stokes' election in Cleveland, black students were organizing "walkouts" at Howard University, one of this nation's prestigious black universities located in Washington, DC. Howard University was founded in 1867 and graduated most of the nation's black physicians, lawyers and doctors. They organized walkouts and staged numerous demonstrations protesting the "white value system" that the university had adopted. They demanded that courses like African American history be added to the core curriculum and formed a Black Power Committee to address these issues.

Homecoming queen candidate Robin Gregory wore her hair in an Afro hairstyle to make a statement in favor of the black consciousness movement at Howard. Paula Giddings describes the night the homecoming queen was announced:

> The lights went down. The candidates went back. Then you heard the curtains open. And you heard the crank of the revolving stage begin. And as the stage revolved and turned around toward the audience, the light began to come up at the same time. Well, before you saw Robin, you saw the way the lights cast a silhouette on the curtains, and you saw the silhouette of her Afro before you saw her. Well, the auditorium exploded. It was a wonderful moment. People started jumping up and screaming and some were raising their fists, then spontaneously a chant began. The chant was "Umgawa, Black Power, Umgawa, Black Power," and a chant was created. People started to march to the rhythm of "Umgawa, Black Power," and there was a line that went all the way around the auditorium, and more and more people joined the line. I did too as it went around the auditorium. And finally out the door and into the streets of Washington, D.C., past the campus and still chanting, "Umgawa, Black Power," and that was really the launching of that moment at Howard.

> (Hampton and Fayer 1990: 435)

The chant provided a unifying element to the black consciousness movement at Howard University. This act lead to the conference entitled "Towards a Black University" in 1968.

The Federal Bureau of Investigation leader, J. Edgar Hoover, launched a counter intelligence program called COINTELPRO, which considered the Black Panther Party a threat to the United States security. He set out to bring down the organization and discredit its leaders. Huey Newton, a high level leader in the party was arrested for allegedly shooting a policeman. Huey Newton, Bobby Seale and 30 other Black Panther members staged an armed protest on 2 May 1967 on the steps of the California State Capitol in

Sacramento. The protest interrupted an address that Governor Ronald Reagan was giving outside. The Panthers, draped in black clothing, gloves, sunglasses and berets, made both the Governor and the attendees of the speech wonder their purpose and fear their actions. In front of live media, leader Bobby Seale addressed the public with these words:

> The Black Panther Party For Self-Defense believes that the time has come for black people to take up arms against (police) terror before its too late . . . a people who has suffered so much and for so long in this racist society has to draw a line somewhere.

(Trikont Records 2002)

During this period, songs like "Say it Loud, I'm Black and I'm Proud" were very powerful. This call and response song became somewhat of an anthem for the Black Panther Party. They published a manifesto that called for black determination and preservation and placed emphasis on blackness and black history.

The struggle for civil rights, equality and freedom began with peaceful resistance, although black youths in the ghettos became frustrated with being submissively peaceful. They felt victimized by the government's tactics, by wide-spread poverty, overt segregation and police brutality. They believed that they would not be able to stop white police terror and racism if they carried on by demonstrating through peaceful means. By 1968 there were over 4,000 Black Panthers patrolling American cities. They protected blacks against police abuse, set up breakfast places for school children and organized donations of food and clothing. Many poets, musicians and pop stars supported the movement through their art. Scott-Heron, The Last Poets, The Staple Singers, Curtis Mayfield and Marvin Gaye were just a few famous entertainers who gave a voice to "black power." Since the late 1960s the lyrics of numerous soul, funk, reggae and hip-hop songs had been inspired by the struggle of the Black Panthers.

According to "Our Own Voice" Black and Proud Website:

> When Jesse Jackson concluded his opening remarks at the Wattstax Festival in August 1972, he called upon the crowd to rise and join him: "I am somebody" he insisted in typical preacher pose and the audience echoed his words, "I may be unskilled, but I am somebody." The crowd bellowed back its approval after each phrase. "I am black, beautiful and proud," Jackson continued in an ever more impassioned voice. The audience shouted back even more enthusiastically. "I must be respected." It was black America's core demand and the message of hundreds of soul lyrics. The charts were overflowing with the new black self assurance: "Say it loud, I'm black and I'm proud" an Afro-styled James

Brown shouted out of the radio speakers. The Staple Singers asked to "Respect Yourself." And Curtis Mayfield confirmed "We're a Winner." Besides, for the first time there were voices emerging in black pop who dared to pronounce poverty, discrimination and fraud by the political system openly. The socially and economically underprivileged had learned during the era of the Black Power slogans, that you could define yourself through songs, raps and words.

(Trikont Records 2002)

As previously mentioned, Hoover launched a successful plan of dealing with the Black Panthers and many of the leaders were harassed, jailed, and shot. Others chose to leave the country and live in exile.

Stokely Carmichael, a hero of the party, became the honorary prime minister for the Black Panthers. Carmichael discussed in his book *Ready for a Revolution* the idea of faith among the people, a faith that would transcend all wrong and allow the creator to take retribution on the guilty. W.E. Dubois, a black intellectual, said of the spirituals: "the most beautiful expressions of the human spirit this side of the seas" (Carmichael 2003: 290).

Carmichael stated:

> . . . so my "people" were strong in faith and certain of their ultimate deliverance. For in faith all things are possible. And overarching this narrow world was the infinite grace and certain justice of God's purpose, the gradual and unchanging arc of whose universe curved toward freedom.

(Carmichael 2003: 290)

He also discussed the fact that music was used for comfort with songs like "There is a Balm in Gilead," "to make the wounded whole." Whenever people came together there was singing and meditation. Carmichael commented:

> Never mind that the Klan (a white hate group), or the sheriff's men were driving by flashing their headlights . . . when we sang "Guide my feet, Lord, while I run this race, for I don't want to run this race in vain" or "Go down Moses, way down in Egypt land, tell ol' Pharaoh, let my people go," and "Wade in the water, chillum, God's gonna trouble the water," it was prophecy being fulfilled and history made manifest around us.

(Carmichael 2003: 291)

Conclusion

One can see that music played an important part in the history of the Civil Rights Movement. The power of the music gave strength to the cowardly, hope to the hopeless and healing to the sick. These songs, based in the tradition of our ancestors, carried the movement beyond what was humanly possible. When nothing else worked there was always a song to be sung to lift the peoples' spirits. The mother of the Civil Rights Movement, Mrs. Rosa Parks, passed away on October 19, 2005. She left behind a legacy of truth and justice. She was the first civilian and woman to lie in honor at our nation's capital in Washington, DC. Her act of refusing to give up her bus seat to a white man set in motion a rallying cry for freedom and social justice that was heard across the world. Her actions in 1955 lead to the Montgomery Bus Boycott. The boycott became the first victory against legal segregation in the South and galvanized the Civil Rights Movement. Although her earthly body is no longer with us, we will forever remember her strength and courage in the face of insurmountable odds as we strive to spread peace through mutual respect, dignity and the joy of music.

References

Boyd, H., Davis, O., and Dee, R. (2004) *We Shall Overcome: A Living History of the Civil Rights Struggle Told in Words, Pictures and the Voices of the Participants*, New York: Herb Boyd Sourcebooks Media Fusion.

Brothermalcom.net (2007) http://www.brothermalcolm.net/mxtimeline.html, remarks of 28 August 1963.

Carawan, G. and C. (1990) *Sing for Freedom: The Story of the Civil Rights Movement Through its Songs*, Bethlehem, PA: Sing Out Corporation.

Carmichael, S. (2003) *Ready for Revolution: The Life and Struggles of Stokely Carmichael (Kwane Ture)*, New York: Scribner.

Cooper, M. (2001) *Slave Spirituals and the Jubilee Singers*, New York: Clarion Books.

"Eyes on the Prize" (1995) *America's Civil Rights Years*, Vol. 1–7 [PBS Home Video].

Fisk Jubilee Singers (2003) *In Bright Mansions*, Curb Records [CD].

Galtung, J. (2000) Telephone conversation with Olivier Urbain.

Hampton, H. and Fayer, S. 1990 *Voices of Freedom: An Oral History of the Civil Rights Movement from the 1950s through the 1980s*, New York: Bantam Books.

Kerran, S. (1995) *When the Spirit Says Sing!*, New York and London: Garland Publishing.

Public Broadcasting Services (PBS) (1990) "We Shall Overcome" [Video, 58 minutes].

Smithsonian Folkways Recordings (1990) *Sing for Freedom, The Story of the Civil Rights Movement Through its Songs* [CD, SF 40032].

Smithsonian Folkways Recordings (1997) *Voices of the Civil Rights Movements: Black Freedom Songs 1960–1966* [CD, SF 40084].

Trikont Records (2002) *Black and Proud Volumes 1 and 2, The Soul of the Black Panther Era*, [CD].

Chapter 7: Music as a Discourse of Resistance: The Case of Gilad Atzmon

Karen Abi-Ezzi

The saxophonist and clarinettist Gilad Atzmon is particularly interesting to look at. Atzmon is a vociferous anti-Zionist and a passionate defender of the Palestinians and their right to self-determination. These political views are surprising given that Atzmon was born in Israel and served in the Israeli army whilst doing his military service. For over a decade now he has lived in London with his wife and two young children, although his parents and other relatives still live in Israel.

Today, Gilad Atzmon is a famous jazz musician. He and his band, the "Orient House Ensemble" became known within jazz circles in the mid-1990s. In 2003 they won the best album category at the BBC Jazz Awards for their album *Exile*. Rather controversially, Atzmon was described in one British broadsheet newspaper as "an Israeli who prefers to be labelled a Palestinian, a Jew who calls himself an ex-Jew, a saxophonist and clarinettist, novelist [and] philosopher . . ." (Byrnes 2005).

So how does a chapter which looks at music as a form of resistance connect with the general theme of this book which is about music for peace? This begs the question, can there be a direct jump from war to peace without an intermediary stage of resistance and if so, resistance against what – the self, the other, political structures? Particularly in such a long and unequal conflict as the one between the Israelis and Palestinians, how can someone resist through music? What does "to resist through music" mean? Does the party that is oppressed do the resisting or can any interested party engage musically in such an act? If someone who is a member of the more powerful party in a conflict resists from within, what kind of impact can this dramatic act have?

This chapter stands in stark contrast to the chapter about Yair Dalal. Both Yair Dalal and Gilad Atzmon are Israelis (although Atzmon has since renounced his Israeli citizenship). But they differ fundamentally in the way in which they understand their roles as musicians and the function of their music as it relates to the Israeli-Palestinian conflict. Whereas Dalal was asked to compose the music for a gala event held in Norway in 1994 to celebrate the signing of the 1993 Oslo Peace Accords, Atzmon's music challenges the premise upon which the current peace process is based. In other words, Atzmon's music challenges Zionism and its inherent ideology which is premised on creating an exclusively Jewish state for the Jewish people. Atzmon explains:

> What is Zionism? Zionism is the transformation of the bible from a spiritual text into a legal document into a land registry. This land belongs to me. Why? Because of the bible. So this is actually the most non-spiritualistic, evangelistic reading of the Bible. So it is a very religious movement. You talk about Judaism. They didn't take the love to God, the love to your neighbour which is there in Judaism. They just took the concept of choseness and supremacy.
>
> (Atzmon 2005)

This chapter will look at how Atzmon goes about resisting this project through his music. But first, it is important to briefly allude to the theoretical framework which informs this study or the "lens" through which I look at this whole subject. So let us turn very briefly to a theory of knowledge known as "social constructionism."

How Do We Know What We Know?
The Role of the "Social" in Understanding

Perhaps it is worth starting this section by quoting the Marxist thinker Antonio Gramsci who in his prison notebooks observed that:

> The starting point of critical elaboration is the consciousness of what one really is, and is "knowing thyself" as a product of historical process to date, which has deposited in you an infinity of traces, without leaving an inventory . . . therefore it is imperative at the outset to compile such an inventory.
>
> (Gramsci 1971, quoted in Said 1978: 25)

It is this "infinity of traces" acting as a filtering lens through which the world is understood, that is particularly relevant and informative in this chapter. The possibility that we can view or understand anything objectively is questioned and rejected by social constructionists who argue that words do not mirror the world, but rather *construct* it. This radical idea places a great deal of emphasis on the social, historical and cultural context which determines what is "true" and what is not. Ernesto Laclau and Chantal Mouffe express this idea very well in the following passage:

> A stone exists independently of any system of social relations, but it is, for instance, either a projectile or an object of aesthetic contemplation only within a specific discursive configuration. A diamond in the market or at the bottom of a mine is the same physical object; but, again, it is only a commodity within a determinate system of social relations.
>
> (Laclau and Mouffe 1987)

This particular way of understanding the meaning-making process is particularly relevant for the case at hand, as we shall see below. We now look at the way in which Gilad Atzmon's music can be regarded as a music of resistance, but first who is Gilad Atzmon?

Introducing Gilad Atzmon

Gilad Atzmon was born in Israel in 1963 and was raised in a secular Israeli Jewish family. He did his military service (which is compulsory in Israel) at the age of 18. This coincided with the Israeli invasion of Lebanon and so he found himself in Lebanon for part of his military service. It was this event that he points to as being a turning point in his life (Atzmon 2005). He questioned why Israel had invaded a neighbouring Arab state; an act of aggression that he could not square with what he had been brought up to believe was Israel's place in the Middle East and with the role and function of the Israeli army or the Israeli *Defence* Forces (IDF). When he got back to Israel, he read voraciously about the history of the country, the formation of the state of Israel in Mandate Palestine in 1948, the plight of the Palestinians who had lived in that land and the estimated 750,000–900,000 Palestinians who had been dispossessed between 1947 and 1948. That war, the first Arab–Israeli conflict, is known as the War of Independence to Israelis and the *Al Naqba* (the catastrophe) to Palestinians, highlighting how the same event can be seen in such different ways by different groups of people. Atzmon reflects:

> When the war broke out and I was in Lebanon [1982], this was the first time I asked myself, where do the Palestinians come from? This is something no one understands. The Israelis don't really understand the scale of the *nakba*. They don't think about it. They are trained not to think about it. This is part of the supremacist ideology that Jewish thinking is imbued with and it is the wrong understanding of Judaism.
>
> (Atzmon 2005)

Disillusioned, Atzmon traveled to England. As he explains:

> Eventually I couldn't stand being there [in Israel] anymore so I thought I'd just leave. The interesting thing is that it happened here. Why did I get so involved, here in the UK? I think that I learned more and more about the Palestinian crisis, about what really happened in Sabra and Shatila [the Palestinian refugee camps in Beirut where an estimated 2,400 Palestinian civilians were massacred in September 1982], what happened in the *nakba*. The Jewish narrative is a big lie from beginning to end.
>
> (Atzmon 2005)

It was at around this time that his musical career began to take off. As he explains on his website, it was when he met fellow Israeli musician Asaf Sirkis that he decided to form a band, which he rather provocatively called the "Orient House Ensemble" (Orient House being the main Palestinian headquarters in occupied East Jerusalem). As Atzmon notes, "I think that when I established the "Orient House" it was my way of putting meaning into music" (Atzmon 2005). Playing in a band and working with Israeli drummer Sirkis, Atzmon "recovered an interest in playing the music of the Middle East, North Africa and Eastern Europe that had been in the back of his mind for years" (Atzmon 2005).

Atzmon's album *Exile*, released in 2003, is perhaps the best example to date of what he calls his "socially motivated" activism. For him, "Exile is where I started to crack the Judeo mythology; the notion of victim, the notion of chosen, the notion of Holocaust, every notion. And music is where I expanded my attack on the entire scientific technological American stupidity" (Atzmon 2005). *Exile* was voted Best Jazz Album of the year by *Time Out* magazine. On it, he plays with the famous Palestinian singer Reem Kelani and they jointly try to "tell the story of Palestine." One characteristic of Atzmon's music is his use of Jewish soul music and Israeli folk music and other "Israeli traditional and nationalistic melodies" as a starting point. He then reworks them, at times giving them a distinctive Arab, or more specifically, Palestinian flavour. He explains:

> I took Jewish tunes and I Palestinised them and by doing that I'm trying to prove two things; first, I undermined the Jewish victim identity – they are not the victims, they are the oppressors. Second, if the music can be Palestinised so easily – and I say so easily because I am far from being a genius so if I can do it, everyone can do it – so maybe they can be Palestinised as well. And they [Israelis] were horrified. And I achieved my goal.
>
> (Atzmon 2005)

He does this with the track "Al-Quds" for example, which in its original form is an Israeli tune that became the anthem of the 1967 Arab–Israeli war. In "Al-Quds" (the Arabic word for Jerusalem) he reworks it, making it sound unmistakeably Arab (gilad.co.uk 2005). This musical challenge is also a political one which strikes at the very core of the Israeli–Palestinian conflict: the fight for Jerusalem. But here Atzmon is fusing the Arab with the Jewish and in so doing is effectively calling for a one-state outcome to the conflict with one shared capital Jerusalem/Al-Quds.

Political Activism, Music and Challenging Borders and Boundaries

Specific musical forms, tunes and melodies are recognizable as belonging to a particular culture or tradition. By taking well-known Israeli tunes and reworking them, often overlaying them with Arabic instrumental sounds, Atzmon is making a clear political statement. But this will not be discernible to all who listen to his music. This gap between what is intended and what is received by the listener is an interesting relationship that is worthy of some examination.

As was noted above in the section on the importance of the social group in the meaning-making process which deposits in each of us an "infinity of traces," this means that different people relate to Atzmon's music in different ways. As a jazz musician, his artistry and imagination appeal predominantly to some, whilst for others, it is the message that is encoded within his melodies that resonates most. This means that there is a complex "filtering" process taking place with the meaning ascribed to Atzmon's work resting neither with Gilad nor the listener but within the discourse. For some, Atzmon's music is a music of resistance, whilst for others it is just good jazz music. Norman Fairclough provides a good definition of what a discourse is. A discourse he writes is:

> widely used in social theory and analysis, for example in the work of Michel Foucault, to refer to different ways of structuring areas of knowledge and social practice. Discourses in this sense are manifested in particular ways of using language and other symbolic forms such as visual images (see Thompson 1990) [Thompson J.B., *Ideology and Modern Culture* (Cambridge, Polity Press, 1990)]. Discourses do not just reflect or represent social entities and relations, they construct or "constitute" them; different discourses constitute key entities (be they "mental illness," "citizenship" or "literacy") in different ways, and position people in different ways as social subjects (e.g. as doctors or patients), and it is

these social effects of discourse that are focused upon in discourse analysis. Another important focus is upon historical change: how different discourses combine under particular social conditions to produce a new, complex discourse.

(Fairclough 1992: 3–4)

It is important to note that although most of Atzmon's music does not involve lyrics. As a self-proclaimed "socially motivated artist," the struggle against political Zionism can often be found in some aspect of his music, be it in the choice of name for his band, his choice of names for some of his albums or the way in which he peppers his live performances with references to the Israeli-Palestinian conflict. Atzmon explains:

> To stand up on stage every night and to dedicate the last tune to Jenin [a Palestinian refugee camp in the West Bank] is shit. It's hard like hell. Sometimes I want to laugh you know. And I'm not in the mood. And I'm doing it because this is my duty. It's not a political duty, it's an artistic and emotional duty to play it. People are dying there. Alright, you had a great night. Remember. And it's not necessarily my most authentic, genuine thing to do. To explain Jenin without explaining what it is, is pretty silly because many people don't know or manage to forget. So I have to do it. It is very embarrassing and consuming to do if you're not exactly in the mood. But anyway I have a band behind me and even if I am not, they will help me. We help each other. You're playing it every night. I've been playing the Jenin number for two years. It's not easy.

(Atzmon 2005)

Atzmon has his own website and receives many e-mails from fans but also from critics, frequently Zionists, who object to his political message and the way he goes about communicating it:

> Some used to write to me. Many used to threaten me. I am open to dialogue. I learnt that dialogue with Jewish people can lead to confrontation because of the way I present my politics. I don't give them a lot of chance . . . I'm not afraid of communicating with Jews. But there is a very narrow set within the Jewish grouping that can engage in a fruitful dialogue with me. Why? Because I reject Zionism. But I reject the Jewish Left as well and this is very hard for many of them to take.

(Atzmon 2005)

It is significant that he has written two novels which also address the Israeli-Palestinian conflict. His first, the *Guide to the Perplexed* published in 2001, is a scathing parody of the Israeli-Palestinian conflict. It was translated and published in England but was also distributed in Israel for only two weeks before it was banned. His second novel published in 2005, *My One and Only Love* was described in the *Observer* as "a biting satire on Jewish identity, Zionist politics and sex" (Nicolson 2005). His published writings cannot be seen in isolation from his music or his music from his writings. It is the totality of this "systematic set of relations" which comprises a discourse of resistance (Laclau and Mouffe 1987: 82).

Music, Politics, Resistance and Change

Music as a form of resistance addresses fixed, dominant structures which through their hegemony constitute the status quo. Atzmon's music, by reinterpreting and reinventing something new from two distinct forms, Israeli-Jewish and Arabic-Palestinian traditions of music, creates a third way. This third way is a musical demonstration of that which is possible. The challenge, at least as I interpret it, seen through my own particular lens, is not for the two music forms, and by extension the two peoples, to be shut off and separated from each other (the Separation Wall comes to mind here) as the Zionist project calls for, but rather to celebrate the infinite possibilities that have yet to be imagined in coming together.

This message, rendered through music, is a challenge to the dominant political international vision of how to "resolve" the Israeli-Palestinian conflict as outlined in the Roadmap (a performance-based roadmap to a permanent solution to the Israeli-Palestinian conflict). Atzmon, by drawing on the essence of Jewish culture and tradition, one repository of which is music, is speaking to the Jewish people through a shared language, a distinct and distinctive musical tradition:

> I started in *Orient House* [his first album] by raising the simple question: How can the people [Jews] who make this kind of music, turn so nasty? What happened to this tradition? Where did it go wrong?
>
> (Atzmon 2005)

His appeal for a coming together with Palestinians, significantly, not in a relationship of domination (read occupation), but in one of equality, is anathema to many supporters of Zionism. The foundation stone of Zionism as a political project is precisely the opposite. It calls for the creation of an exclusively Jewish state for the Jewish people:

> Your nationality is supposed to be a geographic concept. You are German because you were born in Germany. I was born on land that was called Palestine

for two thousand years. The concept of Israel is ideological. So as long as I don't accept the ideology, I'm not Israeli.

(Atzmon 2005)

The maintenance and propagation of the status quo depends on continuity, stability and a reproduction of that which exists. Jazz music from its origins has been a musical form that has resisted tight, constraining, set forms of thinking about and playing music. In jazz, Atzmon has found a language through which to interrogate political systems that he saw around him in Israel; a language of exploration, finding new ways of being, living and communicating with oneself and with "the other" or as he puts it, "I want people to be disorientated" (Atzmon 2005). Much of Atzmon's music is pensive and self-interrogatory. As he notes, he had to begin by interrogating the context and situation he was born into. He saw much injustice was done to the Palestinians and "witnessed and empathised with the daily sufferings of the Palestinians" and spent twenty years trying to resolve for himself the tensions of his background. Finally, disillusioned, he moved away from Israel and went to England to study Philosophy (gilad.co.uk 2005).

Michel Foucault wrote:

> There is irony in these efforts one makes to alter one's way of looking at things, to change the boundaries of what one knows and to venture out away from there. Did mine actually result in a different way of thinking? Perhaps at most they made it possible to go back through what I was already thinking, to think it differently, and to see what I had done from a new vantage point and in a clearer light.

(Foucault 1985: 11)

Could this be a minimalist definition of what Atzmon, the political activist, through his music, sets out to achieve? Is jolting people out of their stupor, re-sensitizing them by presenting them with the *unfamiliar*, the function or at least one function of a music of resistance? If we believe, as Gergen does, that "the degree to which a given form of understanding prevails or is sustained across time is not fundamentally dependent on the empirical validity of the perspective in question, but on the vicissitudes of social processes (e.g. communication, negotiation, conflict, rhetoric)"; and that significantly, "perspectives, views, or descriptions or persons can be retained regardless of variations in their actual conduct," then a challenge at a discursive level as music is, a "social process" may have a vital role to play (Gergen 2003). As Donna Gregory has noted rather succinctly, "we do shape our world somehow in accord with our discursive structures; therefore, changing the latter might help us to change the former" (Gregory 1989: xvi).

Conclusion

Gilad Atzmon is one of many musicians and artists who challenge Israel's continued occupation of the Palestinian territories and the oppression of the Palestinian people through their work. What is particularly interesting about Gilad Atzmon is the fact that he was born in Israel, was brought up in a secular Jewish home but came to see the great injustice done to the Palestinian people. Atzmon has taken his critique of Zionism to what he sees as its logical conclusion. If the Zionist slogan, "a land without a people for a people without a land" was wrong, in other words, if as we now know, the British Mandate of Palestine was in fact *not* empty but populated with Palestinians who had lived there for around 2000 years, then for Atzmon, the option of a two-state solution makes no sense. As he puts it, "why should Palestinians be given Gaza and not Jaffa, Tel Aviv and Haifa?"

What marks Atzmon out is the fact that he has refused to separate his music from what he sees to be his "social commitment" or even tone down his political statements. As such, he admits that he has lost contracts, particularly in the United States where his views are unacceptable to many, especially within the music business. "I am paying a very dear price for it [for being openly supportive of the Palestinian struggle]" (Atzmon 2005).

Atzmon's listeners can be divided into at least three groups: those who appreciate and enjoy his music on the level of the aesthetic, being totally oblivious to the political message carried in his music; those who enjoy his music, understand the political symbolism with which he imbues much of his music and are enraptured with his music precisely because it chimes with their own political views; and thirdly those who may enjoy his music but are put off because they disagree with his politics. The politics of his music becomes a sort of Morse code or symbolism which only the politically initiated can engage with. For example, in the tracks where he fuses traditional Jewish soul music or Israeli folk music with Palestinian folk music, he is voicing his resistance to separation along ethnic lines as is dictated by the tenets of Zionism. Through his literal and metaphoric breathing of life into two distinct musical forms, Jewish and Palestinian folk, he is bringing them together so that at times they sway together, dance, evolve, interlock, dialogue, interweave and spiral into a new form of musicality – or "musikality" as Atzmon would perhaps put it. The two musical forms exist independently, but a third way is also possible Atzmon suggests, and it can be a very pleasing new, fresh, innovative and invigorating musical form. Can it or should it also be a political form or possible outcome for the protracted Israeli-Palestinian conflict? As Cynthia Cohen notes in this book,

> Once we begin to explore the meanings of musical expression not as inherent in texts (i.e. in terms of composers' expressions) but rather in terms of the experiences of the perceiver as he or she interacts with texts and performances, it becomes obvious that what audience members bring TO the musical encounter – the sensibilities, relationships, attitudes, historical resonances, etc. – will contribute a large measure of its meaning.

There are many who are critical of Atzmon and the way he has chosen to go about challenging Zionism. Many Israelis say "unlike Gilad, we have chosen to try and bring about change from inside Israel," implying that perhaps doing the work from within is harder. Other Israelis find his political views and his sharp, abrasive and uncompromising manner unpalatable and are therefore unable to engage with him or his music at any level. For other Israelis and non-Israelis alike, his music brings hope because it challenges stereotypes which present the conflict as one between two supposedly monolithic blocs, Palestinian and Israeli. Atzmon, through his music has managed to carve out a space from which to challenge the status quo in Israel. Whether this is seen as something positive or negative will largely depend on one's politics.

Atzmon clearly believes in art as an arena for social action or social activism. He believes that aesthetics is the most effective way to bring people – or at least some people – to some kind of social awareness and through this awareness to social engagement and action.

References

Abed-Rabbo, S., Mezvinsky, N., and Tekiner, R. (eds) (1989) *Anti-Zionism: Analytical Reflections*, Vermont: Amana Books.

Atzmon, G. (2005) Interview with author, London.

Atzmon, G. (n.d.) http://www.gilad.co.uk

Byrnes, S. (2005) "Talking jazz," *The Independent* (25 March).

Dobbing, H. (1970) *Cause for Concern: a Quaker's View of the Palestine Problem*, Beirut: Institute for Palestine Studies.

Fairclough, N. (1992) *Discourse and Social Change*, Malden, MA: Polity, Blackwell Publishers.

Foucault, M. (1985) *The Use of Pleasure: The History of Sexuality, Volume Two* (translated by R. Hurley), New York: Random House.

Gergen, K.J. (2003) "Knowledge as socially constructed," in M. Gergen and K.J. Gergen, *Social Construction: A Reader*, London: Sage.

Gramsci, A. (1971) *Prison Notebooks*, quoted in E. Said (1978, 1985) *Orientalism*, London: Penguin.

Gregory, D. (1989) "Foreword," in M. Shapiro and J. Der Derian (eds) *International/Intertextual Relations*, New York: Lexington Books.

Laclau, E. and Mouffe, C. (1987) "Post-Marxism without apologies", *New Left Review*, no. 166.

Nicolson, S. (2005) "With anger in his soul," *The Observer* (13 March).

Chapter 8: Unpeaceful Music

George Kent

UN Secretary-General Kofi Annan said, "music leaps across language barriers and unites people of quite different cultural backgrounds. And so, through music, all peoples can come together to make the world a more harmonious place" (Annan 2004). Surely, music does bring people together, sometimes. But we should be wary of music fundamentalists who think music is all good all the time. Have they never heard the booming cannon of the "1812 Overture"? Or Richard Rodgers' "Victory at Sea"? Some music may help to make some kinds of peace some of the time, but, like many other good things, music has a dark side as well. There is music that celebrates war, viciousness, hate, and humiliation. Music does have the power to heal, but we need to see that it also has the power to hurt. Music can bring us together, and it also can divide us.

Repellent Music

Music is peaceful or unpeaceful not because of the inherent character of the music itself, but because of the way it is used. To illustrate, in England a chain of grocery stores "is experimenting with playing classical music outside its shops, to stop youths from hanging around and intimidating customers" (*The Economist* 2005). According to another report:

> To clear out undesirables, opera and classical music have been piped into Canadian parks, Australian railway stations, 7-Eleven parking lots and, most recently, London Underground stops.
>
> (Timberg 2005)

Both accounts say the efforts have been successful. When music is used to repel rather than attract, that use of music is unpeaceful. Other people might think the music is good, but that is irrelevant. Where Homer's sirens used songs to lure men to their deaths, that too surely was unpeaceful, no matter how beautiful their songs might have been.

Nationalistic Music

A good way to study nationalistic sentiments in music is through national anthems. Why is it that anthems tend to be so highly militaristic? The United States' "The Star-Spangled Banner" begins:

Oh, say can you see by the dawn's early light
What so proudly we hailed at the twilight's last gleaming?
Whose broad stripes and bright stars through the perilous fight,
O'er the ramparts we watched were so gallantly streaming?
And the rocket's red glare, the bombs bursting in air,
Gave proof through the night that our flag was still there.

Pride in the nation's military might is also reflected in France's "La Marseillaise," originally named, "Chant de guerre de l'Armee du Rhin" (Marching Song of the Rhine Army). In English translation, it concludes:

Drive on sacred patriotism
Support our avenging arms
Liberty, cherished liberty
Join the struggle with your defenders
Under our flags, let victory
Hurry to your manly tone
So that in death your enemies
See your triumph and our glory!

New Zealand's anthem places much less emphasis on military might, and instead implores, even in its title, "God Defend New Zealand":

In the bonds of love we meet,
Hear our voices, we entreat,
God defend our free land.
Guard Pacific's triple star,
From the shafts of strife and war,
Make her praises heard afar,
God defend New Zealand.

New Zealand's militarism is limited to defending itself against direct invasion:

Peace, not war, shall be our boast
But, should foes assail our coast,
Make us then a mighty host,
God defend our free land.

So, New Zealand will defend itself if it is directly attacked, but it is not going to go into anyone else's space to defend itself. There is militarism in these national anthems, but it is not directed at any specific other.

Insurrectionary Music

Much music is simply irrelevant to those in power. Much of it is subservient, and serves power (cf. Said 1991: 64). Music also can have an insurrectionary quality, challenging those in power. The challenge may be delivered in the content of the lyrics that are voiced, but often insurrectionary music challenges through its contrast with the music of those who dominate. Some analysts see jazz, for example, as having been born as insurrectionary music. Jacques Attali speaks of how the exploited "can still use their music to shout their suffering, their dreams of the absolute and freedom" (Attali 1985: 8).

The meaning of music always depends on its context, but that meaning may be uncertain. Daniel Barenboim argues, "a performance of Beethoven, under the Nazis or under any kind of totalitarian regime, whether left or right, suddenly assumes the call for freedom, even becomes a very direct criticism of the policies of the regime..." (Barenboim and Said 2002: 44). He seems to feel that Beethoven's music is inherently insurrectionary. Perhaps not. The video, "Great Conductors of the Third Reich: Art in the Service of Evil," suggests that instead of being challenged, those who control the context might turn the music to their own ends:

> As a collection of performances by famous German conductors in Nazi Germany, this video provides an unnerving look at both how Nazi Germany tried to exploit culture and at the artists who essentially consented to turn their art into Nazi propaganda. Containing footage of concerts Karajan gave in occupied Paris, as well as Furtwangler conducting before a backdrop of swastikas, this video provides a truly startling and surreal look at classical music in Nazi Germany.
>
> (Synopsis at Rotten Tomatoes 2005)

If Barenboim were correct, how would we account for the fact that, "According to Hitler and Goebbels (Hitler's second in command), the three master composers that represented good German music were Ludwig van Beethoven, Richard Wagner, and Anton Bruckner" ("Nazi Approved Music" 2005).

Whether or not music is peaceful depends on context, but it also depends on how it is heard. If it is used to glorify evil, it is not peaceful.

Is insurrectionary music unpeaceful music? Insurrectionary music that challenges evil and is on the side of justice is peaceful, so long as it does not advocate violence. Of course music itself cannot tell us which side represents true justice.

Hateful Music

Music that expresses hate for others is not hard to find. In 1864, during the civil war in the United States, the Democratic Party's presidential campaign promoted a "new national anthem" called "Nigger Doodle Dandy" that was – and still is – highly offensive to African Americans (Loewen 1995: 148).

The hatefulness that it represented is not just ancient history. Panzerfaust is a neo-Nazi group with its own record label and streaming audio broadcast on the Internet. Its Project Schoolyard USA targeted its hate music to school-children, and distributed free Panzerfaust compact disks to children. Panzerfaust's decline is described at Anti-Defamation League (2005). Some of its products may be found at Free Your Mind (2005) which features a CD called *Downright Hateful*.

A Canadian band is called "Rahowa," which is short for Racial Holy War. Its tune, "Third Reich," sings:

> You kill all the niggers, and you gas all the Jews,
> Kill a gypsy and a Commie, too.
> You just killed a kike, don't it feel right?
> Goodness gracious, Third Reich.

> (Herbert 2001)

There is lots of hate music out there. The white supremacist group Stormfront has a Music and Entertainment section (Stormfront 2005). Some of this sort of material has been popularized under the heading of "gangsta rap," ably ana-lyzed at Wikipedia (2005). On 20 October 2005 ABC News did a segment on "Young Singers Spread Racist Hate," as described at ABC News (2005). These singers were described in Buchanan (2005).

Sometimes hateful music is deliberately used to stimulate soldiers to act. In Michael Moore's film, *Fahrenheit 9/11*, we learn that US Army tanks in Iraq are equipped to play compact disks for the soldiers as they go into battle. One review quotes some of the film's lines:

> "There were a lot of innocent civilians that were killed," admits one soldier, just before the camera cuts to another, who exults, "It's the ultimate rush" when you have a good song playing in the background during a raid.
>
> For one troop, the Bloodhound Gang's "Fire Water Burn" is just such a perfect song, and to illustrate, he spews lyrics: "The roof, the roof, the roof is on fire,/We don't need no water let the motherf**ker burn./Burn motherf**ker burn."

(Fuchs 2004)

What makes music peaceful or unpeaceful? I embrace the Galtungian vision that peace is not about the absence of conflict, but about the handling of conflict in mature, productive ways, and not in violent ways (Galtung *et al.* 2002).

Music that is combative in tone may nevertheless be peaceful if it seeks justice and if it uses nonviolent means in that pursuit. When world music is seen not merely as "an ecumenical, border-effacing aesthetic" but as "a counterforce to contemporary *neo*-imperialism" (Shapiro 2004: 71), it is combative but not violent; thus it is peaceful. "Victory at Sea" is unpeaceful because it supports naval violence, not because of the merits or demerits of the cause that violence supports. In Galtung's terms, one must seek peace through peaceful means.

Attali says, "All music, any organization of sounds is . . . a tool for the creation and consolidation of a community, of a totality" (Attali 1985: 6). Thus music, like other forms of communication, is a means for building community, building empathy among people. How can we reconcile this idea with the reality that there is also unpeaceful music and, indeed, unpeaceful communication of all kinds?

In hate music or war music the musicians play primarily to their mates, their friends, their allies. The purpose is to build solidarity, whether among racist politicians, neo-Nazis, or combat soldiers. Soldiers generally are motivated not so much by hate for the enemy as by the need for approval by their peers. Similarly, racists and neo-Nazis also act hatefully mainly to win the approval of their cohorts.

In hateful music, as in any other, there is a kind of reaching out, but it is always a reaching out to friends and allies. The difference between ordinary and hateful music corresponds to the distinction economists make between *cooperation* and *collusion*. In simple cooperation or collaboration, two parties work together in a way that produces some sort of extra benefit for them. In collusion, however, the cooperation that takes place between the two parties is at the expense of some third party. For example, when two large corporations secretly work to fix prices in their industry, they do so at the expense of consumers. Collusion is similar to conspiracy, a term that implies that there is cooperation, but it is cooperation at someone else's expense.

Hateful music strengthens ties between the collaborators, but at someone else's expense. Thus, a racist ditty sends a message of fellowship to fellow racists. That is more important than the message communicated to the targets of the racism. Similarly, rousing war music like *Victory at Sea* sends its message not to the opponents but to fellow soldiers and allies. If music builds solidarity among some groups by being hurtful to others, it is unpeaceful.

In contrast to nationalistic music, "We Are the World," conveys the message that we are all one, universally. Our merit is based not on invidious comparisons with others, but on joining with others to constitute *us*, together. There is a whole collection of songs about unity at Songfacts (2005), but that is not the concern of this chapter.

Capitalist Music

Exploitation within the music industry is illustrated in the popular film, *The Harder They Come*, which tells about the abuse of a reggae superstar by unscrupulous record producers. There is also the exploitation of the consumers of music – those who pay for it – in various forms.

Modern consumerism is not based simply on an economics of meeting wants and needs. In producing and marketing music recordings:

> the industry, at the same time as creating the object of exchange, must also create the conditions for its purchase. It is thus essentially an industry of manipulation and promotion, and repetition entails the development of service activities whose function is to produce the consumer: the essential aspect of the new political economy that this kind of consumption announces is the *production of demand*, not the *production of supply*.
>
> (Attali 1985: 103)

In Attali's view, "the value of the object is not in the work itself, but in the larger whole within which the demand for commodities is constructed."

Like many others, the music industry produces a great deal of income for many people, but its contribution to meeting fundamental needs is meager. The music system, especially that for popular music, reinforces global inequities, and diverts resources away from where they are most needed.

In this commodification process there is a systematic trivialization of music. In music, as in many other sectors of public life, there is a fundamental social tension between diversity and standardization. In today's music it is standardization of forms that prevails.

Apart from its content, there is a dark side to music in its industrialization and commodification:

> Fetishized as a commodity, music is illustrative of the evolution of our entire society: deritualize a social form, repress an activity of the body, specialize its practice, sell it as a spectacle, generalize its consumption, then see to it that it is stockpiled until it loses its meaning.
>
> (Attali 1985: 5)

There is insurrectionary music, but politically it is a minority voice. The globalized music industry serves dominant power:

> Even though the modern musician, because he is more abstract, gives the appearance of being more independent of power and money than his predecessors, he is, quite the opposite, more tightly tied in with the institutions of power than ever before . . . he has become the learned minstrel of the multinational apparatus. Hardly profitable economically, he is the producer of a symbolism of power.
>
> (Attali 1985: 116)

Music can contribute to peace, but that contribution is limited so long as it is held captive by those in power. Most music is now a commodity, sold in bulk. But there are openings, free spaces in which music can be used in a way that fulfills its potentials. As Edward Said put it, "a very important part of the practice of music is that music, in some profound way, is perhaps the final resistance to the acculturation and the commodification of everything" (Barenboim and Said 2002: 168). This book demonstrates one path of resistance, the use of music in the cause of peace.

References

(Web addresses were last accessed on November 9, 2005)

ABC News (2005) "Young Singers Spread Racist Hate," http://abcnews.go.com/Primetime/print?id=1231684

Annan, Kofi (2004) Secretary-General's introductory remarks at lecture on "Why music matters" by Professor Leon Botstein, President of Bard College and music director and principal conductor of the American Symphony Orchestra, http://www.un.org/apps/sg/sgstats.asp?nid=1166

Anti-Defamation League (2005) "Feud Puts Future of Hate Music Label In Doubt: Panzerfaust Apparently Out of Business," http://www.adl.org/extremism/panzerfaust_update.asp

Attali, Jacques (1985) *Noise: The Political Economy of Music*, Minneapolis: University of Minnesota Press.

Barenboim, Daniel and Said, Edward (2002) *Parallels and Paradoxes: Explorations in Music and Society*, New York: Pantheon Books.

Buchanan, Susy (2005) *The Gaede Bunch: Neo-Nazi Stage Mom April Gaede and Her Singing Twins are Poised for Stardom, of a Sort*, Southern Poverty Law Center, http://www.splcenter.org/intel/intelreport/article.jsp?aid=539

The Economist (2005) "Classical Music and Social Control: Twilight of the Yobs," *The Economist* (January) 8:50, http://findarticles.com/p/articles/mi_hb5037/is_200501/ai_nl8258241

Free Your Mind (2005) http://www.freeyourmindproductions.com/

Fuchs, Cynthia (2004) "Reel Movies, Fahrenheit 9/11: The Roof is On Fire," *Reel Images Magazine*, http://findarticles.com/p/articles/mi_hb5037/is_200501/al_nl8258241

Galtung, J., Jacobsen, C. G., and Brand-Jacobsen, K. F. (2002) *Searching for Peace: The Road to Transcend*, London: Pluto Press.

Herbert, Bob (2001) "High-decibel Hate," *New York Times*, August 20:21, http://www.rickross.com/reference/hate_groups/hategroups2.html

Loewen, James W. (1995) *Lies my Teacher Told Me: Everything Your American History Textbook Got Wrong*, New York: Touchstone Books.

"Nazi Approved Music" (2005) *A Teacher's Guide to the Holocaust*, http://fcit.coedu.usf.edu/holocaust/arts/musReich.htm

Rotten Tomatoes (2005) http://www.rottentomatoes.com/m/great_conductors_of_the_third_reich_art_in_the_service_of_evil

Said, Edward (1991) *Musical Elaborations*, New York: Columbia University Press.

Shapiro, Michael (2004) *Methods and Nations: Cultural Governance and the Indigenous Subject*, New York: Routledge.

Songfacts (2005) http://www.songfacts.com/additionalSearches.lasso?about=More%20songs%20about%20unity

Stormfront.org (2005) http://www.stormfront.org/forum/forumdisplay.php?f=33

Timberg, S. (2005) "Halt, or I'll play Vivaldi!" *Los Angeles Times*, February 13, 2005.

Wikipedia (2005) "Gangsta Rap," http://en.wikipedia.org/wiki/Gangsta_rap

PART III

Healing and Education

Chapter 9: Music Behind Bars: Testimonies of Suffering, Survival and Transformation

Kjell Skyllstad

Incarceration is one of the most depressing experiences imaginable. Freedom is mostly a concept until you lose it. Suddenly your life is no longer your own. You belong to the state, which means that every little aspect of your life is under the control of someone else [. . .] You've already lost the respect and trust of your community, and even being released doesn't change that very much. Essentially, once you've been jailed, you become eternally branded as unwanted: refused decent housing, rejected for employment, unable to care for yourself, let alone your family.

(Jones 2005)

This is the beginning of a letter headed "Music Behind Bars" that inspired the writing of this chapter. It was written by an inmate, Ralph Jones (pseud.) while serving a long term sentence in a prison in the USA.

Words alone cannot measure up to the pain and suffering inflicted by prison systems, which in many countries around the world are still built on the principle of retributive rather than restorative justice. The letter from Jones points to how this mentality is also mirrored through the ways in which societies react to ex-convicts.

Through the ages, music and song have developed as vehicles for the expression of the pain of the prison experience, and as a means of survival, often creating new musical forms and genres, like the blues. But, as the letter goes on to show, music also fulfills other functions:

Reducing tension, connecting people and bringing peace
Increasing empathy and reducing animosity
Providing an outlet for creativity and self expression
Connecting with past life, bringing back happy memories
Offering training to make music after release.

(Jones 2005)

Beginning with a closer look at songs from different times and places mirroring the harsh realities of prison life, we will try to explore these various functions of music behind bars, both in an individual, social and finally, political context.

A Voice of Compassion

Fifty years ago a new voice was heard when Johnny Cash recorded his first song in a Memphis studio, following in the footsteps of looming figures on the blues arena like Huddie Ledbetter (Leadbelly) who first recorded for Alan Lomax at the Lousiana State Penitentiary.

Ledbetter (1889–1949) had himself spent two long stretches of time served in prisons and on chain gangs, by most considered the real birthplaces of the blues. Born out of suffering and deprivation the blues has become one of the richest repositories of knowledge about the tragic history and human costs of slavery. Through its long documented history as the main form of American expressive arts it affords a critical understanding of the wider social realities from which it sprang, including not least the practices of the judicial system.

Cash had early wanted to sing and record in a prison, but Columbia Records was reluctant to support such a project. It would not be an exaggeration to see all his creative output as a social statement, mirroring the harsh realities of life. It all lead up to Cash becoming an ardent advocate of prison reform. A biographer of Cash said:

> Among everything else and perhaps above everything else, Folsom was also a social statement on behalf of disenfranchised peoples, as potent as any such statement in the roiling 1960s, for by appearing in front of America's modern-day lepers and recording and releasing what came of it, he unapologetically told his listeners that these locked-away men deserved his compassion, if not the liberation, that the 1960s offered.
>
> (Streissguth 2004: 13)

Raised in poverty, Johnny Cash on the backdrop of prison life and the burning issues of the day reflected the universal longing for acceptance, for understanding and not least for love. With deep psychological insight he gave voice to the troubling problems and intense longings of inmates – for love and freedom.

In 1968 Columbia Records finally gave the go-ahead for a concert at Folsom Prison in Folsom, California. Cash saw his prison concerts (there were to be 30 of them) as a chance to connect with convicts. He was to be one of them, sharing their suffering, remorse and longing. The dark topics were often treated with a sense of humor, also evident in the tension between text and music, reminiscent of the folk ballad.

Many of the songs directly address prison life: "25 minutes To Go" records the last 25 minutes of a convict on death row. "Give my Love to Rose" describes an inmate released from prison after ten years, who never made the journey home. And in "The Wall" a suicide is disguised as an attempt at escape. Cash said:

> I mean, I just don't think prisons do any good. They put 'em in there and just make 'em worse, if they were ever bad in the first place, and then when they let 'em out they're just better at whatever put 'em in there in the first place. Nothing good ever came out of a prison. That's all I am trying to say.
>
> (Streissguth 2004: 42)

In releasing the record, Columbia Records, knowingly or not, contributed to the widespread public picture of all inmates as unrepentant die-hards. After Cash sings the line, "I shot a man in Reno just to watch him die" in "Folsom Prison Blues," the prisoners are heard cheering loudly. The jubilation is however added during the post production, as Michael Streissguth confirms. The prisoners in fact stood in complete silence and the applause broke out only after Cash had finished the song.

Voices from the Prisons of Spain

> The story of *Dos Gritos de Libertad* (*Two Cries of Freedom*) is incredible; José Serrano & Antonio El Agujetas were in prison when the "Confederation Andalouse des Peñas de Flamenco" had the idea to organize a competition of Flamenco singers in the Spanish prisons – they won and made this amazing album: *Two Cries of Freedom: Gypsy Flamenco from the Prisons of Spain*.
>
> (Calabash Music 2007)

Victor Hugo called Esmeralda a "Gypsy" in his novel "The Hunchback of Notre Dame," but since then we have learned to use the term Rom instead. However, the Roms are still suffering from discrimination in most parts of Europe, and many of them find themselves behind bars in Spain.

An important study of Rom prison songs of Spain has been published by José Calvo González of the University of Malaga (González 2003). This study was done on the basis of collections made by folklorists during the last part of the nineteenth century. González sees the "Carceleras" (Rom prison flamenco songs) in a historical context as major elements in the formation of Rom identity – which González has termed "identity of the suffering."

In their disjunct poetic language these narratives or micro-histories, according to González, mirror the prison experience through a rich spectrum of expressive content. At the base we find the *plaint* directly bearing on the suffering sustained by a marginalized and distressed people. Through these songs the Rom prisoners re-vindicate their claim to dignity and freedom, while asking mercy in a tone of unbroken will and self-esteem rather than submission.

In a thematic analysis of the large collections of prison songs Gonzalés attempts a categorization around a variety of themes, many of them recurring in the songs of prisoners from numerous countries and periods. Among the categories discussed are songs about the experience of being detained, incarcerated and sentenced, reflecting on punitive traditions and power display. Other songs describe everyday prison life, with stories of surveillance and inspections, disciplinary reactions and maltreatment. Finally, there are individual stories of suffering and recounting of tales of exclusion and marginalization.

A content analysis affords a deep insight into the alternative value systems of a marginalized and dispossessed group. This mosaic of forms and themes of Gypsy prison songs, according to Gonzales, reveals an informal "submerged justice system," in conflict with the established system of retributive justice. It seems that the early collectors of songs were aware of this conflict and saw their work as a means of voicing protest against the Spanish administration of justice, raising public awareness and paving the way for prison reform. In short, giving convicts a voice.

Recently this voice got a chance to be heard by a large audience through a national contest initiated by the various state provincial governments (juntas) and the state accredited national flamenco clubs (peñas) in 1997. It was open to all incarcerated prisoners in Spanish jails, with the chance of winning the ultimate reward of 5000 pesetas and a reduction of their prison term. One hundred and fifty inmates from jails in Malaga, Valencia, Madrid, Alomorca, Barcelona, Ocana, Cuenca and Jaen responded by sending in demo cassettes. For the final selection thirty finalists were escorted by the Spanish Guardia Civil to the Cordoba prison, and got a chance to perform with the foremost flamenco instrumentalists and shouters (jaleos).

The great success of the project prompted the organizers to bring the winners José Serrano and Antonio "El Agujetas" – both members of the Rom community – chained and under armed guard, to José Delgado's famous recording studio in Granada. José Serrano had served 18 of his 25-year prison term for a gang-related homicide, for which Rom customs required the youngest to take responsibility, while Antonio "El Agujetas" had been sentenced to 23-years for a drug-related crime. On account of their popularity in Spain and the big success of the recording, they were both put on provisional parole under electronic supervision (Reachout International Records 2007).

A Call for Empathy

In order to fully understand the prison systems of today and the terms of incarceration under which convicts serve time, it is useful to cast a look at history. On a recent visit to the Irish city of Cork and its old City Gaol to look for song material, I got a glimpse of the hardships of prison life. A vast majority of inmates were detained for petty crimes, like stealing clothing or bread. Being poor was equated with being a criminal. (A useful historical account of prison life in Cork can be found in John L. O'Sullivan 1996.)

Van Diemen's Land (Tasmania) – a name uttered in fearful anticipation or recalled in gruesome remembrance in Irish and English convict songs of the 19th century – was once the home to over 12,500 convicts living under the most horrendous conditions of severe punishment. The gaols (jails) in Ireland and England were overcrowded, and the crime rate was increasing due to severe economic hardships and high rate of unemployment. The message of the transports to New South Wales and Tasmania was that crime would be punished most severely.

The songs narrate the long and painful journey from the musty gaols and prisoners' depot of Cork and Dublin across the sea to face the hardship of Tasmanian prison life. As many as one in four died at sea. Arriving at Port Arthur, a wet and inhospitable place at the Tasmanian coast, the survivors had to erect their own prison, each cell containing enough space for a narrow bed and room to open the locked door.

According to the records, of a total of 25,000 women and girls, transported through the years to New South Wales and Van Diemen's Land, about half, often transported with their children, came from Ireland. One song tells their fateful story:

From "Female Transport"

They chained us two by two and whipped and lashed along
They cut off our provision if we did the least thing wrong
They march us in the burning sun until our feet are sore
So hard's our lot now we are got to Van Diemen's shore

We labour hard from morn to night until our bones do ache
Then every one they must obey their mouldy beds must make
We often wish when we lay down we ne'er may rise no more
To meet our savage Governor upon Van Diemen's shore

Like most of these ballads the appeal for empathy ends with a final warning:

Come all young men and maidens do bad company forsake
If tongue can tell our overthrow it will make your heart to ache
Young girls I pray be ruled by me your wicked ways give o'er
For fear like us you spend your days upon Van Diemen's shore

(Australian Folk Songs 2007)

It seems that Irish prisons still have a long way to go if their aim is the prevention of crime. A report *Re-integration of Prisoners* published by The National Economic and Social Forum in Dublin gives an estimate of 77 percent of prisoners re-offending on release, and recommends that effective measures should be taken to promote re-integration through education and vocational training, making career guidance available to all prisoners. "There was a call for a change in the primary focus of imprisonment, from detention and security to rehabilitation and re-integration [. . .] It was felt that rehabilitation and re-integration strategies should be put in place from day one of a prisoner's sentence" (National Economic and Social Forum Report No. 22: *Re-Integration of Prisoners* 2004: 104–6).

The following examples intend to demonstrate how music could be accommodated in a program of re-integration.

Rediscovering Cultural Roots

Native Hawaiians comprise a disproportionately high percentage of the populations of the state prison populations. A coalition of organizations concerned with Native Hawaiian inmate rights (PONO) estimates that Native Hawaiians comprise 70 percent of Hawaii's adult inmate population. To alleviate overcrowding problems, a large number of inmates have been shipped off to mainland facilities, where they are subject to racism and alienation. The Corrections Corporation of America (CCA) has long resisted giving the inmates permission to conduct religious services in line with the doubts expressed by state officials in Hawaii that the Hawaiian religion still existed. True, Christianity has taken hold as the dominant faith among Native Hawaiians, but the older traditions have survived with a multiplicity of deities honored, like Lono, Kane, Ku, Kanaloa or the volcano goddess Pele. It was also feared that such meetings could be a cover for gang and drug activities. In 2003 the Native Hawaiian Legal Corporation sued in federal court on behalf of Native Hawaiian inmates, accusing officials of violating their constitutional rights, and scored a provisional victory. Traditional worship can help restore a sense of "ho'oponopono" (to make thing right) and get back in touch with their culture, and so help break the vicious circle of violence (Sodetani 2004).

After attending the celebrations for King Kamehameha I, who united the island, our source Jones sent this description of the importance of the ceremony, where music plays an important part:

> The men look forward to Hawaiian holidays with excited anticipation. It's the opportunity to sing along with island favorites and, for an hour or so at least, feel transported back to the sweet sounds of the islands. The experience brings a glow to the faces of men who normally face the day to day grind of prison life.

> For Hawaiian inmates, music is as much a part of the day as food and recreation. Does it make them a little more peaceful in nature? Or is their nature expressed by their love of music? Regardless of which is cause and which is effect, the impact and importance of music is evident and ever present.

> (Jones 2005)

Creating Empathy for Victims

In his letter, Jones sees a place for music in increasing empathy and reducing animosity. In the end a prison music program aimed at removing emotional blockages could prepare the way for the development of empathy with the victim, leading to apology and reconciliation on both the individual and social level. Creative initiatives led by competent music therapists could, in my opinion, pave the way for a more comprehensive program of restorative justice even within the predominant system of retributive justice practices. In his chapter Vegar Jordanger reports promising results from using music therapy-inspired methods in facilitating dialogues among the warring factions in the Black Sea/Caucasus region. The Guided Imagery method aimed at what Jordanger describes as "reweaving of life tapestries" that have been torn apart by tragedy could hold great promise for projects aimed at both the healing of victims and the rehabilitation of offenders.

A positive development towards restorative justice, reported from Hawaii, involves a music-based initiative. *The Honolulu Advertiser* reported the story of Brian Wong who, together with nine other inmates at the Kulani Correctional Facility, used donated equipment to record ten songs written by Wong during his eight years behind bars, songs voicing a prisoner's regrets about his past and fears about his future. The article reports that proceeds from sales of the CD will be donated to the Crime Victim Compensation Commission, a state panel that distributes payments to crime victims to try to ease their hardships. "For prison inmate Brian Wong, music has become a way of giving something back to the victims of crime." Within the framework of giving offenders the opportunity to acknowledge their offences and make amends, music could have a definite role to play in awakening empathy for victims (*The Honolulu Advertiser* 2005).

Music for Rehabilitation and Transformation

A growing movement for prison reform in many countries has led to an understanding of the way arts programs can contribute to the rehabilitation effort. In the UK The Unit for Arts and Offenders (UAOP) is the national umbrella organization for the arts in restorative justice. It was renamed "Anne Peaker Centre for Arts in Criminal Justice" in 2004 to honor its founder. Their *Directory of Arts Activities in Prisons 2003* records 76 individual artists and organizations involved in 650 arts projects in UK prisons during 2002. Half of these took place in institutions for young offenders. All reported progress in the development of

- creativity
- cultural diversity
- self-expression
- skills in the art forms
- self-esteem/self-confidence.

One initiative registered by UAOP was the musical project *Fair's Fair* at the Askham Grange open prison for women, situated about seven miles west of

York. This project was inaugurated by the Irene Taylor Trust, a registered charity committed to encouraging and establishing the use of music as part of a rehabilitative, educational and therapeutic process within the criminal justice system, and in other areas of social disadvantage. From August 1996 to March 2000, the Trust undertook 24 highly successful music-based training and performance projects across the UK, working with nearly 500 men, women and young offenders and with children who have suffered emotional deprivation and chronic abuse.

The objective at Askham Grange was to give women prisoners a chance to work alongside professionals and each other, to produce and perform a high quality musical. It was hoped that the project would:

- Raise self-esteem
- Improve self-confidence
- Encourage team-work
- Give the women a chance to be part of their community
- Give the women responsibility for something as a group of people.

The project ran from March through May 2000. The women then went on to tour the show to four other women's prisons. The project report relates:

> This project provides evidence that the experience for prisoners of touring a show to other establishments is highly beneficial in terms of building self-confidence, self-esteem and allowing the possibility for people to re-assess their view of themselves.
>
> (Directory of Arts Activities in Prisons 2003)

The musical project was a follow up of a full scale production of Shakespeare's *Julius Caesar* with an original musical score at Bullingdon prison for men, lasting seven weeks and involving more than 50 prisoners. The published research report documents some remarkable behavioral outcomes:

> 94 per cent of participants did not offend during the time that they were involved in the Julius Caesar project. There also was a 58 per cent decrease in the offence rates of participants in the six months following the project, compared to the offence rates in the six month period before the project began. As a result of the Julius Caesar project a permanent drama group was established at Bullingdon.
>
> (Directory of Arts Activities in Prisons 2003)

Music in Prison and Freedom

In 1991 a trail-blazing project was initiated by the music therapist Venja Ruud Nilsen at the Breitvedt Women's Prison in Oslo, "Music in Prison and Freedom," paving the way for investments in mobilizing musical resources in prisoner rehabilitation on a national scale. The main objective, according to the project initiator (Nilsen 1996: 11–16) was to improve the inmates' chances of mastering everyday life after served time. Each inmate was given the opportunity to play drums, bass, organ, guitar or to sing individually or in groups. The musical objectives of the initial project were for the prisoners:

*   To facilitate the pleasurable experience of playing an instrument and making music with others
*   To use music to consciously explore, master and change their emotions
*   To develop access to aesthetic enjoyment
*   To develop personal creativity through composing songs and instrumental pieces.

The social aims were:

*   To strengthen social skills of cooperation, responsibility, patience and accepted behavior
*   To nurture the development of identity and self-confidence, fostering a positive and realistic image of self
*   To develop faculties of concentration, coordination and related motor skills
*   To help develop positive social networks through music activities and a new perspective on the use of leisure time.

The project has three phases of activity:

Phase 1: Music activities in prison
Phase 2: Music activities following release from prison
Phase 3: Permanent free time music projects.

Just like prisoners elsewhere, the inmates at Breitvedt Prison have a background of mistreatment, failure in school, humiliation, social discrimination and low self-esteem following drug or alcohol abuse, often reinforced through their immigrant status. The average age of prisoners is 31 years, and around half of them are serving time for drug-related crimes. One third of these women, and two-thirds of inmates below 21 years of age, demonstrate self-aggressive behavior (attempting to hurt themselves).

The feelings of these women upon entering prison are mirrored in the songs they compose, like "The Black Sheep":

I've been mistreated, I've been replaced.
Got no money, and no place to call my home.
I can't hide it, it's in my face.
The pain is growing, harder, faster every day

Refrain:

I have been trying hard, and I'm trying now, but I'm
Still the black sheep of the family, I never
Change the way I am.
Still the black sheep of the family, I always
Gonna be the same.
I have been trying hard, and I am trying now.

In the song "Confused" the prisoner relates her background:

My childhood was no good, that's why I try to forget.
Using all kinds of drugs, then I'll take care of myself.
But it's just an illusion, I don't see any lights.
Cause all I can see, is darkness in the deep, deep night.

In the song "Movin' on" the prisoner tells about longing and a determination to change:

I don't wanna live, and I don't wanna die
Cause most of my life, has been based on a lie.
And that's how I feel, 'cause I ain't got nobody.
So tell me please, how I can keep movin' on.

Refrain:

I want you to know, just who I am
'cause I'm no longer, no longer the same.
I've changed so much and I'll guess you have too,
But if you're out there, I'll know what to do.

(CD *Real Life*, Norsk Musikkråd 1.utgave. Song texts expressly authorized for publication in this book by the inmate.)

Under the auspices of the Norwegian Music Council and financed by the Department of Justice, nine prisons around the country are now involved in the music program "Music in Prison and Freedom," with 20 more of Norway's total of 43 prisons on the waiting list. It testifies to a strong belief in the mission and positive results obtained.

The Prisons Transformation Programme

In the letter that prompted the writing of this chapter, the convict described the harsh realities in a men's prison:

> You're with 1,200 or more men who have little or no education, job skills, or motivation for change. The rule is simple: dominate or be dominated. Whoever is more muscular and more aggressive wins. Tension is always high, violence steadily lurking behind the surface ready to explode at any time.

> (Jones 2005)

Nowhere is this picture more applicable and calling for concerted action than in the prisons of South Africa. The Prisons Transformation Programme was born from The Centre for Conflict Resolution at the University of Cape Town in 1998 with an initial focus on imprisoned youth in Pollsmoor prison. The BBC program *Killers don't Cry*, first broadcast on Sunday 29 April 2001 gave impressive evidence of the place of music in transforming a prison confronted by destructive conflicts between gangs of convicted killers and their members.

The program told the story of the "28 Gang," one of the "Numbers gangs" originating in the violence of white rule. It was founded in 1906 as a revolt by 28 black prisoners as a way to defy and protect themselves against the atrocities of the white prison regime. The leader, or General, as he calls himself, had at the beginning of the project served 34 years in this high security prison. Like the other gang members he was heavily tatooed, as nobody expected ever to be released. He admits to having killed more people – mostly fellow inmates – than he can remember, beheading and mutilating their corpses. He describes how, together with other gang members, he cut out his victims' hearts and confesses to have eaten them in a ritual to possess their strength. It is difficult to imagine how this hardened criminal could in any way react to a rehabilitation program, especially one led by a woman.

But miracles can happen. One of the most impressive scenes of the film is where Joanna Thomas from Cape Town's Centre for Conflict Resolution during the Change is Possible project forces the gang members to confront themselves, their actions and emotions, for the first time in their lives. Playing the "Nessun Dorma" excerpt from Puccini's opera *Turandot*, the convicts, including the Leader, break down in tears. This again leads to a symbolic manifestation of reconciliation between rival gangs.

Epilogue

Some closing words from our friend Jones could in a very concentrated way sum up our exploration of the place of music in giving prisoners a voice and, as our examples have shown, prepare the way for a successful re-integration into society:

> Music plays an important role in keeping the peace behind bars. It keeps people's minds off the negative and provides a healthy outlet for creativity. It increases empathy and reduces animosity. With additional research and funding, music could be utilized even more purposefully to amplify the opportunity for self-expression and enjoyment.

(Jones 2005)

References

Australian Folk Songs (2007) "Female transport," http://folkstream.com/038.html

Calabash Music (2007) http://joseserranoantonio.calabashmusic.com/

Dayton, Kevin (2005) "Profits from inmates CD will help crime victims," *Honolulu Advertiser*, June 24, 2005.

Directory of Arts Activities in Prisons (2003 Edition), The Unit for Arts and Offenders (UAOP), http://www.apcentre.org.uk/

Downs, Lawrence (2005) "The Blessings of Lono. A vision of paradise in an Oklahoma prison," *NY Times Editorial Observer*, Feb. 15, 2005.

Gonzáles, C. (2003) *El Canto por Derecho*, Ayuntamiento de Malaga, Área de Cultura, Malaga.

The Honolulu Advertiser (2005) http://the.honolulu.advertiser.com/article/2005/Jun/24/In/In22p.html

Jones, R. (2005) Personal letter sent to the author in June 2005.

Nilsen, V.R. "Musikk i fengsel og frihet" (Music in prison and freedom), *Nordisk Tidsskrift for Musikkterapi* (Nordic Journal of Music Therapy) 5 (2).

O'Sullivan, John L. (1996) *Cork City Gaol*, Cork: Ballyhead Press.

Reach Out International Records (ROIR) (2007) *Two Cries of Freedom: Gypsy Flamenco from the Prisons of Spain*, [CD] http://www.roir-usa.com/8246.htm

Sodetani, N. (2004) "Culture behind bars: a nation within. Hawaiian inmates struggle to practice traditions," http://www.hawaiiislandjournal.com/2004/06b04b.html

Streissguth, M. (2004) *Johnny Cash at Folsom Prison*, Cambridge, MA: Da Capo.

Chapter 10: Healing Cultural Violence: "Collective Vulnerability" through Guided Imagery with Music

Vegar Jordanger

Introduction

The Dalai Lama once said:

> Learning to forgive is much more useful than merely picking up a stone and throwing it at the object of one's anger, the more so when the provocation is extreme. For it is under the greatest adversity that there exists the greatest potential for doing good, both for oneself and for others
>
> (Eckel quoted in Braithwaite 2002: 1)

> The condition which makes mercy possible is the admission of defects and fallibility in oneself!
>
> (Alapack 2005: 67)

Spiritual leaders such as Gandhi, Bishop Desmond Tutu and the Dalai Lama are re-educating the West about the nature of evil and healing. The more evil the atrocity, the greater the opportunity for grace to inspire a transformative will to resist tyranny with compassion. Today, worldwide initiatives invite people from different sides of warring conflicts to engage in dialogue, specifically to promote the conditions for reconciliation with co-constructive, conjoint work towards a stable peace. Fixed contradictory positions, backed by heavy emotional blocks, typically scupper attempts at genuine dialogue. How to overcome them? What will open the dialogue to a level where locked and entrenched positions might yield to discussion of basic interests and real needs? Can we find keys to create conditions to address the roots of emotions that hinder progress and thereby co-generate a transformative process?

Music researchers and practitioners such as Gary David and Angela Micley used music extensively and intensively as a tool for dialogue and reconciliation. They found that music facilitates positive outcomes in situations where limited conventional verbal and more purely cognitively-oriented approaches simply fail. The author's first-hand experiences in using methods inspired by music therapy in facilitating dialogue in the Black Sea/Caucasus region will be shared in this chapter. They are in the form of an eye-witness testimony of the beneficial power of music to dissipate disruptive emotional tensions and thus create a flowing, positive atmosphere that allows for creative collaborative work.

The aim of this chapter is not to "collect stamps," cataloguing a long list of cases where music approaches have successfully created conditions for dialogue. Rather, we will explore in depth a particular case in Crimea, during which Guided Imagery and Music (GIM) was introduced at a critical phase of a dialogue with Chechen, North Ossetian and Russian participants (a more comprehensive analysis of this and other group process cases involving "collective vulnerability" as well as of the music used in this session is under preparation. For more information see www.buildingpeaces.org on research). The purpose of this chapter is to understand the processes that took place. Specifically, we want to demonstrate the transformation of group emotional tensions into a flowing "moment" called "collective vulnerability" by Neimeyer and Tschudi (2003). We will also clarify the contributions of David (2005) and Tomkins (1992) to a theoretical understanding of these processes.

Conflicted and wounded family relationships, social crime, and global war manifest the same basic impulse: to strike back. Such retaliation often fuels long term cycles of hostilities and violence. We call it revenge. No single recipe has been concocted to help humans transcend such "eye for an eye" patterns. However, we can appeal to certain institutions and some concrete historical examples of authentic restorative processes, "moments" when all parties with a stake in the violent conflict came together and collectively came to terms with the aftermath of violence and wounded relationships. The Truth and Reconciliation Commission's (TRC) work in post-apartheid South Africa is a shining proof of the validity of this approach. It shows the possibility of entering processes that address the needs of both victims and offenders in ways conducive to individual and community reconciliation and healing. It took a spiritual leader of the stature and quality of Bishop Desmond Tutu to lead this *collective level* healing process. To transform the deep psychological wounds experienced by black, colored, and white citizens of apartheid South Africa, Tutu explicitly draws upon sub-Saharan indigenous traditional conflict transformation practices. Based on the concept of *Ubuntu*, he designed the enormously challenging work of the Truth and Reconciliation Commission (TRC) (Boneza 2004). *Ubuntu* means that "a person becomes a person through other people," and it expresses a deep, emotionally anchored sense of connectedness with all living beings. This cultural concept was one of the keys to the success of the TRC (see also Tutu 1999). In short, the TRC created conditions for positive transformation for many victims of brutal violence and loss. People who had lost close relatives and family members found mercy and reconciliation, as the Dalai Lama says, bringing out "the greatest potential for doing good, both for oneself and for others."

The good-hearted, charismatic leadership of Bishop Desmond Tutu and Nelson Mandela included the capacity to unite former enemies through their rhetorical art, symbolically powerful speeches and gestures. Tutu and Mandela were not only singing, they were also dancing (Alterhaug 2005). Does this mean that the engagement of opposing parties in dialogue and processes of conciliation, restoration and healing can only be accomplished by rare leaders with remarkable moral authority or spiritual aura? Or have they shown us a "way," so that other (impartial) third parties might facilitate dialogues between parties in conflict?

There are a huge number of situations wherein responsible statespersons and diplomats, or paraprofessionals, like graduate students and young professionals, must design the setting to orchestrate genuine conversation (for instance see the Nansen Academy's Balkan Dialogue Project: http://www.nansen-dialog.net). Negotiations between Israelis and Palestinians, Indians and Pakistanis, Northern and Southern Irish are examples of conflict situations in which third parties have a major responsibility to facilitate the processes of communication and designing the setting for the dialogue. Can the capabilities and human powers of exceptional leaders be transferred to common people? Can we identify the possibilities, repertoires and communication skills that any mature, trained and well-intentioned participant or facilitator might access to quicken stalled, stalemated, conflicted negotiations? What transformative tools might facilitators use whenever faced with emotionally demanding tensions that threaten to sabotage group communication? When tension is highest, what is the proper way of handling the situation?

Music as a Tool to Transform Negative Emotions: The Crimea Case

> Music is the art form par excellence of the affects just because it can duplicate these subtle, complex, ever-changing combinations of affective components by analogy, through variations in sounds which both mimic and evoke affects.
>
> (Tomkins 1962: 191)

In *The Psychology of Art*, Vygotsky endeavoured to demonstrate that art is a means of transforming the individual – an instrument which calls to life the individual's "vast potential, so far suppressed and constrained"(1925: 18). Later he says that the view of art as ornamentation of life:

> fundamentally contradicts the laws of art discovered by psychological research. It shows that art is the highest concentration of all the biological and social processes in which the individual is involved in society, that it is a mode of finding a balance between man and the world in the most critical and responsible moments in life.

> (ibid.: 316)

Guided Imagery and Music (GIM) is a technique inspired by music therapy. What follows is a report on a seminar in Crimea, which the author facilitated, in which GIM was employed to resolve very intense and emotionally demanding episodes at a certain phase of a dialogue seminar. Firstly, we will provide a general background and describe neutrally the "how" of the GIM session. Then the author, as a participating facilitator and observer of the process, will report the responses of the participants to the experience of listening to specific musical pieces. This account will also include participants' feedback based upon in-depth studies on conflict and emotions at this dialogue seminar, undertaken by two master students. A theoretical elaboration follows, identifying what happened at various levels during the music session leading to "collective vulnerability," transformed emotions and flow. Next, we evoke relevant psychological, musicological, and philosophical research to help clarify the assumptions underlying the theoretical argument in the previous section. Proceeding to a meta-level, we will discuss further implications of the study.

Thirteen students and young professionals from Chechnya, North Ossetia, and Russia participated in the music journeys during the dialogue seminar in Crimea in September 2004. Attending also were two facilitators and two master students from Norway, and one local Ukrainian interpreter.

We find the roots of the Russian-Chechen conflict in the eighteenth century when the Russian Empire increasingly expanded southwards. In 1784 *Vladikavkaz*, meaning "to rule the Caucasus," was established as a principal garrison in the North Caucasus. In 1944 Stalin, using an alleged collaboration with Nazi invaders as pretext, deported the entire Chechen and Ingush populations to Central Asia and Siberia. Using the most conservative estimate, over a third of the Chechen and Ingush population lost their lives as a result of the deportation and ensuing exile (Tishkov 2004). In 1994, and then again in 1999, violence erupted. Thousands of soldiers and combatants – Chechen and

Russian – lost their lives. These bloody wars, that have been referred to as the second genocide of the Chechen population, have terrorized and traumatized the remaining civilian population. The people, both Chechens and Russians, are the main victims of this gruesome and violent conflict. Unfortunately, the media simplistically portrays the wars as a conflict essentially between Chechens and Russians, thus creating fear and distrust.

The background for doing a GIM session was the need to deal with a rather emotionally demanding session on identity. The exploration of issues of identity dynamics of individuals embedded in prolonged conflicts is fruitful insofar as it allows participants to open up for understanding. They would discover that identity is not a fixed and "naturally given" reality, but a socio-culturally constructed phenomenon, continuously redefined and developed in multiple ways. In this particular dialogue seminar, with emotionally mature participants with a well-developed understanding of human relations, we used the following combined pedagogical approaches to address identity issues:

- rational verbal understanding of social identities (manipulation of identities, links to enemy images/stereotypes)
- the creation of identity groups (mixed and carefully balanced representation) using competitive exercises and name creation.

Firstly, we worked with identity issues on a predominantly abstract level. We encouraged participants to verbally express their insights on identity issues (e.g. how dictators and leaders in war manipulate identities in mobilizing people for war). Then we split into two groups. The two groups then engaged in a series of competitive exercises and name creation taking place in an atmosphere of joy and excitement. However, without being aware of it, the participants gradually formed two new identity groups. They eventually identified with their new "in-groups" and became completely immersed in the new identity groups: the Tigers and the Lions. We formed these two identity groups randomly, the only criteria being that the groups were balanced regarding national identities and gender. At least for the time being, the Tiger/Lion dichotomy overruled the national Chechen/Ossetian/Russian identities and also the identity-unity of the dialogue group as a whole. We here see the mechanism Tajfel has explored extensively in his now classical "minimal group" studies (1978).

Becoming completely immersed in the group energy of the new identity groups resulted in concrete physical behaviors. Group members failed to take into full consideration the well-being of all the participants. This realization was a hard pill to swallow for this group of fine representatives of future leaders of the North Caucasus. The remarkable ease with which they found themselves seized by the energy flows of the spontaneously formed identity groups, created cognitive confusion and emotional ambivalence. Thus, these normally well-balanced individuals found their well-developed sense of moral responsibility and critical judgment contextually and temporarily limited. There was a striking contrast and unpleasant incongruence between the impressive rational insights about the nature and manipulation of identities that the participants had just unearthed, and the emerging group behavior.

An emotional demand presented itself as a result of this discrepancy between the insights at the verbal level, and the behaviors at the more sponta-neous unreflective, high-energetic group level. However, the potential also was high for learning about identity processes – linking their own experiences to similar processes at community/national/international levels. This was also a great opportunity to form new identities and relationships (after having broken up/neutralized the ordinary ethnical/national identities). Everything hung in the balance. Subsequent handling of the emotionally demanding experiences could have gone either way. Here was the place to fully unfold the creative potential of the GIM exercise.

The Guided Imagery with Music (GIM) Procedure

Returning from lunch after that demanding identity session, instead of intro-ducing the planned role game in exploring reconciliation, we switched focus and we launched the GIM session. At first the participants required an appro-priate background to interpret and position the GIM session they were to take part in. I gave a brief introduction on the important role artistic expressions can play in promoting peace. Then I said that I would like to introduce the group to a music exercise that I had learned from a music therapist working for peace in South America. The music journeys began.

To lead the GIM, I told the participants that I would play approximately six pieces of music. While listening to the music they should pay special attention to the images that came to their mind. I also said that they had the choice to close their eyes or keep them open. I then asked for one minute of silence as a sign of remembrance, sympathy, and respect for those who had suffered in the recent terror attacks, including the tragedy in Beslan, but also in Chechnya where an unknown number of children have suffered and lost their lives dur-ing the last decade.

I then played the following pieces of music:

- Modern-classical song by Souad Massi from Algeria
- Traditional Chinese music
- Soundtrack with sounds from nature
- Traditional music from Laos
- *Om Namo.* An emotionally charged song by Deva Premal
- J.S. Bach. *Concerto for violin, BWD1041, Allegro* (Western classical music from the eighteenth century).

The selection of pieces of music I structured is not linked to the cultural history of the Russian/Caucasian region, except perhaps the Premal song, in Gypsy minor, a mode well familiar to people in Russia and the Caucasus. In addition, I presumed the participants did not regularly listen to the music selected. Also, they did not understand the lyrics of these pieces. These matters curtailed any systematic differences in the participants' responses to the music.

The setting for the seminar, thence the place where we listened to the music, was a beautiful garden at a private hotel situated a few hundred meters from the Black Sea. Sitting in the shadow of a pavilion, we were actually outdoors surrounded by flowers, with the blue sky above us. Since we were fortunate enough to manage to rent a hi-end stereo set, the sound quality of the music was superb. After one or two pieces of music (lasting about two to five minutes), the participants had the opportunity to share their experiences – their music journeys. And they were very willing to do so. For example, when listening to the Chinese traditional music, one participant described in detail her "internal landscape" of images accompanying the music, comprising a Chinese wedding with red lamps as prominent decorating features. Another participant experienced similar images but reported these in a chronological order where specific images corresponded to particular sequences of the music – more like a film accompanying the music. In subsequent studies it would be useful to collect and record such reported image data in a systematic and detailed way. (For an informative account of GIM see chapter 15 in Bunt and Hoskyns 2002.)

The Participating Observer's Experience and
Interpretations of the Music Journeys

We cannot help but transform our experience – Freud's emblem for this is dream-work – and we cannot help but express ourselves.

(Phillips 1998: 11)

From the very beginning, responsiveness to the music clearly characterized the group as a whole. From my perspective, the majority of participants seemed fully absorbed in it. It seemed that there was absolutely nothing else in this world they would rather do than listen to the music. It took them to places they had never been before, or where they had not been since their childhood (as one participant explicitly reported to me after the session).

The music "peak experience" reached its climax when the Deva Premal song was played. I sensed emerging within the group an incredibly deep emotional energy. The group as a whole reached a new level of experience, which was apparently unprecedented or rare for each individual. The repetitive patterns of Premal's singing began to reach a climactic point. I intuited and anticipated that the music could very easily and quickly be transformed to a major trauma trigger. The Chechen girls in particular seemed very close to tears. Later, two of them told me that at a certain point of Premal's music, images of Grozny after the massive bombardment of the city during the first Chechen war, and similar images appeared in their minds. The purpose of music listening in this setting was *not* group therapy with individuals that had suffered relatively intense trauma. This was not the place for initiating long-term therapeutic sessions dealing with deep-rooted individual trauma. At this point, I felt that I should not, at least not in this setting, let the repetitive patterns take the group even deeper down, and I resolutely picked the Bach CD and played the Allegro. An abrupt change of group mood followed the harmony of Bach's Allegro. Relief came, and a high-energetic calmness filled the shared space, accompanied by a joyful mode of curiosity and flow.

Spontaneously, after the music stopped, one girl said she wanted to paint. I suggested a theme for the painting. She and other participants might paint how they envisioned their desired societies for the year 2024. Furthermore, I asked them to be as concrete as possible, describing life in the domains of culture, sports, politics, education, family life, and others. In further studies, from the viewpoint of methodology, it would be useful to gather data from all relevant modalities. It would be interesting to look at the drawings participants made spontaneously or as a part of a group task just after the music peak journeys. An even more specific way of probing affect before, during, and after a peak experience of "collective vulnerability," would be to gather data from facial expressions – arguably the primary site of expression of affect (Tomkins 1992). Also, patterns of changes of body postures and movements – including spontaneous dance movements would be interesting to measure systematically. From my own experience, I remember that during the musical peak experience in Crimea, I sensed that accompanying the experience of heightened awareness my body naturally assumed a balanced posture where the angles between the head, the neck and the back were felt to be optimal.

After the GIM session, the group worked very creatively for the rest of the day and the following days. The whole group dynamic changed; the group stayed on that "positive wave" even in subsequent demanding conflict analyses, where the emotional temperature indeed became high. It seemed that the group tacitly knew that it could allow itself to reduce to a minimum self-imposed censure during the conflict analyses. This common "collective vulnerability" music peak experience they had shared united them precisely on a level deeper than mere disagreement on the verbal discursive level of conflict analysis. In retrospect, what I have referred to above as the climax of the music peak experience was the unique and pivotal moment. The incredibly deep emotional energy emerging in the group was decisive for how the group process unfolded even beyond the dialogue seminar itself. In fact, this "moment" was not limited to a sudden onset followed by an immediate offset. The sudden availability of the incredibly deep emotional energy, taking place in an eye-blink, lasted beyond the blink. It sustained. Using my own experience of sharing the emotional field of the group, I gaged that the crux of this peak experience lasted for somewhere between 30 and 60 seconds (this estimation is based on a relatively precise quantitative measurement of the music peak experience based on re playing the Premal song and a re living of the experience). Several observers/participants and I have identified these unique moments as critical for the subsequent phase of positive emotional flow within the group. I conclude that these unique moments generated a transcending power on the group's emerging experience of "collective vulnerability." In her master thesis Stine Dalsøren reports that, based on interviews with the participants, they see the "music journeys" as having a critical importance for the transformation of difficult emotions to "collective vulnerability," creativity and flow (2005). The other master student, Silja Skjønberg, also studying this case using questionnaires, interviews and participatory observation, confirms these findings (in process).

Theoretical Elaborations on "Collective Vulnerability"

What follows is a closer look at the interpretations of the music peak experience, and also an articulation of the assumptions underlying the phenomenon I have referred to as a shared experience, at the group level, of "collective vulnerability."

The following assumptions underlie my theoretical argument:

Assumption 1: The significant phenomenon that leads to the transformation of negative emotions in this case, is the very saturated emotionally meaning-making at the group *collective level*. Individual differences in experiencing the music, based on personal or cultural differences, do not play a key role in relation to what is studied here.

The background for this claim is that:

Assumption 2: Firstly, the participants have an approximately common mental and emotional state of mind as a starting point for experiencing and responding to the music.

Assumption 3: Secondly, due to fundamental properties of music and the mind and body's musical faculties, the music's sound patterns (including pitch, rhythm, and pulse) may resonate directly with basic human affects.

And, possibly the most fascinating and seemingly counter-intuitive assumption:

Assumption 4: The emotions experienced at the *collective level* are primary to the "individual visual content" of the mental images that manifest during the music journey.

And, finally, our main general assertion:

If organized and facilitated properly, GIM may create conditions for the experience of music journeys allowing for a "now we are all in the same boat" feeling; a state of "collective vulnerability" where negative emotions, particularly unacknowledged shame and anxiety, may be transformed into positive emotions and possibly a state of flow in the group.

Collectively: universal affect and (similar) emotions / individually: different visual manifestations

First of all, in the above interpretations of the GIM session, the level of analysis is essentially at the group level, the adequate level of analysis for what is studied here. Thus, the next assumption follows logically: individual differences including differences in experiential environmental background and personalities, in relation to what is studied here will not play a significant role. In effect, the emotions experienced when listening to the music are on a certain level, shared universal emotions. Experienced at the *collective level*, they are in some respects primary to the emerging mental images of the participants. At the individual level, these images show differences concerning their visual perceptual content, but more fundamentally they are perceptual manifestations or products of the emotions the music triggers. These emotions vary little from individual to individual.

We also may add that if an individual in this group is initially less emotionally involved than the group as a whole, the affective amplification at the group level will amplify this individual's emotional involvement. Affect and emotion are contagious. The affective amplification at the *collective level* functions as an additional amplification of affect in each individual. There is here an isomorphism between emotional amplification at the individual and *collective level*. Indeed, Donald Nathanson has proposed that there is no difference between the internal affective contagion that makes each affect trigger more of the same affect within one individual, and contagion from the outside, from other people. He argues that it is the receptors for internally derived affect that register the "music" of affect from other people (Nathanson 1992: 69). The receptors Nathanson has in mind here are those that transmit information back to the brain about the "affect program" that is currently operating – like hair on the head or the body; a breath of air blowing over erect hair feels quite different from "relaxed" hair, and will call further attention (back to the brain) to the fact that the individual is frightened.

"Collective vulnerability"

When the participants were allowed to share their experiences of the music journey and thereby reveal their emotions, therefore also articulating their emotions, the other participants received confirmation that they had experiences with similar emotional patterns (despite differences in visual perceptual content). This united the participants. Moreover, listening to the Premal song evoked a common emotional experience that, in this context, strongly accentuated our common suffering and perennial vulnerability to unpredictable risks and dangers. This particular group by no means had in common a "we are all small under the starry night sky" feeling, on a more or less abstract hypothetical level. Rather, concrete common experiences were at the fore of the participants' consciousness when entering the GIM session. These included the recent terror acts in the region shortly prior to the dialogue seminar, culminating in the Beslan terror acts, and more recently the shame experienced by the participants in the Tigers and Lions identity group behavior. Also it is a reasonable expectation, as we have already mentioned in passing, that the Hungarian Gypsy minor scale of Premal's *Om Namo*, would be familiar to the listeners. This musical mode is prevalent in Eastern Europe and Russia, including the North Caucasus. Of itself, typically it triggers a deep-culturally conditioned feeling of sadness, sorrow, and loss. The Hungarian Gypsy minor is a scale typically associated with Eastern and Central Europe, though it has moved into Western music with use by composers such as Franz Liszt and Bela Bartok. The scale is pentatonic in usage (five tones) though it contains seven distinct pitches. In terms of Western scales it is best thought of in terms of a harmonic minor with a raised fourth degree. What gives it its "color" is the presence of two augmented seconds between degrees three and four, and between degrees six and seven, giving it an Eastern or Oriental feel.

This background is at least one condition that made possible that the hi-end performance of Premal's songs evoked a "now we are all in the same boat" feeling. This state of "collective vulnerability" is the platform that allows for the transformation of negative emotions, particularly unacknowledged shame and anxiety, into positive emotions and a state of flow in the group. The meaning-making that led to this transformation resulted from both the verbal triggering of recent common real life experiences of loss and suffering, and the culturally conditioned response to the Gipsy minor and the repetitive suggestive patterns of Premal's voice (triggering it), and the whole order of the music experience.

Music, Emotions and Visual Imagery

Gary David has described the relation between sound and music, and affect and emotions as follows:

> [I see] sound as an analogue of affect, and music as an analogue of scripted scenes. I accept Silvan Tomkins's distinction of affect as biological, and emotion as a psychological phenomenon that occurs when scenes found to be similar (on the basis of the affect that motivated some response) are bundled together and as a bundle are made salient because magnified by another affect. Tomkins was as much involved in the mystique of the theatre as with the theatre of life, and therefore defined this psychological formation as a 'script' that operated with specific sets of rules and conditions. Scripts allow memory to leverage meaning within a current experience. By grouping families of past experiences, scripting shapes our feelings about and perceptions of what happens at any particular moment. It is the affect within a script that makes the past feel present. Analogously, music is a way of scripting that brings the sounds of the past into the present. It is the actual sounds heard that make the past feel present. Sounds in a musical script are like affect in the sense that they do not express anything other than their own embodiment. Yet they function as part of the meaning-making process that I call "*musicking*," a term first used in the eighteenth century to indicate the process of making music.

(David 2005)

David further argues that "music and emotion are so similar that it is difficult to distinguish where one starts and the other leaves off" (ibid.). Along these lines Susanne K. Langer writes:

> The tonal structures we call 'music' bear a close logical similarity to the forms of human feeling – forms of growth and of attenuation, flowing and stowing, conflict and resolution, speed, arrest, terrific excitement, calm, or subtle activation and dreamy lapses – not joy and sorrow perhaps, but the poignancy of either and both – the greatness and brevity and eternal passing of everything vitally felt. Such is the pattern, or logical form of sentience; and the pattern of music is that same form worked out in pure measured sound and silence. Music is a tonal analogue of emotive life.
>
> (Langer 1951: 27)

Cohen and Inbar (2001) talk about "emotional schemata," that may manifest in music as well as in other expressive modes, such as the prosodic level of speech, gestures, and facial expressions. In other words, we find music patterns – broadly defined – as a key aspect of the unfolding of emotional experience and expression in a broad range of communicational domains – not only in what we ordinarily refer to as music, or music interactions.

What is the major source of the emotional experience felt while listening to any music performance, for instance the hi-end performance in Crimea? Is listening to music invariably a major source of the emotional experience? Are the musical patterns resonating in the listeners paramount and determining? We can affirm close connections between musical patterns, emotions, motor action, perceptions and sensory imagery. Emotional experience and expression is trans-situational, unfolding in the emotive-musical aspect of speech, gestures, poetry, and visual imagery of daydreams and films. Godøy and Jørgensen (2001) put it this way: "there are associations formed which link musical sound to events in other modalities, such as to vision, various motor-related sensations or to more general emotional images" (Godøy and Jørgensen 2001: 3). Realizing this, they go on to raise the following questions:

> The question in our contexts is to what extent, as well as how, the images, schemata and/or constraints in other modalities can engender, enhance and influence images of musical sound, and conversely, to what extent images of musical sound may trigger images in other modalities. For instance, is it possible to imagine highly emotionally – charged music, e.g. Schoenberg's *Erwartung*, without also arousing emotions, and conversely, can various emotions evoke certain images of musical sound? Does imagining certain kinds of music also engender images of certain kinds of movement, e.g. does imagining a juicy tango also evoke sensations

of dance movements, or does the image of a frenetic drum sequence evoke the images of equally frenetic mallet, hands, and body movements?

(ibid.)

It now makes sense that one young woman spontaneously asked after the musical journey, "Can we paint?" Musical, emotive, visual, and motor schemata are interconnected. Her question was not merely "a more or less random expression of creativity," but evidence of hard wired structures and operators directing the information between the previously mentioned modalities.

Notwithstanding the close links between different modalities such as visual imagery and perception, motor-related sensations, and musical patterns, in our case of GIM in Crimea, the musical affordances in this hi-end performance shaped the group's emotional experience. Music and emotion are very similar; music is the art form par excellence of the affects because it analogously duplicates subtle affective components. These statements accord with our assumption:

- that in the case of Guided Imagery in Crimea, most fundamentally the emotions experienced are similar and shared at the collective group level – shaped by the music patterns
- that the visual images that are triggered are individual expressions of the same affects and similar human emotions at the *collective level*.

Different visual images in this group display the same or very similar emotions. Peculiar personal backgrounds provide correspondingly different perceptual and associative memory-stores. Accordingly, the same or similar affect will activate different imagery corresponding to the individuals' somewhat idiosyncratically established overall memory pool of imagery-emotion complexes – or in Tomkins' terms: "scripts" (1992). We stress that in this case, the difference in "activated" imagery is not to be attributed to systematic sub-group cultural differences. We deliberately chose selections of music to avoid systematically different responses to the music according to participants' different cultural backgrounds.

Affect triggers images. In turn, images trigger affect, just like memory in general, associated with emotional experiences, triggers affect. What kind of affect is triggered by individual images cannot be predicted in the same way as the affect experienced as a direct resonance of musical experience. Whereas in the latter case, we go from biology to biography (culture), in the former we go from biography back to biology. In itself, the triggering of affect is not necessarily a transcendental experience. This is an emotional peak experience involving higher cortical functions. As such they are resources where one may reach new subtle existential insights about oneself, the world and one's place in it. In short, there is no dichotomy between "primitive" affect and "ideal" refined emotions. There is no place for simplistic Cartesianism in the modern science of emotions.

Creating the conditions for trust and dialogue

Our case is merely illustrative or prototypic. In general, given the right circumstances, music can be very efficient in activating or enhancing the degree of shared content of consciousness. A high degree of shared content of consciousness is potentially very useful as it creates a basis for coherent thinking, ease of communication, common understanding, trust, and a new common identity. All this may unfold, nevertheless, only if the group is in accordance at an emotional level (accord, from old French, means, close to the heart). We may now better understand the great potential of music as a resource in facilitating human interaction and unity. Following David and Langer, we consider music as a tonal analog of emotive life. Not only will a shared music experience shape the emotional content of the group level consciousness. If a music performance can also allow for common emotional experiences, like in music journeys in which negative emotions such as unacknowledged shame, anxiety, disgust, and fear may be transformed, the group members will benefit from this beyond the individual level. Ascendant is the experience of deeply felt unity at the *collective level*. If there is no fundamental *emotional* unity at some level, there will be no common ground for trust. Likewise, there will be no ground within which one may talk freely and openly, so that expressing disagreement would not be construed as attacking the adversary but communicating sincerely, respectfully and constructively in an atmosphere of mutual recognition. People may be talking about the same things, doing the same things and apparently experiencing "a high degree of shared content of consciousness." But if there is no real significant *emotional* unity or level of identification, underlying incongruent emotionally backed-up assumptions will be the real operators in verbal discourse and apparent progress in communication is not likely to be sustainable.

Healing Cultural Violence: "Collective Vulnerability," Creativity and Flow

Neither Nelson Mandela nor Desmond Tutu were aiming at erasing all borders; they were not really embracing the idea that humankind should transcend to a kind of cosmic unity where any social categories or distinctions no longer exist. They understood quite adequately the human life-world and the nature of perception, cognition and human relations. Thus, they did not believe in idealistic versions of such "Gaia-like" ideas. On the contrary, they understood that social categories and distinctions will always exist as long as there are human beings on earth. What is needed are facilitating processes to release social categories and identities. Transcending the meaning of formerly frozen social categories and distinctions allows high and low, victims and perpetrator, to meet on higher overarching levels (see also *Grunnriss av en differensiell epistemology*, Johansen, unpublished manuscript).

Music therapy has developed into community music therapy (Pavlevic and Ansdell 2004). How does the collective musical practice we have called "music journeys" relate to these disciplines and traditions? In the case of the Crimea music journeys, we used music as a tool. Normal people from different sides of violent, protracted conflict held constructive dialogues as a part of their work in attempting to build peace on the community/intra-regional level. Music journeys can here be a crucial part of our repertoire in creating conditions for participants to transcend binary verbal thinking and the meaning of formerly frozen social categories and distinctions. What we seek is to allow for optimal combinations of different mental tools – then there must also be rhythm, resonance and music.

If we call the music journey some kind of therapy, it is not a completely apolitical therapy for "sick" individuals. Neither is it a community therapy for healing tensions and inter-relations in those communities. It is more fundamentally a therapy for our limited ways of thinking. Here, the boundaries between education and therapy become blurred. The variety of human mental tools is amazingly rich, yet we are victims of strong cultural-ideological deep-rooted patterns, as June Boyce-Tillman shows in her chapter. We can use music to counter and expand our mono culture of thought that limits our ability to transcend simplistic verbal thinking and has led us astray (in our desperate attempts to keep our self-image, polish our statue; insisting that we are much more civilized than advanced chimpanzees).

In the case of the Crimea music journeys, we emphasized the enormous potential of flow and creativity that may unfold as transcendence takes place within the context of "collective vulnerability." Interestingly, there seems to be a significant relation between the realization of creativity and (effective evaporation of) direct violence. In the Ecuador–Peru conflict over disputed land, Galtung (2005) notes that the successful creative solution of co-owning the piece of disputed land effectively stopped the violence between the parties.

Now, did the creativity in the Crimea music journey case wither or sustain? Actually it unfolded and flourished. The participants developed a *Peace through Art* project. They invited Russian, Chechen, Norwegian and Kenyan musicians for a days verbal and musical dialogue gathering, ending up with a peace concert in Rostov-on-Don, Russia in September 2005 (for more about this project see http://www.buildingpeaces.org). The event was a success and the musicians are currently planning further cooperation, possibly taking tours of the Caucasus and Norway. The creativity that unfolded in the wake of transcendence "collective vulnerability" led to the development of concrete regional peacebuilding projects. That is valuable in itself. Let us suppose that the participants sharing the music journeys would have represented a network of advisers to politicians and parliament members. What if they had been people with significant ties to influential political decision-makers? Then the creative action eventually might have lead to new sustainable solutions to regional or global violent and protracted conflicts.

Cases of "Collective Vulnerability" at Meso- and Macro-Levels?

In the Crimea music journey case, there are no attempts to downplay, avoid directly addressing, or "erase" social distinctions or differences. Rather, the group processes initiated touched directly and involved very deeply the affective layers of the participants. A reconfiguration of human relations resulted. Former social categories, distinctions and identities did not change in their particularity; the overall meaning of these found place in a more total or comprehensive container. Primarily, the relations between social entities changed. The introducing of new information and meaning altered the entire social system. A question arises: to what extent do similar processes take place at the meso and macro levels?

We believe that it is important to examine seriously other cases of "collective vulnerability." In so doing one should pay special attention to the role of the non-verbal and verbal aspects of such processes/experiences. Interestingly, John Paul Lederach, in his book *The Moral Imagination: The Art and Soul of Building Peace*, reports a remarkable case of conflict transformation from Ghana (2005). Not long ago, the century-long cycles of violent conflict between the Konkombas and the Dagombas tribes were brought to a change. Why? A sudden shift took place in a mediation process that initially seemed to be a disaster. In accounting for this turning point, Lederach does not use the phrase we have borrowed from Neimeyer and Tschudi, namely "collective vulnerability." However, just prior to the turning point in this mediation process, Lederach emphasizes that "the attitude, tone of voice, and use of the word *father* spoken by the young Konkomba man" apparently affected the Dagombas chief such that he remained silent before responding to the young man (2005: 9). When he finally spoke, he did so with a changed voice, expressing emphatically his understanding and pity for the suffering of the other tribe that was lacking a chief – whereupon he asked for forgiveness. At this moment, the young Konkomba walked to the chief, knelt and gripped his lower leg, a sign of deep respect. He uttered a single and audible "Na-a," a sign of affirmation and acceptance (ibid.: 10). Lederach further notes that "those attending the session reported that the room was electrified, charged with high feeling and emotion" (ibid.: 10).

How far can one generalize? We document our case and the limited data Lederach provides to exemplify "collective vulnerability" and transcendence. Interestingly, this case from Ghana opens up the possibility that "collective vulnerability" might be a path towards conflict transformation occurring in large-scale settings, with beneficial consequences for thousands of people stuck in protracted violent conflict.

References

Alapack, R. (2005) "Mercy and revenge: fundamental themes in Dostoevsky, Nietzsche and Gandhi," *Psykologisk Tidsskrift*, 1: 67–70.

Alterhaug, B. (2005) Conversation with the author.

Braithwaite, J. (2002) *Restorative Justice and Responsive Regulation*, Oxford: Oxford University Press.

Bohm, D. (1987) *Science, Order and Creativity*, London: Routledge.

Boneza, R.N. (2004) *Peace through Africans' Peaceful Means*, Oslo: Kolofon.

Bunt, L. and Hoskyns, S. (2002) *The Handbook of Music Therapy*, East Sussex: Brunner Routledge.

Csikszentmihalyi, M. (1996) *Creativity: Flow and the Psychology of Discovery and Invention*, New York: Harper Collins.

Cohen, D. and Inbar, E. (2001) "Musical imagery as related to schemata of emotional expression in music and on the prosodic level of speech," in R.I. Godøy and H. Jørgensen (eds), *Musical Imagery*, Lisse, The Netherlands: Swets & Zeitlinger.

David, G. (2005) *Vamp 'Til Ready: Musings on Music and Emotion*, http://www.philosphere.com/article61.html?&MMN_position=61:61

Dalsøren, S. (2005) "Emotions and conflict – a case study of interactive conflict resolution," Master's thesis submitted to the Department of Psychology, Norwegian University of Science and Technology (NTNU).

Fonagy, I. and Magdics, C. (1963/1972). "Emotional patterns in intonation and music," in D. Bolinger (ed.), *Intonation* (pp. 286–312), Harmondsworth: Penguin Modern Linguistics Readings.

Galtung, J.V. (2005). *Resolving Conflicts – Lessons Learned*, posted at http://www.big-picture.tv/index.php?id=65&cat=&a=159 (Sept. 5, 2005).

Godøy, R.I. and Jørgensen, H. (2001) "Overview," in R.I. Godøy and H. Jørgensen (eds), *Musical Imagery*, Lisse, The Netherlands: Swets & Zeitlinger.

Johansen, S.E. "Grunnriss av en differensiell epistemology [Outline to a differential epistemology]," unpublished manuscript.

Langer, S.K. (1967) *Mind: An Essay on Human Feeling*, Vol. 1, Baltimore: Johns Hopkins University Press.

Langer, S.K. (1942, 1951) *Philosophy in a New Key: A Study in the Symbolism of Reason, Rite, and Art*, Cambridge, MA: Harvard University Press.

Lederach, J.P. (2005) *The Moral Imagination. The Art and Soul of Building Peace*, Oxford: Oxford University Press.

Neimeyer, R.A. and Tschudi, F. (2003) "Community and coherence: narrative contributions to the psychology of conflict and loss," in G. Fireman, T. McVay, and O. Flanagan (eds), *Narrative and Consciousness: Literature, Psychology and the Brain*, New York: Oxford University Press.

Nathanson, D. (1992) *Shame and Pride: Affect, Sex, and the Birth of the Self*, New York: W.W. Norton & Company.

Pavlevic, M. and Ansdell, G. (2004) *Community Music Therapy*, London: Jessica Kingsley Publishers.

Phillips, A. (1998) *The Beast in the Nursery* London: Faber and Faber.

Schneider, A. and Godøy, R.I. (2001), "Perspectives and challenges of musical imagery," in R.I. Godøy and H. Jørgensen (eds), *Musical Imagery*, Lisse, The Netherlands: Swets & Zeitlinger.

Tajfel, H. (1978) *Differentiation Between Social Groups: Studies in the Social Psychology of Intergroup Relation*, London: Academic Press.

Tishkov, V. (2004) *Chechnya: Life in a War-Torn Society*, Berkeley and Los Angeles: University of California Press.

Tomkins, S.S. (1962) *Affect, Imagery, Consciousness,* Volume I, *The Positive Affects*, New York: Springer.

Tomkins, S.S. (1992) *Affect, Imagery, Consciousness,* Volume IV, *Cognition: Duplication and Transformation of Information*, New York: Springer.

Tutu, D. (1999) *No Future Without Forgiveness*, London: Rider.

Vygotsky, L.S. (1925/1987) *Psikhologiya Iskusstva [The Psychology of Art]*, Moscow: Pedagogica.

Chapter 11: Music Therapy: Healing, Growth, Creating a Culture of Peace

Maria Elena López Vinader

Introduction

Music therapy provides means for healing and rehabilitation, promotes inner growth, and can thereby contribute to the creation of a culture of peace. Many of the chapters in this volume illustrate the power of music to create peace and harmony. George Kent has also demonstrated that music can be used for unpeaceful purposes. Cynthia Cohen has shown that paradoxically, it can be used as a universal language only in specific settings, one of them being music therapy. In this chapter I will define music therapy and touch upon its origins and current trends. I will explain why I have chosen Logotherapy and A Continuum of Awareness as the main frameworks for my practice of music therapy, in conjunction with the Transcend Method of Johan Galtung, in my work for peace. I will talk about the nature of music, about its integrative and intrinsic qualities that have the ability to reach and connect human beings on the psychological, spiritual and social levels. An explanation of the importance of music based on biology will also be explored. We will see how music therapy can contribute to peace at the individual, family, community and planetary levels. Today music therapy has already been recognized in many countries for its effectiveness in the treatment of illnesses in both individual and group therapy settings. Now we need to find out how much we can stretch its potential for social and even planetary transformation. Can we move towards a "social music therapy," as Olivier Urban mentions in the introduction to this volume? We believe that the work of Music Therapists for Peace provides part of the answer.

Definitions, Historical Background and Trends

Definitions

Music therapy for me is: "the art and science of healing through the use of the power of music, sound and movement as a treatment modality within a therapeutic relationship, with the purpose of rehabilitation and enhancement of the human condition."

Because there are so many definitions of music therapy I will mention one agreed upon by members of the World Federation of Music Therapy. This definition was discussed at the World Congress of Music Therapy in Germany in 1996:

> Music therapy is the use of music and/or its musical elements (sound, rhythm, melody and harmony) by a qualified music therapist with a client or group of clients in a process designed to facilitate and promote communication, relationships, learning, mobilization, expression, organization and other relevant therapeutic objectives, in order to meet physical, emotional, mental, social, cognitive and spiritual needs. Music therapy aims to develop potentials and/or restore functions that sometimes can not be reached through other means of expression. In this way the individual can develop better intrapersonal or interpersonal integration and consequently, a better quality of life through prevention, rehabilitation or treatment.
>
> (Petersen 2005)

Historical background and trends

The use of music as a therapeutic tool is almost as old as humankind and some of its roots can be traced back to ancient Egypt and Greece. In classical Greece, Pythagoras prescribed some specific musical intervals to promote health and Plato linked music to the moral welfare of the nation. Nevertheless, music therapy started as a profession after WWII at the veterans hospitals in the United States and the first educational program was created at Michigan State University in 1944. In 1950 the first National Association of Music Therapy was created in the USA (Boxill 1985).

In the seventies the humanistic approach to music therapy started in the New York area with Doctor Kenneth Bruscia, Gillian Stephens Langdon, Edith Boxill and Barbara Hesser among others.

In England, some of the pioneers in the field were Juliette Alvin, Mary Priestley and Paul Nordoff and Clive Robbins. In Argentina, a well known pioneer is Doctor Rolando Benenzon who started the first music therapy program at the Medical University of Salvador in Buenos Aires in the 1960s.

There are different music therapy programs around the world. Some colleges and universities offer programs at the bachelors, master's and Doctorate levels. However, there is still no global agreement on courses and level of entry requirements for music therapy students.

At present, there are several models or approaches, such as Neurologic Music Therapy (Michael Thaut, Center for Biomedical Research in Music, Colorado, USA), Medical Music Therapy (Chery Dileo, USA), Humanistic Music Therapy (Victor Munoz, Mexico), Plurimodal Music Therapy (Diego Shapira, Argentina) among others. However, five internationally recognized pioneering models were presented at the ninth World Congress of Music Therapy held in Washington, DC in 1999. They are:

The Behaviorist–Cognitive model

This was the main trend in the United States until humanistic psychology came into the picture. It is based on the behavioral sciences, using music as an object to influence behavior. Some music therapists in the area of music and medicine conform to the medical behaviorist approach considering how certain types of music influence bodily reactions. This approach is goal-oriented, using music as a tool for the attainment of behavioral changes. One example is the clinical use of the Orff Schulwerk approach (Gaston 1982; Tyson 1981).

The GIM model

GIM (Guided Imagery and Music) was created by Helen Bonny in the 1970s. By listening to carefully chosen pieces of classical music, the client goes into a deep state of relaxation, which gives the possibility of entering into another state of consciousness which allows the person to heal wounds from the past, reach peak experiences and enhance one's creativity with a music therapist as a guide (Bonny 1978). Special training is required in order to be certified to use this method. Originally created in the US, its popularity has grown worldwide. In his chapter, Vegar Jordanger describes how he has used GIM during a reconciliation session in Crimea.

The Creative Music Therapy model of Nordoff and Robbins

Paul Nordoff and Clive Robbins implemented this method of improvised music therapy in the early sixties in England. Paul Nordoff was a composer and pianist and Clive Robbins an educator who believed in the power of music to help in the treatment of autistic and severely handicapped children. It is based on clinical musical improvisation and on the concept of the "music child," which posits an inborn musicality in each person who responds to the power of music.

This method is performed in dyads of music therapists where one person usually plays the piano while the other assists the child with other percussion instruments, movement, or whatever is required during the session (Nordoff and Robbins 1980).

The Benenzon model

Dr. Rolando Benenzon, a psychiatrist and musician, pioneer in the field of music therapy in Argentina, Brazil and other countries, is the originator of this model, developed in the early seventies. It has a strong psychoanalytical frame. Benenzon believes that one of the delicate problems in music therapy as a paramedical discipline is the training of music therapists (Benenzon 1981: 90). Gabriela Wagner who has worked extensively with him explains about the postgraduate training program:

> This model stands on three pillars: the continuous experience in didactic music therapy, the process of going deeper into the knowledge and expression of sound-music language, and recognizing one's own body as an intermediary object . . . It is based on predominantly improvisational process and verbalization may only increase at its completion.
>
> (Wagner 2006)

The Analytical Music Therapy model of Mary Priestley

Mary Priestley explains her model which she created in the 1970s in the UK:

> Analytical Music Therapy is the name that has prevailed for the analytically-informed symbolic use of improvised music by the music therapist and client. It is used as a creative tool with which to explore the client's inner life so as to provide the way forward for growth and greater self-knowledge. The analytical music therapist will have been trained in the Intertherapy orientation course, having previously or subsequently had personal experience of analysis or analytical psychotherapy . . . The idea is to learn how to redirect the energy so that the healthy part of the person can be reached so as to work with the "mad", dissociated parts of the personality.
>
> (Priestley 1994: 7)

We should note that music therapy, like life itself, is an unfolding process where each music therapist keeps learning about integrating knowledge, experience, science and art and new models develop to better suit the needs of the patient or client. I would like to share some of the theoretical and philosophical context of my own work.

Logotherapy, a Continuum of Awareness and Peace

As previously mentioned, music therapy is always based on one or more specific psychological frameworks. For my practice I have chosen Logotherapy which blends well with the humanistic concept of A Continuum of Awareness, developed by Edith Boxill. Based on these frameworks, different techniques and strategies are used to fulfill each person's needs.

Logotherapy was established by Viktor Frankl (1905–97), a neurologist, psychiatrist, doctor of philosophy, and survivor of four concentration camps. He developed the third School of Psychology in Wien called "Logotherapy and Existential Analysis" (Logos = spirit, meaning), a psychotherapy which helps people find meaning in their lives and to take responsibility for one's actions and attitudes. He gave the name "noogenous depression" to a type of depression due to a lack of meaning in life (Frankl 2000). He also said that meaning can be found in three types of values: experiential, creative and attitudinal. These values can be developed in a music therapy session because of the experiential and creative nature of this modality. A person who can feel and express his/her self through music, is better equipped to respond with strength to adversity. Frankl says that if there is something we could change we should, but it is when we *can not* change the circumstances of our lives that an attitudinal value *could* help.

Frankl's aim was to re-humanize the field of medicine and psychotherapy. Logotherapy gives an excellent foundation (not only psychological but philosophical and anthropological as well) to the practice of music therapy and allows the therapist to make the necessary links and efforts towards creating a culture of peace. One of the main concepts in Logotherapy, besides responsibility, freedom and values, is the concept of "self-transcendence." We acquire self-transcendence when we develop awareness and consciousness of the world around us. Frankl says that consciousness originates in the spiritual unconscious and that it is the voice of meaning . . . *where the spiritual self steeps itself in its unconscious depths, there occur the phenomena of conscience, love, and art* (Frankl 2000: 45). He says that ethics and aesthetics also have their foundation and basis in the spiritual unconscious. In the practice of music therapy we often work with clients or patients facing unchangeable circumstances. An example of this is the case of patients in dialysis treatment that I worked with. Their attitude towards the dialysis machine made a substantial difference. Some felt grateful because it helped prolong their lives while others felt as if they were "chained" without freedom to a machine three times a week. When patients understood that they can develop an attitudinal value from the freedom of the spiritual dimension, so that they can find "meaning" in their suffering, it made a big difference in the outcome of their treatment.

A Continuum of Awareness

The concept of a Continuum of Awareness has its roots in the gestalt therapy of Frederick Perls and client-centered therapy of Carl Rogers. This concept leads to the process of "intrinsic learning." It helps us to understand how learning occurs and it is the framework that I have chosen together with Logotherapy for the practice of music therapy. This is what Boxill says:

> The process of "intrinsic learning" and change as it is developed through a continuum of awareness, is viewed in terms of ever-increasing levels of awareness of self, others, the environment and the self in relation to others and the environment.
>
> (Boxill 1985: 74)

Professor Boxill in her vast experience with developmentally disabled people has implemented music therapy as a "Primary Treatment Modality."

Peace

The concept of continuum of awareness to promote intrinsic learning is not limited to helping people who have developmental disabilities but to anyone who is in the process of self-actualization, and self-transcendence. At this moment in the life of our planet can we say that the people in power are "aware" of the needs, and ecological problems as well as the possibilities which are available to promote a healthy world?

Frankl teaches that what matters is not what happens to us, but how we react to the events in our lives. This means that we can always choose how to react to specific experiences, even unpleasant ones, in order to create something positive and he called this "attitudinal value." This is very much in line with Johan Galtung's Transcend Method, which considers conflicts as a source for productive transformation. Frankl recommends a responsible way of life in which we take full responsibility for the way we react to what happens to us. If a growing number of people could learn how to do that, it would surely contribute to the development of peace.

In a music therapy session we are in tune with the Transcend Method either at the conscious or unconscious level. We help transforming conflicting aggression into accepted musical behavior by entering into a musical dialogue which is always creative and of course "non-violent." When we resonate with empathy, healing can occur and peace can be felt (López Vinader 2004).

As will be explained later in this chapter, the ability to resonate in a continuum of awareness naturally leads to the extension of this modality outside the treatment room towards the promotion of peace at a global level through "Music Therapists for Peace" (MTP). Logotherapy, as well as the Transcend Method added more light and insight towards the work of MTP.

Concerning music, the present author uses it in therapy to awaken inner possibilities for growth and inner peace. Music can "bypass" the mind and go straight to the heart, touching what Frankl calls the "defiant power of the spirit" (Lukas 1996: 161).

Biology, Nature and Music

After bypassing the mind, going straight to the heart and the spirit, where does music lead us? According to some biologists (Hunt 2001), our own bodies are made of a huge combination of vibrations, and we could say that we are not matter, nor energy, but "music," a vibrant combination of both. Our bodies are made of cells which are in constant vibration and "resonating," We also have the rhythm of our hearts and of our brainwaves, as well as the rhythm of other internal organs; we have melody in our voices and movement in our bodies: we move, we have rhythm, we have sound, a language of our own, a language and music from our families, ancestors, and even a "musical unconscious" which we share with all human beings. According to this interpretation, "we are music," and this makes the art of sounds a very powerful tool for therapy. It has also been proved that music can connect neurons in the brain. In a therapeutic empathic relationship we know that emotions of well-being trigger a better response and functioning of the body through the release of endorphins. Another aspect of the nature of music is the inherent musical intelligence which lies inside all of us. Louise Montello talks of an "essential musical intelligence" which can connect us with a realm of possibilities for growth (Montello 2002).

Another aspect of music is rhythm. It helps develop organizational skills and gives structure to the personality of the client or patient. It is a source of energy and group cohesion. This has been used for many centuries, and for the Guarani Indians (whom the author knows very well for living in their territory in the northern part of Argentina) as in many other traditional cultures, the state of trance is always induced by music making where rhythm is essential. They are also very much aware of the music made by nature, the wind, plants, birds and other animals, and this type of natural music plays a large role in their worldview. In today's busy and high-tech world, many people use relaxation tapes which mix music with the sounds of nature to connect with themselves. There is a technique called "entrainment" (an altered state achieved by repetitive rhythm) that is similar to the one described above and it is used in pain management in hospitals.

I often summarize this biological explanation with the phrase: "we are music." The kind of music we produce by our thoughts and actions and its influence on people and society, becomes a crucial question concerning our role for peace. In this sense, the voice plays an important role not only in therapeutic sessions but also in the overall communication of our thoughts and feelings. It is usually the music of the spoken language that reveals the true intention of the message. The power of singing together can never be overestimated because it is a source of union and collective gratification. It is also a source of strength and resistance as we saw in the chapters of Baruch Whitehead and Anne-Marie Gray.

Individual and Family Sessions

Music therapy is all about relationship, communication and empathy. The training to become a music therapist is very important because there are no "recipes" on how to run a session, since each client and each situation is new and different. A high degree of "tuning" of oneself towards one's own feelings, recognizing transference, counter-transference, developing intuition, creativity, unconditional acceptance, love and respect will be important to be able to *really* listen and resonate with deep empathy with the client so that a connection can happen and trust be developed in the therapeutic relationship. This relationship is the basis of healing, of learning, and the starting point for the search of meaning in life.

Different tools and techniques are used to meet the person's needs. However, there are three main strategies developed by Edith Boxill in her work with developmentally disabled people which are useful in establishing contact through music therapy. These are: reflection, identification and a contact song.

I have worked with different populations over the past twenty years, such as blind people, developmentally disabled children and adults, at school settings with children with behavioral problems, with pregnant women and at a medical hospital and in private practice with a varied population. Other places where music therapists work are psychiatric hospitals, nursing homes, special education schools and music therapy community centers.

One of the breakthrough experiences I had while doing my practice as an intern was a session with an autistic blind adult through singing. It was the only mode of communication to reach him and to create awareness of himself, his behavior, wishes and needs.

Working with pregnant women

Working with pregnant women with music therapy is an opportunity to give the best preparation to the new generation coming into this world. It is a kind of "preventive music therapy." I worked in an interdisciplinary team with a gynaecologist, and a yoga teacher.

The physical preparation for delivery played a major role and this was done by the yoga teacher who taught breathing exercises and special body movements. Music therapy provides the space and time for connection with the unborn baby, experiencing the beauty of creation through sound making, learning and exchanging lullabies, visualizing a bright future for this new life. One woman reported that during the music therapy session it was the first time that she had connected with her baby because otherwise she was under too much stress. Husbands were also included at the end of the workshop. It gave the whole "new family" a chance to share, to connect and enjoy music at a different level, releasing stress and anxiety.

The couple could also decide on "special" music to take to the delivery room that was significant enough as to give them strength and company at the moment of labor and birth. Parents who had this experience noticed how much their children were drawn to learn musical instruments and sensitive to sound and music, an element which contributed to creating a healthier environment in the family.

Working at a medical hospital

My experience as a music therapist in the neuroscience department and at the pediatric floor, as well as in the intensive care unit of the Hackensack University Medical Center in New Jersey, was one of the richest and most profound in my career. It was an opportunity to see how the power of music therapy, integrated with the Logotherapy theory, could help people overcome their sufferings. It was also an opportunity to learn about other cultures, to be able to "tune in" with the patients with empathy and caring concern. I could realize the universality of the language of love, music, sound and silence.

For instance, to soothe a child who was crying due to a medical procedure, I would start playing the marimba (a percussion istrument) and the child would stop crying, and even start to smile. For the placement of electrodes procedure, music therapy was also important as it avoided the use of sedation in cases of hyperactive children. The parents also experienced relief when they were able to play music with and for their children. Using music therapy with children in a hospital almost always means dealing with the whole family, and this fact provides a link between the individual and the family unit, expanding the power of music beyond a single person.

Once, I was working in the intensive care unit with a beautiful 16-year-old Polish girl who had been completely paralyzed in a car accident. I improvised a greeting in Polish and we taped songs with the voice of her mother for her to listen to during the day. In working in conjunction with the physical therapist with this patient, she said that when I was playing the autoharp, the patient was very relaxed. In fact, the physical therapist said that listening to the music comforted her as well. She was also experiencing stress, and the natural anxiety that most professionals go through while working in an intensive care unit, and the music was healing her too.

On one occasion, while I was playing for my paralyzed client, she opened her large green eyes, and I could hear a "thank you" coming from her heart. She was "trapped" in her body without being able to move or talk, but I was able to see the power of music to go straight to the heart.

Another instance which requires great sensitivity is at the time of waiting to enter surgery. The whole family is full of anxiety and nervousness and time takes on a new dimension. Five minutes could seem like one hour. Accompanying them with the instruments, singing with the child, or sometimes just playing for them makes those unbearable "waiting" minutes pass more easily. Music has the power to cross the boundaries between individual and family therapy.

Ringing the bell of understanding after 9/11

It was nine o'clock in the morning when I arrived at the hospital and from the eighth floor (where the neuroscience department was located) I could see the smoke coming from both towers. We had to comfort the patients, and be available for them. Going back to the hospital the next day was very painful as many people had lost family members, others were saved as though by a miracle. At the hospital you could feel a certain animosity and suspiciousness towards people of Arabic descent, whether they were patients, workers or visitors.

I took the peace bell (a portable bell made of recycled weapons) with me to the hospital and let its beautiful and soothing sound ring for my colleagues both individually and also in groups. We all needed to center ourselves after such a terrifying event had happened so close to us. The power of sound and the awareness of being able to do something to ease the pain we were all going through was a way for me to contribute to the healing of each individual, but also of the whole group, and at that moment I felt I was a true music therapist for peace.

Adding the Community Level

A pioneer in the work of the Community Center for Music Therapy was Florence Tyson in New York City. She founded the Creative Arts Rehabilitation Center, Inc. in 1963 for mentally ill patients who were discharged from the hospitals. Patients would receive music and other arts therapy services (Tyson 1981).

Nowadays, there are growing number of community music therapy centers in England, one of them is "MusicSpace." Leslie Bunt is a well known music therapist and the director of the charity "MusicSpace Trust" which offers a "space" for music therapy not only to patients/clients with different needs but to music therapists as well. This idea is now spreading to other European countries (Bunt 2002). In Argentina there is a group of music therapists working on prevention through psychosocial programs at schools and community centers mainly with adolescents "at risk" (Pellizari and Rodriguez 2005).

In Appendix 1, the reader will find the experience of Gillian Stephens Langdon which relates to the subject of community music therapy. As we move towards the subject of Music Therapists for Peace, the reader is encouraged to also read Judy Weisman's experience of working with veterans, promoting peace inside and outside the treatment room, in Appendix 2.

Healing the World: Music Therapists for Peace, Imagine: Peace is Possible

Music Therapists for Peace, Inc.

> Music must serve a purpose; it must be a part of something larger than itself, A part of humanity . . .
>
> (Pablo Casals, in Boxill 1997a: 157)

Music therapists have been extending their work outside the treatment room for more than a decade, and lately even more so in response to the trauma caused by war and by terrorist attacks like 9/11 in New York City, and others in Madrid and London. As the field of music therapy was born out of helping veterans who were traumatized, nowadays we are implementing our modality not only towards healing but also towards prevention, by supporting the creation of a culture of peace.

The organization Music Therapists for Peace, Inc. (MTP) was established in order to extend the continuum of awareness concept to respond to the many challenges of this world. Logotherapy has added a philosophical dimension to our work. Being able to promote peace through music therapy is a source of meaning and fulfillment in life.

In April of 1988 the bylaws of the organization were signed by Gillian Stephens Langdon, Edith Boxill and myself. Edith Boxill, as a director, developed activities in New York City with the help of other music therapists as I developed other programs in Argentina. Edith sadly passed away on 11 October 2005. She was a woman with great energy and conviction and she will be remembered as a visionary in terms of the contributions that MTP can offer to create a culture of peace. As the International Director of this organization, my commitment continues to grow as I find other people in the peace movement, and new knowledge such as the Transcend Method on conflict transformation is incorporated to expand our scope of action. The purpose of this organization is as follows:

> MTP's global context and vision offer untold possibilities for consciously using the power of music for the betterment of humankind, for the enhancement of peace in the world on all levels. Its broad scope and depth are being put into action – effecting healing and creating more harmonious relations among the many diverse people(s) of our planet Earth.
>
> (Boxill 1997a: 167)

MTP are engaged in different projects in the educational areas, and related fields, and have presented at major congresses of music therapy, logotherapy, and peace education as well as having participated actively in peace marches, candlelight vigils, and drum circles for peace. MTP works closely with other peace organizations such as T:AP (Transcend Art and Peace Network), IPRA (International Peace Research Association), the Peace Education Center at Columbia University and others.

One of Boxill's main concerns was to help children traumatized by war. She developed a project for the United Nations to send music therapists to affected areas.

Among the different programs it is worth mentioning SAVE. (Students Against Violence Everywhere), a project designed to reduce the violence that is rampant in schools. It empowers students to save their own lives, offering peaceful means of conflict transformation and alternatives to destructive behaviors through music therapy interventions. A pilot project was developed in New York City.

Following in the same direction and in order to reach more students, a course for teachers on "Stress Reduction and Preventing Violence by Creating Harmony in the Classroom" has recently been organized by myself in Argentina. The response from the teachers was very positive since they were able to notice changes in the behavior of the students in terms of learning and better relationships among themselves. Further research on the data provided by this course is currently being conducted (February 2007).

Another program under way is a multicultural exchange program with music therapists from different countries sharing music, languages, and cultures in order to deepen understanding, honor similarities and differences and creat harmonious relations between diverse people. This started two years ago between MTP of Spain and Argentina.

Music therapist Wang Feng Ng has written extensively on the work of music therapists promoting peace worldwide and her findings are published online in a virtual magazine called "Voices," a world forum for music therapists. In an interview with Edith Boxill she shares Boxill's involvement in the Drumming Circle for Peace (DCP) activity as a vital contribution for social peaceful transformation:

> DCP seeks [to raise the] awareness of people(s) of all ages, background, and conditions that nonviolent means of conflict resolution are imperative if we are to survive as a human species . . . in ways that are inspirational, transformational, and enjoyable. *Non violence is key.*

> (Ng 2005)

Imagine: Peace is Possible

"Imagine: Peace is Possible" is a radio program created five years ago by myself, hosted by the University of Misiones, Argentina and available on the Internet. The program is geared to promote democracy, human rights, cultural understanding and, last but not least, to empower people towards becoming active participants in their own lives; instilling hope that it is possible to develop an "attitude" of peace which respects and celebrates life, learning to accept and solve conflicts without violence. The themes have to do with the preservation of nature, peace education, as well as information about local and global events.

Artists, educators, and friends come from abroad to participate in the program. Special collaboration comes with members of T:AP through music, comments and phone calls from Japan, the USA, Canada or Pakistan. Taped conversations with prominent people in the field of peace education or music therapy are also part of the program.

The music is carefully selected for its meaning which sometimes is carried by the lyrics and sometimes by the cultures it represents. Exposure and appreciation of music from other cultures can promote a sense of acceptance, oneness and belonging to our "diverse" human family. Music therapist Even Ruud says: "Belongingness concerns not only our relationships to other people or larger groups or communities but also our feeling of being at home in the larger world, in history and geography"(Ruud 1998: 64).

Sometimes I may play an instrument with the guest or sing a song or invite the audience to a "guided relaxation" with the intention of creating a feeling of inner peace. On 22 November 2005 the day of music in Argentina and other countries (the day of St. Cecile, Patron Saint of Music), we celebrated our 100th program. There was a special "on the air party" with the Director of the radio station Pedro Silva and some friends playing live music on the air. He said:

> The University needs a space like this where open dialogue is practiced, allowing pluralistic views and tolerance, something which doesn't necessarily happen among the faculty members of the University where competition and power struggle seems to be the norm. We are happy to have a program like this . . .

The final sound of the program is a Tibetan singing bowl or the peace bell made with recycled weapons from WWII. It has the shape of a Buddha with a heart on the head which means we need to unite head and heart. It has a beautiful soothing sound and it has been used at many peace vigils and ceremonies. We unite in this sound with our intention for a brighter humanity.

Conclusion

The goal of this chapter was to share the contribution that the profession of Music Therapy is making to the world through healing, and promoting growth and peace. Integrating Logotherapy, A Continuum of Awareness and the Transcend Method gives a substantial base for bringing out people's highest potential for spiritual development.

Johan Galtung's chapter, regarding the interconnections between peace, music and the arts, showed how apparently incompatible differences could be resolved nonviolently with an attitude of integration, empathy and creativity. It is a great example of the transcendent quality of music, art and human values. By developing our higher consciousness, in sync with the rhythm of our hearts, we can all take part in the great symphony of life. Learning to transform dissonance into harmony, we can unfold a melody of hope, unity and creativity for the third millennium.

Appendix 1

This text was written by Gillian Stephens Langdon (a pioneer in the area of New York of the Urban Association of Music Therapy in the 1970s) who has worked for more than thirty years as music therapist at the Bronx Psychiatric Center. She shows that the same therapist can use music successfully at the individual, group and community levels. The main ingredient behind her work is empathy, a concept thoroughly discussed in Felicity Laurence's chapter.

Music Therapy and Empathy in an Adult Psychiatric Hospital

Gillian Stephens Langdon, M.A.

I look across a field and see the large institutional-type buildings rising up. As I approach I can see the high double fences surrounding them. At the door, a guard buzzes me in.

It is a long-term psychiatric hospital in the Bronx, New York City. This is a place for the poorest people who are mentally ill, violent or suicidal. They may have come from their own home, from the streets, or from prison to a short-term hospital and then when it was deemed that they needed more time to recover or the courts wanted them to stay longer, they were sent here. When they were first hospitalized, they were brought by a family member, themselves or the police. They may have been using drugs. They may be 19 years old or they may be 60. This is the end of the line – mentally ill and no money and probably unlikely to recover or be released for months, if ever.

I have worked here as a music therapist for over 33 years. It is here that I have learned to put love into action. Here is where I learned to move from doing good "for them" and creating a career for myself, to growing in empathy and healing. I have been privileged to see differences of language, culture, age and diagnoses melt away through music, to form bonds of laughter, caring and hope.

The main mode of music therapy is empathy. It is meeting another person in music and traveling together through the music toward health. Music naturally draws people together and therefore is a perfect mode for helping bring psychiatric patients back to health and, in many cases, back in to the community.

I work in a "central program" which is for patients who are well enough to come on their own from the wards where they reside. In the music therapy groups, sometimes we sing songs, sometimes we write songs or do "fill-in" songs. There is almost always musical improvisation using percussion, melodic percussion and voice. The whole group creates the music and no one has to have had musical training. I use more or less structure depending on the needs of the group. There is usually an opening song or activity that serves as a warm-up, a middle section that focuses on group and individual needs or a particular feeling that emerges, and a closing activity or song. I normally work with groups rather than individuals because of the tremendous needs and time constraints.

In order to look more closely at the work of empathy I will break it down into three spheres: individual, group and community.

Music therapy and individual empathy

This first sphere can be called individual because this is the focus, yet it can occur in a group. There are two aspects to it: 1. listening in silence, and 2. listening with a musical response. Individual work begins with an awareness by the leader of the individual patient and his or her needs. As a leader, I quiet myself and look at the new group member, whom I have met previously in an interview. I try to really "receive" him or her. I honor them with my heart and I look for their health. This is fostered by the creation of music. In creating music one is creating "wellness."

An example of the first aspect, responding in silence, is with someone with whom I am currently working. He is diagnosed as paranoid schizophrenic and medical tests have discovered that he also has cancer. So far, he has refused treatment for it. He always appears angry. He is continuously muttering to himself or cursing loudly. Sometimes he shouts about a family member, sometimes about the government. Sometimes he will include me or another group member in his tirade. He is usually hunched over.

His body is tense and he often has his hands in fists as if ready to strike out. At times I have asked that the staff remember him from the group because he is proviking the, other group members to such an extent that I am afraid there may be a fight. However, middle aged man has a rich and beautiful voice and it is in his moments of singing that he finds a little peace. Even though he used to refuse to join in at all. Now, sometimes he may stop yelling and if I ask him to try to be quieter, he may say, "I will sing you a song."

Usually when he sings he will look up at me over and over with his intense green eyes. I center myself and receive his song into my heart. I have a feeling of wanting to communicate without words: "Yes. Here you are. I hear your beautiful voice. You are here." The group is surprised by the beauty of his voice and they listen quietly and then clap for him when he finishes singing.

I am hoping that being heard deeply will allow him to increase his trust and help him find a constructive outlet for his anger through creating his own music.

I also hope that, building on this, he will begin to have moments in which how feels at peace even when he is not singing.

In the second aspect, where the therapist's response is musical, there is what music therapists call "clinical improvisation." I join the client's music with my own music, trying to really experience it. Does what the client plays sound soft, fragmented, tense? Is the rhythm irregular or steady? I meet the client's music where it is, usually using a harmonic instrument such as piano or guitar, where I have a wide range of responses available to me. As we "meet" in the music sometimes the client will look up at me in recognition. I will support where he or she feels the music wants to go. Does a fragmented rhythm want to become loud and forceful? Does a quiet, timid sound want to become tender and expansive? I feel it more than I think it. I see how the client responds. If the client responds to where I take the music, then I feel it is all right to continue and we create an improvisation together – a new music of health.

Music therapy and group empathy

One of my overarching purposes is empowerment – to let each client find an authentic voice and find a way to get this across, helping each group member to receive him or her.

Creating music draws people together. First there is rhythm which tends to get people in sync. And then there might be a refrain of a song or an entire song that people know. Yet they have to be listening first. Some people, as in the previous example, have to be heard first before they can listen. As group members begin to feel valued and begin to listen to one another – even if it is music of a different culture (of which we have many) – they begin to be able to create music together.

As a group leader I help to guide the group. There may be many requests at the beginning of the group. "Let's do this! Let's play that!" I want to help the group find its collective voice while at the same time honoring the individual.

So, as the group leader, I help to choose what we begin with based on the "feel" of the group. Are they angry, joyful, resistant? It is from this sense of the group that I begin. At the same time, empathy expands and the group members may be able to act on this themselves, honoring each other and trusting that they will be heard in the group.

I remember one session in which the patients came in quite loud and disorganized. One group member blurted out, "Did you hear? My girlfriend tried to hang herself last night." She was a patient who had made many attempts before. They resided on the same ward and she was a member of this group. It was shocking news. He became paranoid and afraid of hearing the drums played loudly. I asked him what he needed and he said, "quiet music." I sang a peaceful song, feeling his pain. But the group hadn't coalesced yet and, hearing his traumatic news, they began to get out of control, talking loudly, demanding to be heard first. The first patient's concerns became lost in the chaos. I needed to help the group come together. So I began to use structure, as I often do with this group, including singing patients' names at the beginning, following a rhythm of one of the clients and supporting it on the piano, telling the conga player to wait and listen, then listening to his song.

We managed to achieve some order, and a sense of listening to one another. But I was still filled with the ache of the first patient in witnessing the suicide attempt of one of his only friends in the hospital. I held this ache in my heart, and near the end of the group, I asked one of the quieter members what song we should end with. He immediately chose "No Woman No Cry," a song by Bob Marley. I thought, "Yes. This is the answer to this patient's anguish." I began to play on the guitar and sing "no woman no cry . . . I remember when we used to sit . . . No woman no cry." I played from my heart. I did not own the music. I felt it travel through me. The group was silent, soaking up the beautiful consolation of Bob Marley's words: "In this great future, you can't forget your past. So dry your tears, I say. No woman no cry . . . Everything's gonna be all right, everything's gonna be all right." Here was the response to the anguish of the first patient. The patient who chose the song felt it and the entire group was able to feel the concern and the healing and to honor it.

Music therapy and community empathy

I have changed and my work has changed over the years. I have come to trust in the nonverbal, the power of music to heal and the presence of love in the face of silence or fear or sorrow. My experience with the BPC Band has been my most recent journey and continues to be a place of transformation.

The BPC Band was created by a student of mine and when she left she passed the leadership over to another music therapist who is a bass player and a professional musician. I asked if I could be the piano player. When they agreed, I started a new journey of breaking down barriers and creating community – a wider empathy. For the patients it has been an experience of creating community between the members of the band – learning to listen, to respect each other, share their individual talents and work together, performing for their peers and reaching out to the community outside the hospital.

The goal of the BPC Band is to gather musicians within the patient population to rehearse and perform. As it has developed, we have invited group members to return once they were discharged. As such we now have outpatients, inpatients and patients in transition. We perform within the hospital but we have also performed in the community. At the same time, some of the members who are living outside are beginning to reach out themselves, as their confidence builds. Some have joined a community band and are beginning to perform independently while continuing their work with at the band the hospital. It is wonderful to see this dedication and joy spread beyond the walls of the hospital.

For myself, barriers have fallen away in the process of struggling to create and perform music. I think I truly realized this the first time I got angry when one of the group members told me that I had been playing a particular rhythm incorrect for months. I was so angry I almost quit. But then I had to go back and work on it until I got it right. I realized then that I had let go of the feeling of condescension I had been subconsciously carrying. I was just a band member with a hurt ego.

Another time I realized that barriers had melted away was when the band played at a family day event. One of the band member's mother and niece had come too and he said, "Sit with us, you're family anyway."

I should explain that the name of the BPC Band refers to Bronx Psychiatric Center. We keep this name because it is sort of an "in" thing. If you live or work there you know what it means. It is the patients' band. We belong to the hospital.

I have to do some juggling with my different roles and I feel a certain need for self-protection, but our work together in the BPC Band has broken down many false barriers, allowing love and respect to flourish as we enjoy our music and hard work. This translates into beautiful music, laugher and smiling on stage. The patients observing us and dancing with us, partake of the joy and feeling of freedom – because we are *their* band. We are not a hired band to take care of or cheer up the "poor patients" or provide uplifting music for the "unskilled, uneducated, crazy people." Because, with a little support, the patients *are* the BPC Band.

I have also experienced amazing things in music therapy groups. After the attacks World Trade Center in 2001, the patients wanted to sing songs in prayer for the people who died and for the families who lost loved ones. Who would guess that these people, the poorest in New York City, locked up in a mental hospital would be praying for the suffering people in the world.

As can be seen in music therapy in a psychiatric setting, empathy has many aspects: the empathy of receiving the voice of another simply and purely into one's own heart; the empathy of being sensitive and open to the need of a patient in the group which is also communicated within the group, allowing the empathy to expand and guide the group in its musical responses; and, finally, the empathy of letting down barriers to join and support the world of the "patient" and create new communities, as seen in the BPC Band and experience in the creation of prayerful songs for healing in the world.

Appendix 2

Working with Veterans

Judy Weisman, Ph.D.

In music therapy, veterans and I explore music and peace through improvised sounds, military, patriotic and peace songs. I support and validate experiences, feelings and thoughts. Awareness comes and decreases conflict.

In a "Music Therapists for Peace" educational course, held at an American Music Therapy Association Conference, by Professor Edith Boxill and myself, a young veteran was among the participants. I conducted an experiential session regarding empathy. One half of the group was to represent terrorists. The other half was to play the victims. All took musical instruments and turns improvising sounds of war or of being warred upon while acting. Afterwards, in debriefing, the veteran said that when he played a soldier, his sensitivity towards the victims of war was dulled and killing was too easy.

What *is* the effect of military and patriotic songs on veterans?

In informal research I identified which songs had a greater likelihood of leading them to think of war or peace. The military songs were: "The Caissons go Rolling Along" for army and, for navy, "Anchors Aweigh." The patriotic song is played at sporting events and national ceremonies: "God Bless America." I performed these, asking veterans to listen or to (optionally) sing along. Afterwards, I asked: "Did this song make you think about war or peace, or neither?" Less than half thought about war when they heard their military song. A majority felt the patriotic song made them think of peace. Further research is needed with a larger population and controls, on the topic of what the effects were of these songs on feelings/mood/affect.

Some veterans are plagued by terrible memories, which service songs evoke. The pain re-experienced by one veteran grieving caused me to ask everyone for a moment of cleansing, healing silence (part of music) in tribute.

Veterans were arguing about war. Someone mentioned John Lennon. Another: "He's anti-war." "If you don't like it, go someplace else." "I was against that war and am against this war." I decided to play Lennon's beautiful song "Imagine" without words. "Yeah, I liked a lot of his music." The group's tension eased. In another session, a veteran voiced terrible sadness about the men she saw killed in battle. I played "Where Have All the Flowers Gone?" a well known 1960s song reflecting that sadness. Through music and music therapy I was again able to help heal separateness and reduce pain.

References

Benezon, R.O. (1981) *Manual de Musicoterapia*, Barcelona: Paidós Educator (2nd edn).

Bonny, H. (1978) *Facilitating Guided Imagery and Music Sessions*, Baltimore, MD: Monographs ICM Books.

Boxill, E.H. (1997a) *The Miracle of Music Therapy*, Gilsum, NH: Barcelona Publishers.

Boxill, E.H. (1997b) *Students Against Violence Everywhere*, New York: Music Therapists for Peace, Inc.

Boxill, E.H. (1985) *Music Therapy for the Developmentally Disabled*, Rockville, MA: Aspen Publications.

Bunt, L. (2002) Mentioned during the "10th World Congress of Music Therapy" held in Oxford.

Federico, Gabriel (2003). *Musica Prenatal*, Buenos Aires: Editorial Kier.

Frankl, V.E. (1979) *El Hombre en Busca de Sentido*, Barcelona: Empresa Editorial Herder, S.A.

Frankl, V.E. (2000) *Man's Search for Ultimate Meaning*, New York: Perseus Publishing.

Galtung, J. (2000) *Conflict Transformation by Peaceful Means (the Transcend Method)*, New York: United Nations.

Gaston, Thayer E. *et al.* (1982) *Tratado de Musicoterapia*, Barcelona: Ediciones Paidós.

Hunt, V. (2001) "The lost chords found," http://www.bioenergyfields.org/index.asp?SecId=4&SubSecid=35

Khan, Inayat (1979). *The Mysticism of Sound; Music; The Power of the Word; Cosmic Language*, Katwijk, The Netherlands: Servire BV.

López Vinader (2004) "Music and the Transcend Method," *SGI Quarterly Magazine*, No. 37.

Lukas, E.F.J. (1996) *Tras las Huellas del Logos. Correspondencia con Víctor E. Frankl*, Buenos Aires: San Pablo.

Montello, L. (2002) *Essential Musical Intelligence*, Wheaton, IL: Quest Books.

Music Therapy (1987) *The Journal of the American Association for Music Therapy*, Volume 7.

Music Therapy (1988) *The Journal of the American Association for Music Therapy*, Volume 8.

Ng, W.F. (2005) "Music therapy, war trauma, and peace: a Singaporean perspective," *Voices: A World Forum for Music Therapy*, http://www.voices.no/mainissues/mi40005000191.html

Nordoff, P. and Clive, R. (1980) *Creative Music Therapy*, New York: Nordoff-Robbins Music Therapy Clinic.

Pellizari, P. and Ricardo, R. (2005) *Salud, Escucha y Creatividad, Musicoterapia Preventiva Psicosocial*, Buenos Aires: Ediciones Universidad del Salvador.

Petersen, E.M. (2005) "Music therapy and oncology at the National Institute of Cancer," *Voices: A World Forum for Music Therapy*, http://www.voices.no/mainissues/mi40005000195.html

Priestley, M. (1994) *Analytical Music Therapy*, Gilsum, NH: Barcelona Publishers.
Ruud, E. (1998) *Music Therapy: Improvisation, Communication and Culture*, Gilsum, NH: Barcelona Publishers.
Tyson, F. (1981) *Psychiatric Music Therapy: Origins and Development*, New York: Creative Arts Rehabilitation Center.
Wagner, Gabriela (2006) Personal communication with the author by email in January 2006.

Chapter 12: Managing Conflicts through Music: Educational Perspectives

Kjell Skyllstad

Education for Empathy

Responding to a call from the Intermusic Center in 1988, the Norwegian State Concert Agency (Rikskonsertene), involved in a national scheme for promoting musical literacy, started planning for an educational project aimed at preventing ethnic conflicts in Norwegian primary schools. Increasing social tension and incidents of harassment in Oslo's inner city schools with mixed ethnic populations had become the subject of heated public debate and a search for political answers.

A new urgency to explore the complex factors involved in the formation of destructive conflicts in today's world has been created by the experience of social tension accompanying forced and voluntary migrations. The transformation of the public school populations in a multi-ethnic direction calls for new tools in dealing with the educational challenges. It is generally believed that added emphasis on information intended to bridge ethnic divides is the key to a better school climate, replacing harassment and other expressions of conflict by inclusion and cooperation.

The American standard textbook in adolescent psychology, however, emphatically contradicts this belief:

> Various people have attempted to reduce the already measured prejudice in a given group. The logical assumption was that an intolerant person will lose his negative attitudes once he has been given adequate information about, and adequate contact with, those whom he dislikes. The matter is, however, not so simple, because prejudice rests upon emotional rather than intellectual grounds. There seems to be no relationships between knowledge and feeling toward a group, and an already established prejudice is reduced only a little if at all by supplying facts to counterbalance it.

(Cole and Hall 1970: 485)

It was precisely this kind of understanding that led to the focus on musical methodology as an important tool in fostering empathy and tolerance. One conclusion from these findings is that preventive measures must be put in place before prejudicial attitudes have been firmly established. They cannot be based on the communication of information alone, but should confront the irrational and emotional bases of discriminatory attitudes.

Building on the success of their school music program, Rikskonsertene set out to involve competent teachers of music and musicians from immigrant communities, together with artists from countries of origin, in a program of intercultural music education. The project was called the Resonant Community (as a musical parallel to an already existing social project, the Colorful Community).

The following goals for this three year program were formulated:

- To spread knowledge and create understanding for the values that reside in the culture of immigrants by presenting live music and dance for children.
- To counteract racism by contributing to changes of attitude towards various immigrant groups through cultural influence.
- To bring out the musical resources that lie in the various immigrant groups in Norway, as well as to provide external professional support through performers from the immigrants' home countries.
- To ease the process of integration for immigrants through multicultural interaction.

Methodical guidelines were worked out in cooperation with the musicians and teachers involved, with special attention being given to both traditional and innovative approaches and practices originating from countries of origin. Building on the National Curriculum masterplan and new research in educational psychology and music therapy, the following areas were singled out:

- Listening to live performances of music from Asia, Africa and Latin America facilitating a positive response to the cultural heritage of migrant students.
- Organizing music and dance activities, with special emphasis on improvisation, in order to foster group cohesion and integration.

Listening: A Transformative Experience

Music is not in the first place dependent on those stimuli that reach the outer ear, not even the reactions of the inner ear, but of the organizing and transforming reactions of the mind.

(Murcell 1937)

Among the transformative experiences reflected in musical compositions (like Heinrich Schütz's famous motet: "Saul, Saul, Saul, was verfolgst du mich") none is more poignant than the New Testament account of the calling of Paul, the apostle. The story relates how Saul, the aggressive and fanatical persecutor and oppressor, is suddenly overcome by a total and explosive sensual experience of light and sound that completely changes his life.

Abraham Maslow has coined the term "Peak Experience" for such encounters that involve a deep, structural shift in basic premises of feelings, thought and actions. He points to their transformative function, facilitating a sensation of expanded time and place, of becoming part of an enveloping whole. Maslow also describes how these experiences lead to a new relationship with others and a change in world outlook (Maslow 1968: 101).

World literature, including the sacred books and epic accounts, contains numerous stories about the function of music in rehabilitation and person reconstruction, which have prepared the ground for the establishment and rapid growth of modern music therapy. Dr. Kenneth Bruscia, a leading figure in music therapy today, emphatically puts the arts at the center of inner conflict transformation:

> Therapy should facilitate peak experiences, those sublime moments wherein one is able to transcend and integrate splits within the person, within the world. Since the arts facilitate the occurrences of peak experiences, aesthetic endeavors are seen to be a central aspect of life and therefore of therapy.
>
> (Bruscia 1987: 33)

Neuro physiologists explain how such sensory experiences remove emotional blockages through simultaneous neural breakthroughs, leading to permanent encodings in the synaptic structures. Maslow asserts that peak experiences create a demand for reliving the experience. As Piaget has pointed out, each new encounter will then be integrated into previous experiences (Piaget and Inhelder 1974: 134). A single peak listening experience in early age can be seen to trigger a long, often lifelong ongoing process of activating and mobilizing cognitive fields and value systems. Noted psychologists maintain that strong emotional experiences in preadolescence may decisively influence the value orientation of a whole generation.

In young people the listening experience in a social setting is often accompanied by a physical feeling of total involvement. The key to individual and social integration then lies in the dynamics of the human body. We are moved towards sympathy, understanding and togetherness. Within the context of the Resonant Community project it was early decided that dance activities should become a central arena for developing empathic competence. Professor Even Ruud at length discusses the listening process as a peak experience, referring to an interview involving 149 respondents (Ruud 1997: 178–86). Many respondents referred to strong bodily reactions to music. Most significantly, the listening experience was described by many as becoming one with the music, living in expanded time and space, as well as experiencing a strong feeling of community.

Vegar Jordanger of the Department of Psychology at the University of Trondheim and Director of the Building Peaces network has demonstrated the power of listening in conflict transformation. Jordanger builds on the listening methodology of the music therapist Helen Bonny.

Ensemble Playing: A Key to Social Learning

Music is part of the very construction and interpretation of social and conceptual relationships and processes.

(Seeger 1987)

Human life develops through creative interplay, linking artistic and social activities. This view of human development which is held by ethnologists, psychologists, sociologists and historians alike constitutes a firm base for music education.

Throughout the long history of humankind, artistic activities like music, dance, theatre and painting have constituted the explorative space where social relations are formed and transformed and where democratic traditions are developed and maintained. Music ethnologists like Anthony Seeger, through his studies of music traditions among Amazonian tribes (Seeger 1987), has shown how important music making is for the construction of civil society.

In this process, musical forms have been shaped and reshaped to make them effective tools in social construction and reconstruction. The musicologist John Blacking finds that music has been socially most effective "when people made links between its formal structure and social content and their own experiences of life and music" (Blacking 1987: 98) and quoting anthropologist Clifford Geertz: "Art and the equipment to grasp it are made in the same shop." This means that music is interpreted through the same tools that we use to interpret other aspects of our socio-cultural system. This points to a basic musicality inborn in every human being, an indispensable tool for the mastery of life.

Human values and human patterns of behavior are shaped partly as a result of artistic activities. We are all born with a strong possibility of becoming responsible citizens through training in social interaction. Through music making, personal creativity becomes transformed into social energy.

Blacking observed how music making among the South African Venda people in the same process, facilitates a simultaneous and coordinated outlet for individual and social expressivity. The playing of a piece of music that could easily be performed by one musician alone is distributed between the members of a whole ensemble. This practice, which he terms "democratic polyphony," enriches both the social situation and the music itself (Blacking 1987: 99). A similar performance situation is found in the *angklung* traditions of Southeast Asia.

This society building process may be studied through ensemble practices of peoples all over the world, mediating between tradition and innovation and between individual and collective creativity. Research has shown that musical activities, especially in social settings, lowers the concentration of the hormone inducing aggressiveness – testosterone in men together with other behaviour – regulating hormones, thereby preventing social conflicts. In both men and women music lowers the concentration of the stress hormone cortisone. Some tests indicate an increased production of oxiton, a hormone that strengthens social bonding between men and women and ensures greater group cohesion.

Folk music ensembles have through the ages been developed as important vehicles for establishing and maintaining social coherence, especially in local settings across ethnic divides. Political manipulation and historical misinterpretations have in some countries, like the former Yugoslavia and Ireland, caused a kind of musical apartheid, where traditionally shared practices, and even instruments, are now divided up to be used as artistic symbols of exclusivity in the current conflicts.

Realizing this situation, musicians and musicologists have sought ways to support cultural and social reintegration. One such project, named "AZRA" among Bosnian refugees in Norway, was initiated in 1994 by Dr. Svanibor Pettan of the University of Slovenia and myself. It was part of a course for university students at the Department of Music and Theatre at the University of Oslo, entitled "Music in Exile."

After learning to perform some Bosnian music that before the war was shared by all ethnic groups, the Norwegian students were introduced to Bosnian refugee musicians of different backgrounds, and the groups then started teaching each other Norwegian and Bosnian tunes. In the following years the ensemble gave concerts in refugee camps all over Norway and in other European countries as well. The intention was to offer to all Bosnians, regardless of their ethno-religious affiliation, a musical concept with which they could associate and find their bonding communalities anew across the divides.

In many parts of the world the music ensemble is the central educational arena for social learning. The nations of Southeast Asia have been at the forefront in developing ensemble playing as a tool for social bonding and conflict transformation. The most impressive examples are the gamelan ensembles of Indonesia and especially of Bali, where traditionally, every male member is supposed to take part in the weekly music-making sessions, contributing their own musical ideas to the creative process. These ensembles serve an important educational function as children join the groups from an early age, accompanying their fathers. The process of inclusion into adult society is thus promoted through a channel of interactive music making. On the island of Lombok I have experienced how the playing of traditional instruments, indigenous to the island, like the *Gendang Beleq*, is used in the rehabilitation of criminal youth. Big drums are played in ritual duels, allowing opponents to release pent-up aggressive feelings.

In later years the introduction of the anklung instruments into different arenas of music education in Southeast Asia has attracted international attention. This musical methodology aims at giving every child the opportunity to make music in a social setting, developing their powers of group co-ordination. In Thailand, Dr. Bussakorn Sumrongthong, Deputy Dean of the Faculty of Fine and Applied Arts at Chulalongkorn University, has studied the effects of *angklung* playing on integration (see www.intermusiccenter.com). At a yearly camp for children with physical and mental handicaps, "Art for All," arranged by the faculty, small groups of children with various handicaps live together in small cooperative housing units for a week, engaging in creative arts activities under the guidance of nationally renowned musicians and artists.

In the face of conflicts in the local as well as the global arena, the rediscovery of the socially bonding functions of music is a pressing need. The musical ensemble may retrace its role as a central space or workshop for cooperative cultural and social learning, for problem solving, for developing a sense of "collective affectivity" and shared emotions, and for celebrating diversity.

In 1992 I initiated a cooperative project between Norway's Department of Music and Theatre at the University of Oslo and Sri Lanka's Institute of Aesthetic Studies at Kelaniya University. The project aimed at promoting multicultural music teaching and research, resulting in the organization of a five nation (Sri Lanka, India, Thailand, Indonesia, Iran) multicultural music festival. Groups of musicians from both the Singhalese and Tamil communities symbolized the potential of cultural and social sharing through musical dialogues developed from a single theme.

In many cultures, music improvisation works to facilitate person reconstruction and social integration. It is seen as an opportunity to release strong, pent-up or subconscious feelings, promote self-awareness and resolve personal and social conflicts. Music penetrates the emotional defense system so that one finally risks living through negative emotions and as a consequence also risks reestablishing social contact. The effects are much like the results obtained through the Guided Imagery method of music listening.

In recent years ensemble practice and playing has been introduced in prisons as part of a rehabilitation programme. Positive results have been obtained in prison education programmes in Norway like the "Music in Prison and Freedom" project, paving the way for investments in mobilizing music resources in prisoner rehabilitation on a national scale. For a closer look at this and similar programs the reader is referred to the chapter "Music Behind Bars" in the present volume.

A special case of team-building through music in many Western countries may be observed in the way jazz ensembles cooperate in working out a musical concept, which should warrant new focus on the educational possibilities it could offer.

An illuminating article appeared in *Organization Science*. The author, Frank J. Barrett, takes as his point of departure that "the fundamental shift we are experiencing involves empowering people at all levels to initiate innovative solutions" (Barrett 1998: 605).

Barrett considers the jazz ensemble to be an effective training center for collaborative learning. He stresses key characteristics of jazz improvisation that have direct bearing on conflict transformation: the ensemble he sees as a laboratory "creating conditions that encourage members to bring a mindfulness to their task that allows them to imagine alternative possibilities heretofore unthinkable" (Barrett 1998: 210).

No doubt we have here arrived at the very core of creative conflict transformation and peace brokering requiring innovative solutions.

In an educational context a key outcome of participating in improvisational music-making will be the ability to *embrace errors as a source of learning*. Barrett rightly observes that jazz playing contravenes the tendency to construe errors as unacceptable, which often has the consequence of immobilizing people after a breakdown. In the context of conflict transformation this refusal to give up is of extreme importance in those critical moments where negotiations seemingly have come to a dead end. Barrett notices that jazz players are often able to turn unexpected problems into opportunities: "Errors become accommodated as part of the musical landscape, seeds for activating and arousing their imagination." Looking at errors and breakdowns as opportunities rather than failures, they become tools for enhancing innovative action, while "developing an aesthetic of forgiveness, releasing those who make noble efforts, for consequences that could not be foreseen" (Barrett 1998: 611).

In a way, jazz improvisation is based on what Barrett labels "the principle of distribution of tasks." It becomes an effective instrument for promoting "continual negotiation toward dynamic synchronization": "What characterizes successful jazz improvisation . . . is the ongoing give and take between members. Players are in a continual dialogue and exchange with one another." In order for jazz to work, players must develop a remarkable degree of empathic competence. "Jazz members are able to negotiate, recover, proceed, adjust to one another because there is a shared task knowledge." This is a main principle of cooperative learning. Barrett brings out how musicians connect with one another "sometimes experiencing an ability to perform beyond their capacity" (Barrett 1998: 613–14).

Barrett suggests the need for further research initiatives in the field of conflict transformation.

> Studies of jazz improvisation suggest that researchers revisit such familiar concepts as empowerment, motivation and team-building, concepts which have been studied almost exclusively from a cognitive and individualistic perspective. The experience of spiritual intimacy, synergy, surrender, transcendence and flow warrant wider study.
>
> (Barrett 1998: 815)

Building a Resonant School Community

The experiences drawn from a variety of international sources, like those discussed above, together with the positive results of multicultural music projects initiated by myself during the 1970s were incorporated in the planning for the Resonant Community project. In 1989 the official inauguration took place in a special ceremony led by the Norwegian Minister of Culture with the Speaker of Parliament delivering the opening message. As sketched above, the three year Resonant Community project (1989–92) involved 18 primary schools in the

Oslo area with varying populations of immigrant children. The mean for the Oslo area is 30 percent, while inner city areas would have much higher percentages (up to 98 percent). Six of these schools (A-schools) were to participate in an intensive arts education program (music, dance, performing arts) concentrating on immigrant cultures. Six other (B-schools) were to participate in an intercultural school concert program, while the six remaining (C-schools) would function as control institutions.

The target groups were school pupils between the ages of 10 and 12 in Norwegian primary schools, situated in areas with varying concentrations of immigrant pupils, and the families of the children involved. The same pupils were to follow the project for three years (from grades four to six).

The idea was not only to present musical traditions of the immigrant communities, but equally to stimulate participation in interethnic musical activities, a twofold approach of listening and participation essential to educational programs aimed at fostering empathy and contributing to conflict transformation. Students of different ethnic origins were encouraged to try their hand at playing various percussion instruments, forming small classroom bands or ensembles, accompanying dance performances and musical plays. African drumming had already been introduced in Norway through the activities of the Center for African Culture, and leading musicians of West African origin were employed to teach jembe drumming and traditional African village dances.

A generous gift of a full gamelan and piphat ensemble from the Governments of Indonesia and Thailand respectively, has made it possible to introduce multicultural ensemble practice and performance in other social settings as well. In the larger gatherings the whole school population was invited to join in. Sometimes parents were invited for evening performances joining their children in the pleasures of music making and playing musical games from many countries, often originating in traditional rituals of social interaction and integration.

Cultures from three geographical zones were presented. Asia (first year) where the methodical emphasis was put on facilitating new and existing listening experiences, Africa (second year) with a strong emphasis on music making in groups. The third year (Latin America) would then focus on the social and political aspects of music and dance.

During the first year, the emphasis was on *multicultural* activities, mirroring the diversity of cultural traditions, with a focus on the countries of Asia. At the time of the project, inner city areas had received a considerable influx of immigrants, mainly of Pakistani origin and refugees (boat people from Vietnam and Tamils from Sri Lanka). As in many other cities, they had settled in separate districts. In Oslo these districts in popular communication would bear names like "Little Karachi" or "Little Saigon."

The second year, focusing on African cultures, was geared toward *intercultural* activities, where the emphasis was on music making and dancing. Students participated in ever-changing ensembles which enabled them to interact with a great number of partners, affording an outlet for working out both positive and negative emotions. Individual and group creativity were developed through a strong focus on improvisation.

The third year, which coincided with the 500th year commemoration of the Spanish conquest of South America, aimed at a *transcultural* understanding of the dynamics of cultural interaction and change. It also focused on providing insight into relations of cultural and social power in the world and the role of music and the arts in mobilizing for the struggle against cultural and political oppression and environmental destruction.

Workshops for participating artists and teachers were given at the start of the project and later at regular intervals, and background material for teachers and students (including recordings and video material) was prepared. The main concern here is that music be studied in a wide cultural and social context.

The main findings of the composite test program, including questionnaires, reports and continuous participating observation were:

- Considerably greater increase in the A-schools (as compared to the other school models) from 1989 to 1992 in the number of pupils who report that they have no personal problems with harassment or mobbing. This is most marked with the immigrant pupils, indicating a clear connection between the project and improved social relationships in the school. The tendency towards better social relations and diminished ethnic conflicts is confirmed by reports from the teachers.
- Attitudes toward immigration seem to have remained unchanged in the A-schools while there was an increased degree of negative attitudes found among the pupils in the B- and C-schools.
- A greater number of pupils in the A-schools at the end of the project consider immigrants to be honest, law-abiding, industrious and kind, while there were fewer in the other school models.
- Immigrant pupils in the A-schools have strengthened their self-image during the project. The teachers reported that there had been a highly positive development in identity formation and activity level of immigrant pupils.

Conclusion

In my final report as research coordinator the following summing up and recommendations could encourage follow-up and necessary remedial action:

> On the whole, the project has created a basis for growth, for triggering the inter-cultural processes which are necessary in creating a cooperative society and to avoid disruptive cultural collisions. It is important that such initiatives be implemented at the ages seen as critical for the development of individual attitudes, and therefore can stimulate the participation of the new generation in a dynamic and democratic interactive society.
>
> [...]
>
> The Resonant Community is a small, but significant attempt to finally prepare the way for the school to fulfill its obligation and responsibility to our new citizens. It is hoped that this can prompt institutions of music education and music life in general to follow. I am thinking of the entire spectrum of institutions, from municipal music schools to colleges and universities.
>
> [...]
>
> Multicultural music education bases itself on the ability of music to cross boundaries and communicate between cultures. This crossing of boundaries means that we finally begin to accept the artistic expressions of other cultures to be of equal value with our own cultural heritage. The aesthetic subjects can, in this way, lead the way to a necessary re-evaluation and restructuring of the content and methods in an intercultural direction. This will require a revision of teaching materials and curriculum plans in all subjects with the goal of removing mono-cultural bias and hidden value manipulation. But in a wider context, this should lead to a necessary re-evaluation also of the total social milieu which gives nourishment to prejudice.
>
> (Skyllstad 1993: 18)

The study of conflict formation and transformation through the artistic media has led to a revision of the very concept of conflict itself. It has led to a new understanding of the different levels of conflict and their relationship in the social, political and cultural sphere. Many of the conflict areas that students encounter in school – conceptual conflicts, conflicts of ideas and interests – will also face the students in adult society. The way these conflicts are met creatively in school can prepare students to become active participants in the day to day interactive processes of democratic society.

References

Barrett, F.J. (1998) "Creativity and improvisation in jazz and organizations implications for organizational learning" *Organization Science*, vol. 9, no. 5.

Blacking, J. (1987) *A Common Sense View of All Music*, Cambridge: Cambridge University Press.

Bruscia, K.E. (1987) *Improvisational Models of Music Therapy,* Springfield, IL: Charles Thomas.

Cole, L. and Hall, I. (1970) *Psychology of Adolescence*, New York: Holt, Reinhardt & Winston.

Maslow, A.H. (1968) *Toward a Psychology of Being*, New York: Van Nostrand Reinhold Company.

Piaget, J. and Inhelder, B. (1974) *Barnets Psykologi*, Copenhagen: Hans Reitzel.

Ruud, E. (1997) *Musikk og identitet (Music and Identity)*, Oslo: Universitetsforlaget.

Seeger, A. (1987) *When Suya Sing. A Musical Anthropology of an Amazonian People*, Cambridge: Cambridge University Press.

Skyllstad, K. (1993) *The Resonant Community Fostering Interracial Understanding through Music. A Summary Report*, Oslo: University of Oslo.

PART IV

Stories from the Field

Chapter 13: Working in the Trenches: Surviving Conflicts through Folk Music and Tales

Rik Palieri

Since the beginning of time music has inspired many emotions, from love, to war and in some cases peace. In some rare instances the music itself was able to not only create a feeling of peace, but actually to stop violence. In this chapter we will explore through story and song how some musicians have been able to use their music and stories not only for enjoyment and entertainment but as tools to achieve peace. As I have learned the art of story telling through my own family, I would like to start by sharing a few personal stories that illustrate how I have been able to use stories and songs to help overcome a few battles in my own life, and then share a few more stories showing the power of music to move people to stand up against injustice, and even against war. Exclusive interviews with Utah Phillips and Pete Seeger follow, and I conclude this chapter with a few reflections.

Five Real Life Stories: Music for Family, Harmony, Justice and Peace

Fathers and sons

I grew up in a working class town in central New Jersey, with ethnic roots from Italy, Poland and Germany. I had what you might call "a rough childhood." When my father was young he was an angry and violent man. He worked the midnight shift at a lousy factory and then, just to keep the bills paid, had to work a part-time job as a hardware salesman. Working those two jobs left my dad little free time as he was always working or sleeping. Even though he always brought in the money to keep up with the bills, our home life suffered. My mother got tired of being alone and started hitting the bars and night clubs and sometimes did not come home for days. The heavy work load, combined with a failing marriage, created a monster and when he exploded it was like a volcanic eruption. I often caught his wrath and was thrown into walls, down stairs or used as his punching bag. As I was an only child at the time and a young boy, he always hit me with a closed fist saying that I should "Take it like A Man." As time passed and my parents worked on their marriage and had more children, most of the violence stopped but we never had much of a life together and in fact, when we were in the same room we hardly spoke to one another. It was on a Father's Day years after I left my parents' home that I realized how distant my father and I were. The longer I pondered our situation, the more I realized that it went far beyond just my father and me. This kind of estrangement went all the way back to my father and his father and even my grandfather and his father. As I thought back to all the fights and arguments that we had while I was growing up, I realized I was carrying around too much baggage from my childhood, and it was time to unload. Now was the time to break the chain. I went down into the basement, grabbed a pencil, and set my thoughts to paper and then put it to a simple tune.

Fathers and Sons

By Rik Palieri

Fathers and Sons, since time began,
Iron clad hearts weighing a ton.
A shake of the hand – a slap on the back,
Old memories from a worn leather strap.

Chorus

The hardest thing for a father to do,
Isn't swinging an ax or tying little shoes,
So open your heart let your spirit shine through
By showing your son your love.

My Father & me would never agree,
Fussing & fighting since the day I was three.
Agiant of steel, who just couldn't feel
How to show his son his love.

Chorus

The autumn winds blew as the young child grew
As he cursed at a man, that he never knew.
While doing the chores, he cursed him much more
& never gave his father his love.

Chorus

Too many days have come and have passed
And the days of my childhood are out of my grasp.
Now my father & I both want to cry,
Thinking back on the time that we were denied.

Chorus

After I finished writing the song, I knew that I had to sing it for my father, as I felt that perhaps music was the best way to heal these old wounds.

It was only a short time after the song was written that I got that chance. During one Thanksgiving in the 1980s my family came up from Florida. They had came North to bring in the holidays at a gathering at my Grandma's house. As the kitchen filled with the sweet aroma of Polish sausage and cabbage, everyone was busy setting the table and preparing for the big meal. Before we sat down to eat, I told my parents that I had planned something special. When I nervously picked up my guitar the room was still filled with noisy dinner chatter. But as I sang, the room quieted down with my family listening to every word. When I finished, they were all sobbing around Grandma's kitchen table. As the last notes of my guitar still rang through the kitchen walls, my dad came over and gave me a hug and said "Son, I'm sorry. Though we can't change the past, we can try to make the future better." With everyone still in tears, I sang a few more songs before we ate. Singing this song became a major turning point in our relationship.

As the years passed I continued singing this song and I had some remarkable results. I found it was a great way to address this difficult topic and even in a few cases reunite families. Perhaps the most successful reunion came about after I sang the song over the radio. It was on another Father's Day when I was doing a live radio program on Vermont Public Radio. After I sang my song, the in-studio phone rang. An older man was driving in Montreal, Canada and heard my song and was so moved that he pulled over and called his father. He said, "I had not talked to my dad in ten years but after hearing your song I decided that I would take the risk and make the call. My father was so happy to hear my voice and we have already made plans to meet. Thanks again for writing that song!"

That first experiment made me realize the power of music and how it can in a small way change lives. The next time I had the chance to test this idea was when I ran into a problem at an airport.

Musical bus ride

I was returning from a tour in Alaska, and was ready to fly home out of Bellingham, Washington. Once I started checking in, I noticed there was a big problem. The check in attendant was throwing up her hands as she had to tell everyone that all the planes were having problems and they would not be able to fly that day. You can just imagine the stress that this caused. It was then suggested that a bus would be provided that would take us to Seattle and perhaps some of us would be able to make our connections. Everyone was worried as we only had an hour and a half to make the connecting flight and the bus had not even arrived at the airport yet. When the bus pulled up, the driver said in a nasty tone, "They just pulled me out of bed, after an all night shift, and they expect me to perform a miracle and get you to Seattle in time to catch your flight. Good luck." Needless to say, everyone was in a bad mood. I was loading my stuff into the bus, and had slung my banjo over my back when the bus driver said, "What? Are you going to play that in my bus?" "Well I really did not plan on it," I replied. "I was only kidding," said the driver. But I started thinking about it and reached inside my case and pulled out the banjo. A worried angry woman said, "Well what if I don't like it?" "Then tell me and I'll stop," I replied. The bus drove off and the tension inside the bus was horrendous. Then I started plucking away at the old standard "Blue Skies" (a neat version I learned from Pete Seeger) and, in a few minutes, I noticed everyone was humming along. A few more minutes went by and I heard a few voices singing. I started to sing too, and before long the whole bus burst into song and even the bus driver himself sang along in his big bass baritone. One song led to another, and everyone seemed to have a request. "Do you know 'You are my Sunshine'?" Soon photographs appeared, pictures of vacations, family members, little newborn babies and old friends.

Everyone laughed and sang, with food being passed around the bus, and before long the airport was in sight. The bus driver called, "We made it with time to spare" and everyone clapped their hands. Then he said, "We would never have done it without the help of our banjo player" and shouts of approval rang through the bus. The bus stopped and, as we all got out, people exchanged addresses and invitations, a few exchanged hugs and we all went our separate ways. As I was leaving, the bus driver said, "This was the best ride I ever had. Thanks for your music." A few weeks later, back in the hills of old Vermont, my mailbox was filled with letters of reminiscences of that "musical bus ride."

This next story relates how music can sometimes overcome the harshest weather conditions and create a warm peaceful feeling on even the coldest winter days.

Way below zero: a rose for peace

It was in February of 2003, I had just come back from a long tour overseas. I was planning to go to New York to join the protest against the war in Iraq, when I got a last minute call, asking if I could sing at a local gathering at the Montpelier State House in Vermont. The organizer said, "There are a lot of people here in

Vermont who cannot go to the big protest in New York, but still want to protest the war. Will you join us, and sing a few songs in the program?" As his words rang in my ears, I thought of that old slogan, "Think Globally, Act Locally." I decided that it was more important to stay here to support my community.

On the day of the protest, it was way below zero fahrenheit, without the wind chill. It was one of those days when you were warned to stay inside. When I arrived, a group of brazen volunteers were hard at work digging through the ice and snow, desperately trying to find the electrical hook-up to get the PA up and running. A small podium was quickly set up and I was asked by one of the organizers to start the program by playing an old melody on a Native American flute. As I stood on the snow covered steps and played an ancient melody, I could see people pouring out of their cars. As my final notes cracked through the winter air, the speakers took the stage and the rally began. As the speakers rallied the crowd, the snowy State House lawn quickly filled up with colorful banners and chanting from the few thousands of dedicated protesters who were there to let their voices be heard and be counted. When I looked out at the crowd bundled in heavy coats, hats and gloves, I could see lot of old gray haired "peace-nicks," but there were also many young faces. I realized that they, just like me, knew that it was important to be here. So, despite the chilly winds, we braved the cold, lifted our voices, played our instruments and sang out about our opposition to this unjust war.

Because of the extreme cold, the stage program hurried along so that no one had to stand out in the weather any longer than was necessary. One performer after hearing the wood on his guitar crack told me, "this will go down as one of the craziest things I have ever done!" When it was my turn, I felt my cold, red fingers burn as I strummed the strings of my banjo with my bare hands and then sang a new song that I had just composed for the event:

Rose for Peace

By Rik Palieri

Sometimes in life my friends, this old world seems hopeless
When all your dreams go up in smoke and you start to lose your focus
When the mountains seem too high and the road too long
That's the time to lift your voice and keep your vision strong

So, plant a rose for peace today and peace will come tomorrow
Hope and pray for better days without war, pain or sorrow
Work each day in your own way, return the love you borrow
Plant a seed of hope and dream, the road to peace will follow

Let the sunshine through the clouds and chase away the darkness
Let the light within you now, restore your faith and purpose
Keep your eyes upon the prize, keep your spirit strong
The only way we can change the world, is to keep on keeping on!

So, plant a rose for peace today and peace will come tomorrow
Hope and pray for better days without war, pain or sorrow
Work each day in your own way, return the love you borrow
Plant a seed of hope and dream, the road to peace will follow

After I finished my song, everyone on stage joined together to sing, "Last Night I Had the Strangest Dream" by Ed McCurdy. As we played and sang together you could almost forget about the cold and frostbite, while our voices filled the frozen State House lawn with a feeling of hope and optimism. Someone looking from afar would wonder why on earth anyone would be out in weather like this. The only answer I can give is that throughout my life I have been with many others in all kinds of weather, standing up for things we believe in. For many of us it is part of the life blood of a long standing tradition, to sing and speak out.

There are other stories that I have come across over the years that also show how music can work miracles and sometimes even stop violence.

Overcoming racism with a song

This next story came from my mother-in-law, Christel Fuchs Holzer. Christel has been a peace activist most of her life and this story came from the days she was an organizer for the American Friends Service Committee in Brattleboro, Vermont back in the early 1970s. My mother-in-law was heavily involved with the peace movement when she heard that the Klu Klux Klan were coming to town to try and start a branch of their organization in the peaceful hills of Vermont. The Klan had planned a large rally in the town. They were able to get a permit to set up a stage and were also receiving a lot of attention from the press. Christel and her friends were very upset and soon were on the counter-attack. They planned their own rally to protest the Klan. The day of the Klan's speech came and the protesters gathered around the park as the Klan, dressed in their white robes, filled the stage. As the Grand Wizard started spouting out his words of hate, some of the once peaceful protesters became so angry they started shouting, with some even throwing rocks. At once, the Police jumped up and arrested the rock throwers which delighted the Klan and helped them to incite the crowd. Then it happened. One protester stood bravely and loudly and started singing "We Shall Overcome." Others joined in and soon the whole park was reverberating with the power of the song. The singers sang so loud and proud that they began to drown out the Klans' PA system. The Klan tried in vain to turn up the PA but the singers' voices were too powerful. Then the protesters joined arms and encircled the stage, moving closer and growing louder until the Klan finally gave up and realized that they had been beaten. They then jumped into their VW van, moved out of town and were never seen again.

> We shall overcome, we shall overcome,
> We shall overcome some day
> Oh deep in my heart, I do believe
> We shall overcome some day!

Christmas truce 1914

One of the most powerful stories of all took place in France in 1914, during WWI. The war had just started and both armies were new to trench warfare. The soldiers were facing each other, locked in mortal combat. Sometimes only a short stretch of as little as 60 feet of no man's land separated their bloody trenches.

It was December 24, Christmas Eve, and soldiers on both sides of the trench received gifts of food, drink, new warm clothing and letters from home. The presents helped the soldiers forget for the moment about the war, but none would ever guess that the greatest gift of all was still yet to come.

By evening the British troops started hearing the singing of Christmas carols from the other side of the trench. Later they saw lights sparkling in the night as the Germans began lighting the candles on their Christmas tree. Taken off guard, the British troops were surprised to see two Germans waving a white flag out in the middle of the no man's land. The officers of both armies met and declared a truce to bury the dead.

Then the two armies celebrated together, sharing food, singing songs and even played a flare-lit game of soccer. The truce was said to have lasted for several days and according to one story, some of the regiments had to be replaced as they refused to fire at each other after the truce was over.

For many years this story was almost unknown and thought to be just a myth. Songwriter John McCutcheon heard the story and put it to verse, to share it with the world. He then met a few of the soldiers who had actually been there, and who verified that the story was true.

I have learned a great deal from two of my friends, folk singer and rebel-rouser Utah Phillips, and singer-songwriter and peace activist Pete Seeger. I would like to end this chapter with a bit of wisdom from two of my mentors, and a story from Pete's sister Peggy.

Singing for Peace: Utah Phillips, Peggy Seeger and Pete Seeger

When I considered writing this chapter I was hoping to find many stories to share. If the topic was just using music as a tool toward building a better world, I could have filled an entire book for all the dedicated and hard working musicians who are involved in peace work. But when asked the question, "Can you tell me a story when your music has actually stopped violence or calmed a moment of confrontation?", I found that while our dream is to build peace through music, in reality the stories of it actually happening are few.

I found out that most of the stories came from our elders, who were involved in earlier political struggles related to unions and civil rights. I have selected three singers who have built their lives around working to build peace: story teller, union organizer and peace activist U. Utah Phillips, traditional balladeer and writer of womens' issues, Peggy Seeger, and her half brother, internationally known singer and songwriter Pete Seeger.

Interview with U. Utah Phillips (Nevada City, California, USA, June 9, 2005)

Today U. Utah is almost a mythical figure. With his long white beard, work shoes, big overalls and WWI buttons pinned to his wide red suspenders, he has become like the Mark Twain of the left.

He has been traveling the USA for decades, riding freight trains, planes and automobiles, singing in concerts and on picket lines, spreading his music throughout the land. When I asked him about how he got started in peace work he began with this story:

> *Utah*: My great teacher of music and nonviolence was Fred Hansen. Fred was a member of the IWW (Industrial Workers of The World), he was a very old man, and spent many years working on the docks. In Houston, Texas he had a reputation as a peace maker. When there was a strike on the docks and strike relief ran out and it was raining, of course tempers would start rubbing raw. Of course the word went out in the strike: "no booze, no guns, no violence," to get an injunction to break the strike. But as I said, sometimes tempers would rub raw and sometimes one of the workers would pick up a brick and decide to throw it at a company guard. And that's when Fred would get everyone singing. Because he knew that when people were singing together they [weren't] throwing rocks and

they [weren't] throwing bricks. That lesson stuck with me and many times came in handy.

One time when I was in Antioch, Ohio, at a strike, the janitors were out on strike over wages hours and conditions. And the students went out in sympathy, so the whole college was shut down. I was down there early in the morning, it was quite cold and there was a fire barrel burning near police barricades. The pickets were in front of the police barricades with the police mounted on horseback. They came to try and move the pickets, to try and break the line. So I got everyone singing. We were singing "We shall not be moved." Everyone was adding in new verses and singing with their arms linked. I was at the end of the line playing my guitar, everyone had their arms linked so there was no display of fists or anything like that. The cops trying to come around on the end of the line knocked over a police barricade on me and knocked me down and it fell on top of me and my guitar (that is why I got the big scratch on the front of my guitar). I put the barricade back up and we just kept on singing. And finally, the police backed off and our barricade continued. I guess they knew that they weren't going to be able to break it.

Rik: Did you see any effect on the policemen's faces when you started singing?

Utah: I think the policemen were puzzled, I think in previous pickets there was a lot of cat calling, a lot of yelling, a lot of verbal abuse ... and here it wasn't, it was just a blank statement that we were not going to go anywhere. And people were laughing and singing. I think they (the police) felt better about it, they felt less antagonism.

Rik: Woody Guthrie used to have a sign on his guitar saying that "This machine kills Fascists," and Pete Seeger has inscribed around his banjo head, "This machine surrounds hate and forces it to surrender." So how are you able to use your music for peace and working towards social change?

Utah: Well the sign on my guitar says "This machine kills time!" Well you know I don't play it as much as I used to. I sing all kinds of songs, Rik, but my real joy is getting people laughing and singing together. I am mostly a story teller. Like if I tell about the Spokane free-speech fight or about the Lawrence textile strike, these stories are where these people came together armed with only their sense of degradation of human beings and in face of enormous odds prevailed, nonviolently.

The Spokane free speech was won by the solidarity of the workers out there on the street. It didn't take any ballot boxes, and it didn't take any political parties. [It's] direct action, nonviolent direct action. You know, I believe so strongly in that. The man you know, the man with a capital M (police) can exculpate violently. The cop on the beat with a hand gun or with a hydrogen bomb and everything in between can always say: "Come up that road (of violence) with me; come up that road with me."

You can go so far up that road of armed struggle that you get killed. So no, you have to take the road, he doesn't own that road that he doesn't know anything about, that road of peace. And you say: "Come on up that road, come up that road, that road of nonviolence" and you know you got to be able to make that stick. Because that cop is committed to wearing a gun and the ability to use it when he feels it is necessary. He has to be able to absolutely understand that you are not going to attack him or mean him no harm at all.

You got to be able to make it stick; you got to be able to be knocked down, by a mounted policeman and stand up and keep on singing.

Well, like when I was traveling on a bus in the Northwest on a tour. I was on the buses during the first Gulf War because I said my car doesn't run on blood! I was sitting on a stool in a diner in Idaho Falls waiting to get back on the bus to Pocatello, when the fellow sitting next to me saw my peace button and knocked me off the stool. I discovered then that you know if you are really a pacifist somewhere on the way to the floor. And if you pick yourself mad, boiling mad, ready to fight, you have some work to do and if you get up and shake hands with the fellow and say I think we need to talk about this, then you are probably doing ok.

A short story from Peggy Seeger (Philadelphia Folk Festival, USA, August 28, 2005)

Peggy has been for years at the forefront of the political and topical song movement. Her work on BBC Radio, with her late husband Ewan McColl is legendary, as is her commitment to working for human rights. I was performing at a recent festival where both Peggy and I were on the bill. While we were standing in line, chatting, I told her about this book project and asked her if she could recall a time when, with her music, she was able to stop violence. At first she could not think of an instance, then she shared this short story:

I think it was in Lancaster, or Morecambe, in the UK, back in 1968, during the student strikes that began in Paris and moved out over Europe and thus England and Scotland. Our universities were in turmoil, most of it quite chaotic and leaderless. Ewan and I made up a couple of songs about it all and we were thus quite popular at some of the students' meetings. This particular one was meant to be ended by 11 or so, but it went on and on. Four or five policemen came to turf out about 150 students. The students were by this time hyped on choruses and beer and they started to hoot and howl. I don't know if they would have gotten violent . . . they weren't like the miners in the miners strike or the poll tax objectors in Maggie Thatcher's time.

But the police were outnumbered by the students who, good-naturedly, hauled the cops into their midst, surrounding them, including them in the company, offering them drinks and the 1960s equivalents of high fives. The police were mostly young as I remember, with (as usual) an older officer with them. These ones were all encouraged to sing and drink. Ewan and I rolled into an innocuous song (Down in the Valley? I'm a Rover? Leaving of Liverpool?), and wonder of wonders, the cops began to sing! … And to enjoy it as well. Then Ewan and I closed the evening down and we all left feeling good. Everyone's needs had been met.

For my final interview I was able to visit with one of my mentors and friends, singer-songwriter Pete Seeger.

It took a bit of work finding time in Pete's busy schedule but after a few phone calls and letters we were able to find a few hours when Pete could sit down and talk. Pete was eager to talk about music for peace as it is something he has been working towards all of his life.

Now at the age of 86, Pete is still busy, plucking on his banjo and singing for the things that he believes in.

Interview with Pete Seeger (Beacon NY, USA, July 27, 2005)

Rik: Pete, there are a few things that you have written during your life when the music has taken on a different power, I would like to talk about this because in my chapter I am addressing those times when musicians were actually able to use their music to stop a violent act. Can you tell us about when you and Woody were traveling as "The Almanac Singers"?

Pete: I know exactly what you are talking about. It was in June 1940. I only met Woody a couple months earlier and he must have been smiling to himself at my New England ways. I was from New England, he was from Oklahoma, "that Seeger the strangest man I ever knew, he don't drink, he don't smoke, he don't chase girls." Ha!

However, I could accompany him and any song he played. I didn't have to listen to it twice; I could see the chord change coming, hear the chord change coming, so he let me tag along with him. We went out to visit his wife and children in Oklahoma, no Texas, panhandle of Texas, flat as a billiard table. And on the way there in Oklahoma City, we sang for a little meeting, they were trying to organize a union of oil workers, digging oil wells, small meeting maybe fifty people. And there were women and babies there, children people didn't have money for babysitters, and the women wanted to come and see what this union business is all about.

The organizer, Bob Wood was his name, he leans over and says see if you can get them singing. There are some men standing in the back. It's an open meeting, we don't want to turn anyone away but they haven't taken off their overcoats, they're just standing against the back wall. And we did the crowd singing, and later on we found out that the men had come to break up the meeting, they had clubs hidden underneath their overcoats.

Rik: Pete you have traveled a lot, not only through the United States and Canada but throughout the world. And you've seen a lot of tension in the world and I recall there was a time when you were in Israel and that you were actually traveling back and forth, you were doing some concerts in Israel and then you went to Palestine, is that correct?

Pete: Not exactly. I had never been to an Arab country and I asked my manager to leave a few free days so I visited Lebanon. So I rented a cheap hotel, walked down a busy little alley in a street, when I heard someone shout "Pete Seeger, is that you?" Well, it was a young Arab doctor on a vacation, visiting his family in Beirut. He'd actually been born in what now is known as Israel. But in the war of 1948, the radio said: "Leave your home, the War is coming to your town, when we've pushed the Jews into the ocean then you can come back." Well, of course the Jews were not pushed into the ocean, and Egypt, Jordan and Syria and I don't know what other Arab nations were involved, and they were defeated. And this young Arab doctor grew up in Lebanon, he got a good education because he got a scholarship to a medical school in the United States.

And when he found out that I was going to Israel he said, "Pete, I don't want to see war, no sensible person does, but believe me there is going to be war, unless Israel realizes how bitter the Palestinians feel, they feel like their homeland has been taken from them." And, "So don't mention you're going to Israel next week or you might not get there, in fact, you very probably won't get there."

But when I was singing this in Lebanon I said, "I sang this song Guantanamera." I said, "the man who wrote this song was in exile from his homeland in Cuba. And I dedicate this to exiles all around the world. Exiles of nineteen years (that meant the Palestinians) and exiles of two thousand years." The Romans exiled all the Jews, and most of them never got back, they just kept the memories that some day, some day maybe we'll get back our home. It's in their songs.

A week later in Israel I could be more frank. I sang for twenty thousand people, sang the song "Tzena, Tzena, Tzena," they all knew it and sang it with me. Then I sang "Guantanamera" and again I dedicated it to exiles of 2000 years and exiles of nineteen years. Afterwards, a man backstage said to me, "you are very brave." I said, "What do you mean?" – "well" you don't know how tense things are here; Well, about a week later the six day war broke out. And again it was a disaster.

However, I came back and wrote an article "Jews and Arabs I love them both, both beautiful traditions and sooner or later, whether it's this decade or this century, they will be getting together because the alternative is no human race on earth."

Rik: What about some of the historical uses of music that you recall, when people were able to use music to solve problems?

Pete: Oh my gosh, one of the great examples was the Abolition Movement. There were white people up North who said "Slavery was wrong" and there was a great family called the Hutchinson Family who got in their stage coach and horse and wagon, went from town to town singing:

Roll it along through the nation
Freedom calls for emancipation

Great old tune! They sang abolition songs and then of course a song called "John Brown's Body" came along. And the wife of a leading abolitionist put these words to it: the battle hymn of the Republic: and such a good song that it is still sung later.

There are other examples; they (people) put Union verses to old church tunes. Way back in the nineteenth century they had a song, "I'll overcome, I'll overcome, I'll overcome Someday" and black and white coal miners in Alabama sang it as "We will overcome, we will overcome."

Back in 1946 a woman, one of 300 hundred women tobacco workers who were on strike, she liked to sing this song in what they call slow meter or long meter, which means you sing it so slowly that anybody who knows how to do harmonies can sing along, whether they are a bass singer, or alto or soprano.

I learnt it from a white woman who learnt it from her. I printed it as "We will Overcome" in 1947. I tried to play a banjo to it . . . ha! But it didn't really work out.

It wasn't till the Civil Rights Movement in 1960 that they worked this out, great African American rhythm in 6/12 . . . And changed the words to "We shall Overcome," and that's the way the song spread. It wasn't just a song, it was *the* song! And I recorded it in '63; it was *the* only record that I ever made that was sold in any quantity and the song went around the world.

Rik: You were also telling me a story, a very old story from Wales, do you remember it?

Pete: Oh yes, the Welsh people love to sing in the Welsh language and sing the old melodies from thousands of years ago. Way back, some king I suppose, maybe five or six hundred years ago, was invading Brittany (part of France but there are a lot of Celtic people). The Brittons are really Celtic people, they like to speak Britton, which is a Celtic Language. And along come these invading English soldiers. The officer said: "Charge!" They said: "how we can charge them when they are singing our song?" They recognized the old melody!

Rik: I know that a lot of people look at music as entertainment, they look at musicians as entertainers. So what drives someone from being just an entertainer to really starting to use their music to bring people together?

Pete: I long felt that some music helps us forget our troubles. Some music that has words that will help us just make fun of our troubles. But some of the greatest music throughout history has been music that helps us overcome our troubles.

Who knows, I think that if there is a world here in a hundred years some of the greatest songs will be songs that somehow manage to get sung by people who had been very angry at each other but it's such a good song they all join in.

When I am standing on a stage and I look at a sea of faces, I realize that people there are of different religions, of different ethnic backgrounds. Maybe someone over here had a grandfather who was trying to chop off the head of the grandfather from someone from over there. If those grandfathers should see them all singing together, they'd say, "Why did I fight so hard?" Good question! We're going to learn how to work together somehow and singing together will be part of it.

Conclusion

Music hath charms to soothe a savage breast,
To soften rocks, or bend a knotted oak.
(William Congreve 1670–1729, "The Mourning Bride")

Music hath charms to soothe the savage beast,
And therefore proper at a sheriff's feast.
(Rev. James Bramston 1694–1744, "A Man of Taste")

The main theoretical framework of this book is peace as constructive conflict transformation, and this chapter has shown that in some cases, music has tremendous power to help transform conflicts peacefully. I think the stories show how we musicians can try to use our musical talents for more than just entertainment, as a tool for building and creating peace.

If music cannot always calm down a furious animal, as James Bramston was hoping, at least it can move one person's heart towards nonviolence, as William Congreve declared. In this chapter I have shown that sometimes, it can even save a whole crowd from useless suffering.

Chapter 14: Art for Harmony in the Middle East: The Music of Yair Dalal

Olivier Urbain

While I was putting together the team of writers for this book in October 2004, Kjell Skyllstad recommended his friend Yair Dalal, and this was the beginning of a wonderful correspondence and friendship. This chapter is based on several online interviews with Dalal, numerous phone calls, and live discussions during the four days of the Toda Institute Conference in Madrid in May 2005.

The Construction of Identity in the Middle East

Ever since the establishment of the state of Israel on 14 May 1948 life has been very hard for both Palestinians and Israelis. For almost 60 years, many people have tried to offer nonviolent solutions through diplomacy, politics, culture and the arts, apparently to no avail. Recent developments such as the Gaza pullout of August 2005 and the democratic elections for the Palestinian Authority of January 2006 are noteworthy, but there is no indication that they will lead to sustainable peace in the region. Palestinians in Gaza were on the verge of starvation in June 2006 (World Food Program 2006). The Israeli attacks on Lebanon in July and August 2006 and the rationale for this war, have made the situation much worse, and as of February 2007, frequent clashes between members of Hamas and Fatah are crushing hopes for a quick development towards peace. Most Israelis feel insecure and under threat. Needless to say, this insecurity and violence would not plague the region if Jews and Arabs were getting along. For several decades, one musician has offered an interesting and controversial solution, namely going back to the common roots that all people in the desert used to share, before the appearance of either Jews or Arabs, thousands of years ago.

Yair Dalal believes that these two peoples have so much in common that there is no reason to argue or fight along cultural identity lines. He thinks it is better to rebuild one's identity on a larger basis, and widely declares that he is an "Arab Israeli Jew." He is one of the best oud players today, the oud being a typically Arab instrument. He is also a master of the violin, which has been a favored musical instrument in Jewish communities worldwide for centuries. We will use social constructionism in order to examine the intricacies of Yair Dalal's life, work, and project for peace, agreeing with Karen Abi-Ezzi that our cultural identities are constructed on specific interpretations of reality. It should be possible, at least in theory, to rebuild one's identity on new ground, if one is aware that all cultural identities are first and foremost constructed. Music can be useful in this endeavor, by helping us bring out a deeper and broader feeling of identity.

For instance, in his chapter about Guided Imagery with Music (GIM), Vegar Jordanger shows that it is possible to construct a new cultural identity if one reaches deep enough within oneself, with the help of music therapy methods, in order to reach a point called "collective vulnerability."

This chapter will highlight episodes in Yair Dalal's experiences and biography that explain why he affirms his identity as an "Arab Israeli Jew," how his philosophy of peace is translated into his musical work, and some facts of history that confirm, and others that negate, his theory of the "common roots" between both peoples. The last section will show where two seemingly contradictory projects, that of Yair Dalal and of another brilliant Israeli musician, Gilad Atzmon, converge under the lens of social constructionism.

The Cultural Identity of an "Arab Israeli Jew"

What is the meaning of Yair Dalal's declaration that he is an "Arab Israeli Jew"? We can understand that he is an Israeli citizen, but how can he be an Arab and a Jew at the same time? The answer is simple: his whole family is from Iraq. Dalal was born in Israel of parents who had recently emigrated from Baghdad. Some of Abraham's descendants established themselves in what is now Iraq, and for centuries until 1948, many Jews had been living with Arabs, like Arabs, and actually as Arabs. If the preceding sentence does not make sense, simply replace "Arabs" with "Europeans" and it will become clear.

European Jews have been living as Europeans for centuries, and despite countless persecutions, they were an integral part of the cultural and social life of Europe. Ethiopian Jews live in Ethiopia, and Chinese Jews live in

China, and some of them move away from their ancestral homes. As Dalal himself says:

> I was born in Israel in 1955 to parents who emigrated from Iraq and lived in temporary settlements in the new state of Israel. My parents, like most Jewish immigrants from Arab countries, spoke Arabic and still do. It is actually the first language that I heard as a child. The land which is now Iraq, known in the Jewish tradition as Babel, is where the oldest Diaspora took place, as early as 550 BCE, and this gave my family a rich cultural heritage. It is as members of this traditional branch and with this cultural background that my parents started their new life in the then recently established state of Israel.
>
> (Dalal 2006)

Dalal's linguistic, musical and cultural education was a rich mixture from the beginning:

> As a child, I was surrounded by Arabic-speaking people, and I was exposed to Arabic music. Arabic and Hebrew seemed very similar to me, and both were effective and enriching for my education. It is only after I entered school that Hebrew became my main language. Music was all over: Hebrew songs, Arabic music, Russian, Klezmer and Classical European music, people were singing and playing in the open air at parties during holidays, radios were playing loud, this was the atmosphere in Israel in the 50s and 60s, it was naive and romantic.
>
> (Dalal 2006)

Thus, Dalal refers to himself using the improbable and controversial title of "Arab Israeli Jew." However, Dalal's childhood was fraught with challenges and frustrations. Being raised with children of European descent was quite a challenge for an Arab-looking boy, and some rather traumatic events were also at the origin of Dalal's philosophy of peace and identity construction:

> I think that it came to me because as a child I suffered from humiliation being a small boy born in Israel to Iraqi parents. Most of the people in our neighborhood and in school came from European countries – I was different by my color and culture, I wasn't accepted by the other children like I wanted to.
>
> (Dalal 2005)

Dalal affirms his right to be both an Arab and a Jew, to be the complete Yair Dalal, without having to choose between one half of himself or the other, as countless former Yugoslavs were forced to do in the 1990s during the dismantling of their country:

> I know it sounds difficult, but this is who I am. I am a Jew and I am proud of it. I was born in Israel to an Iraqi Jewish family, and our culture, language, food, and

many additional attributes are common to the Arabs. Similarly to being a Spanish Jew, I am an Arab Israeli Jew, and I live peacefully with this fact. My hope is that this can be an example to live in peace.

(Dalal 2004)

For Dalal, the meaning of peace is in its Arabic (Salaam) and Jewish (Shalom) roots:

Peace in Hebrew is "shalom," shalom comes from the root "shalem," which means complete, entire, whole, this is the meaning of peace – to live as ONE. My definition of peace goes back to my childhood. Since I was very young I believed in peace among people.

(Dalal 2005)

To be at peace with himself, he needs to be the whole Yair Dalal, not an Arab or a Jew. This gives him a unique perspective on how to deal with the Jewish–Arab conflict through music.

Yair Dalal's Music for Peace

There are at least five ways in which Dalal's philosophy of peace is shared through music: performing Babylonian music, masterfully playing both the oud and the violin, mixing Jewish and Arab music, organizing concerts with musicians from both backgrounds, and sharing his views through interviews.

Performing Babylonian music

After many years of research and musical training, Dalal became a master of Babylonian music. He is inspired by the Babylonian musical tradition that goes back thousands of years and is equally enjoyed by Arabs and Jews. One good example is the song "Samai Wachi Al'Naharein" composed by Salim Al-Nur, on the album *Asmar* (Najema Music 2005). The chosen instrument for this type of music is the oud, which was born in the area of what is now Iraq and Iran about 3,500 years ago. Contemporary Jews and Arabs are still composing new songs in this style, for instance Salim Al-Nur and Dalal himself. Performing Babylonian music can be a way to celebrate the common roots of both peoples.

Playing both the oud and the violin

The oud is a typically Arab instrument, and the violin a typically Jewish instrument, and Dalal plays both masterfully. Many of the best Iraqi oud players of

the first half of the twentieth century were Jews. They were forced to leave Iraq
for Israel in 1948, just like Dalal's parents. During his childhood, Dalal's home
was always full of expatriates and immigrants, some of them Jewish Iraqi oud
masters, from whom he learned to play the instrument. The oud is more than
3000 years old, and it spread throughout the world, adopting different forms,
to become the lute, and later the guitar, and many other instruments:

> The Oud first appears in Mesopotamia during the Kassite period (1600–1150
> BC) with a small oval body. A larger variety, similar to the instrument's present
> day dimensions, appears at Alaca Huyuk in Anatolia dating from the Hittite New
> Kingdom (1460–1190 BC). Today, the Oud is known as *ut* or *ud* in Turkey, *laouta*
> in Greece, *udi* in Africa and *barbat* in Iran. In Arabic, the word means "wood,"
> "twig," "flexible rod," and also "aromatic stick."
>
> (Armenian Heritage 2006)

As thousands of fans can attest, anybody hearing Dalal play the oud would be
convinced of his thoroughly Arabic origins. However, he plays the violin
equally well and in an interview he shared the reason why he started learning
the violin:

> Back to my childhood, my parents used to take me to Iraqi parties and on one of
> these occasions I met a great violin player, his name was Daud Akram. He was a
> blind man with dark glasses covering his eyes, and his music and personality
> impressed me greatly. I was four years old at the time, and the sound of his vio-
> lin entered deeply into my soul, and I decided that I wanted to play the violin.
> After a long struggle with my parents they agreed and sent me to study at the
> Conservatorium.
>
> (Dalal 2006)

Mixing Jewish and Arab music

The song "Through the Mist of Your Eyes," an original composition by Yair
Dalal from the album *Asmar*, is a harmonious mixture of Arab and Jewish
music, and is sung in both Jewish and Arabic. For the unsuspecting listener, it
sounds like a song in one specific style and sung in one single language. It is one
of the numerous examples of songs combining both musical and linguistic cultures.

Another example is a sequence of three songs on the same album, a Jewish
prayer, a Maqam and a traditional Iraqi song, forming a rare combination.
Usually the prayer is in Arabic, followed by the Maqam and song. This
sequence is formed by the last three songs of the album:

- "Prayer for Peace," in Hebrew for *Yom Kippur*, sang by Maureen Nehedar
- "Maqam Dashti" sang in Iraqi style (Yair Dalal) and Persian style (Maureen Nehedar)
- "Ya Aziz Al Rouh" – a pasta (a traditional Iraqi song).

Dalal learned Arab music not only from the Iraqi Jews visiting his home, but also directly from the Bedouins:

> The Bedouin music that is an integral part of his style has an accentuated melodic line, a reserved but extremely emotional expression. There are no electronics used to design or create additional atmosphere. Dalal has preferred to remain as authentic as possible, even choosing to record in a tent. Bedouin music and culture is slowly being eliminated, and this is an attempt to preserve at least a small repertoire of Bedouin music from the Negev. Dalal's reserved personality goes well with the Bedouins' modest behavior, and their friendship dates back many years. When others were traveling to India in the '70's, Dalal traveled the Sinai and Negev deserts with his camel and violin. It was back then that the strong bond with Bedouins and their culture was founded.
>
> (Backroads Music 2006)

Performing with musicians of both backgrounds

According to an article about Israeli musicians on the website of the Israeli Ministry of Foreign Affairs:

> In the early 1990s, Dalal formed an ensemble called "Al Ol" which plays a mixture of Jewish and Arab, eastern and western music. Al Ol is composed of traditional instruments such as clarinet, flute, violin and guitar, which are played alongside the ûd, tampura, and darbuka. Dalal has initiated several projects with Palestinian musicians. His upbringing has had a significant impact on his work, and he has drawn much inspiration from leading Iraqi Jewish musicians in Israel. In his six* CDs, Dalal's message is politically-oriented: global peace and Arab-Israeli peace are possible. Only by a deep recognition of the other and its uniqueness and difference, is it possible to create human, social and political harmony. Dalal's first international exposure came in December 1994, at the Shalom-Salaam concert held in Oslo to mark the first anniversary of the signing of the agreement between Israel and the Palestinians.
>
> (Ministry of Foreign Affairs 2006)
> (* As of June 2006, Yair Dalal had produced eight CDs.)

For this concert, Dalal brought forty Palestinian and forty Israeli children to have them perform together. This was the result of intense and difficult

negotiations, and the public was deeply moved. However, as we have seen in
the introduction to this chapter, and as is mentioned in the last section, a negative interpretation of this event is also possible.

Sharing his message through interviews

Several groups try to use music to build friendship and mutual respect between
Arabs (especially Palestinians) and Jews (especially Israeli Jews), such as the
group Atzilut, who define their music as a "Jewish/Arab Cultural Bridging
Project" (Atzilut 2006). What sets Yair Dalal apart is that this cultural bridge-
building is constantly happening within one single individual.

Dalal's philosophy of music and peace in this context is clearly stated on the
back cover of his 2005 CD entitled Inshalla Shalom, recorded live in Jerusalem,
a collection of folk songs from the Middle East:

> Inshalla Shalom was recorded live at a concert in Jerusalem with Jewish and
> Arab musicians. This album is dedicated to the folk music of the Middle East;
> songs that date back dozens of generations. These are the songs which all of the
> people of the region grew up with. Arabs, Jews, Christians and Moslems – peo-
> ple of all nationalities and tribes who share the same musical culture.

> Peace, Inshalla (with God's help), will be sung like a folk song that sends its sim-
> ple and honest message to all, regardless of religion, race or nationality. Amen.

(Najema Music 2005)

About the Common Roots between Jews and Arabs

Dalal cannot reject his Arab cultural roots, nor his physical appearance. The
title of the album Asmar means "brownish," a nickname given to Dalal's father
by his friends back in Iraq, before Dalal's birth (Backroads Music 2006). Nor
can he reject his Jewish ancestry. He therefore created an idyllic past, the common past of all Jews and Arabs, in Mesopotamia, Sumer and Babylon, the culture of the people of the desert. Let us take a close look at some of the myths
and facts of history concerning the common ancestors of both Jews and Arabs.
Some seem to confirm Dalal's theory, and some seem to contradict it.

In his "Postscript on Later Arab History," Robert Brow, author of the
online book *Ishmael The Arab 1866–1729* BC, mentions the close ties he believes
have linked Jews and Arabs from the beginning of their history. According to
him, there is enough evidence to establish that the two sons of Abraham,

Ishmael and Isaac, were indeed the ancestors of the Arab and the Jewish people, respectively:

> Using dozens of texts from the first book of the Jewish Bible we have pictured Ishmael as the ancestor of the Arabs. Genesis was written in its present form at least a thousand years before Egypt became a Roman province. And it certainly does not look like a book of legends. We have noted a totally self-consistent framework of dates, and the very careful genealogies of five groups of Arab tribes whose origins are closely connected with Ishmael and his twelve sons.
>
> (Brow 2006)

There are only about 13 million Jews in the world today, but about two or three hundred million Arabs. This numerical discrepancy can be explained by the way in which both groups started growing:

> Whereas the Jewish descendants of Isaac tended to be exclusive and closely tied to the land of Canaan, the Arab vision was to include any who would join them. In addition to the twelve tribes descended from Ishmael's sons (**Genesis 17:20**), other tribes connected more or less closely with Abraham joined themselves by marriage (**36:2–3**) to the Arab brotherhood. We have pictured this beginning to happen through Ishmael's personal vision, but it took a long time to come to fruition, and there were setbacks.
>
> (Brow 2006)

Both Arabs and Jews were originally Sumerian, but spoke an Aramaic language:

> In previous chapters we have noted that communication between Israel and her Arab neighbors was possible because they had the common language which Abraham and his sons learned in Canaan. Modern scholars call this language West Semitic, but according to the biblical terminology this was a Hamitic language (**Genesis 10:6, 15**) which had displaced the previous Sumerian (Shemitic) language that Abraham had spoken in Ur (**Genesis 10:21–24, 11:10–32,** see the Introduction to this book). This meant that both Jews and Arabs were originally Sumerian by race, but they spoke the language of Canaan, which was a dialect of the Aramaic language that was understood all over the Arab lands.
>
> (Brow 2006)

We might therefore be tempted to dream of idyllic times before Abraham, when there were no Jews and no Arabs, and when all the people of the desert were harmoniously united as one family. A few words of caution are necessary here. First, there is no irrefutable proof that Abraham has ever existed, and that his two sons were at the origin of the Jewish and Arab peoples. These are famous legends, but on the other hand, from a social constructionist point of view, when so many millions of people believe in these legends, they acquire much more power than any scientifically proven facts, and they have a huge impact on people's daily lives and the shaping of societies. We therefore need to take them into account.

The second problem concerning this idyllic past is that chances are that this peaceful "pre-Arab–Jewish split" paradise only existed for brief periods of time. The first civilization, Sumer, was organized into competing city-states that were soon fighting with each other regularly. Around 2300 BCE, Sargon I conquered Sumer and established the Akkadian empire, the world's first empire in the area of ancient Mesopotamia, effectively putting an end to Sumerian civilization. We can only imagine the amount of violence his efforts involved. Then around 1800 BCE, the Amorites moved into Mesopotamia and soon Hammurabi, the king of Babylon, conquered the Akkadians and ruled all of Mesopotamia. That means that by the time Abraham appeared in Ur, the whole region had already been replete with fighting and violence. Nonetheless, we can understand Dalal's project as a desire to go back to the greatness of Mesopotamia (without the violence), taking pride in the establishment of the first civilization including the first writing system and irrigation technology by the Sumerians, the Code of Law by Hammurabi, and many other achievements.

One thing is certain, music had already an important place in Sumer, the first human civilization, and it only makes sense to use music as an effective medium to evoke the common heritage of both Jews and Arabs:

> The discovery of numerous musical instruments in royal burial sites helps illustrate the prominent role music played in Sumerian life and religion. Musicians and their instruments appear frequently in the artwork and archeological artefacts of Iraq's deep antiquity.
>
> While the exact music from ancient Mesopotamia can never be recovered, Iraq has produced intriguing written evidence supporting the existence of sophisticated music theory and practice in Sumerian, Babylonian and Akkadian cultures. A family of musical texts inscribed in cuneiform tablets reveal a wealth of musical information about specific tuning modes, string names and hymns. These written documents demonstrate that musical activity was being recorded a thousand years prior to the rise of ancient Greek civilization, a culture commonly credited with the earliest development of musical documents.
>
> (Williamsound 2006)

Since the Sumerians are credited with the oldest writing system, the cuneiform, it is only natural that the oldest recorded songs in the world were also found in Mesopotamia.

Comparing Yair Dalal and Gilad Atzmon

Earlier in this volume, Karen Abi-Ezzi observed that her chapter "stands in stark contrast to the chapter about Yair Dalal." Indeed, Dalal supported the Oslo initiative by participating in a Nobel Peace Prize gala concert in 1994 whereas Atzmon denies the right of the State of Israel to exist, and claims that the entire country should be called Palestine, and ruled by Palestinians.

Atzmon's view is based on the past before 14 May 1948, when there was still a possibility to establish a Palestinian state ruled by Palestinians. Gilad Atzmon projects himself into this virtual past, and brings it back today in his musical work. He believes one of the keys to peace in the Middle East is for Israelis to become "Palestinised":

> I took Jewish tunes and I Palestinised them and by doing that I'm trying to prove two things: first, I undermined the Jewish victim identity – they are not the victims, they are the oppressors. Second, if the music can be Palestinised so easily – and I say so easily because I am far from being a genius so if I can do it, everyone can do it – so maybe they can be Palestinised as well. And they [Israelis] were horrified. And I achieved my goal.
>
> (Atzmon 2005)

In contrast, Yair Dalal does not contest the existence of the State of Israel at all, and he affirms his identity as an "Arab Israeli Jew." He goes back to a past much older than Gilad Atzmon's, tapping into a period more than 4000 years ago. This position also requires a lot of courage: Dalal is banned from performing in some Arab countries because he is an "Israeli," from some Muslim countries because he is a "Jew," and from some Israeli radio programs because part of his lyrics are in Arabic, and sung in Arabic.

Both of them are challenging some aspect of the status quo, and both are playing an important role for peace by shaking the foundations of the constructed cultural and national identities that have torn the Middle East apart for decades.

Conclusion

In his studio in Jaffa, Dalal sometimes plays music that can be heard outside. Passers-by are often attracted by the sounds of the oud or the violin, and come closer to see who is playing. Arabs are surprised to see a Jew playing their music, and Jews are surprised to see an Arab-looking person playing theirs. Things become even more interesting when both Jewish and Arab visitors meet at Dalal's place, each attracted by some part of his music. Sometimes these encounters lead to meaningful dialogues, and even to the development of friendships, contributing in some small way to peaceful conflict transformation in the Middle East.

Yair Dalal's life and musical work, his cultural identity as an "Arab Israeli Jew," the fact that he is perfectly fluent in the music and languages of both peoples, his family background and biography, do not really give him a choice concerning his musical mission for peace. He might not have the solution to all of the Middle East's miseries, but he is definitely part of the solution. So are hundreds of excellent musicians who show us that as complex as the protracted conflict between Jews (especially Israeli Jews) and Arabs (especially Palestinian Arabs) is, music can help people to find varied responses. Yair Dalal's music allows us to build a better appreciation of the common roots of the peoples in the region, and it gives us hope that they might one day find a way to once again share their ancestral lands.

References

Armenian Heritage (2006) "History of the oud," http://www.armenianheritage.com/daoud.htm

Atzilut (2006) Homepage of the musical group Atzilut, http://www.atzilutmusic.com/

Atzmon (2005) in K. Abi-Ezzi's chapter in this volume.

Backroads Music (2006) "Feature artist: Yair Dalal," http://www.backroadsmusic.com/catalog/feature_artist/dalal.html

Brow, R. (2006) The Robert Brow "Model Theology": "Ishmael the Arab 1866–1729 BC," by Robert Brow, http://www.brow.on.ca/Books/Ishmael/ Ishpost.htm

Dalal, Y. (2004) Interview with unknown person in Spain, obtained from Yair Dalal's manager by email.

Dalal, Y. (2005) Email to the author.

Dalal, Y. (2006) Email to the author.

Israeli Ministry of Foreign Affairs (2006) "Sounds from the South," *The Israel Review of Arts and Letters* 2001/112, http://www.mfa.gov.il/MFA/MFAArchive/2000_2009/2002/7/Sounds%20from%20the%20South

Jordanger, V. (2006) see his chapter in this volume.

Najema Music (2005) *Inshalla Shalom* [CD].

Williamsound (2006) "Musical traditions of ancient Iraq: the Gold Lyre of Ur, c. 2650 BC (BCE)" by D. Irvine, http://www.williamsound.com/gold_lyre_music_info.html

World Food Program (2006) "WFP warns of growing destitution among Palestinians," http://www.wfp.org/english/?ModuleID=137&Key=2128

Chapter 15: Music and Peacemaking in Educational Contexts

June Boyce-Tillman

Introduction

In this chapter, I am concerned with the way in which we communicate Values to our students in educational contexts through music making activities. Because much of the musics that make up our Western music curricula and concerts with children are "masterpieces" from Western culture's past, the values that we are presenting may also be Values that we have abandoned in the wider society like those of colonialism, particularly in relation to intercultural borrowing. This chapter uses the analytical frame set out in my previous chapter to examine various projects I have carried out in educational contexts that attempt to set out different value systems for the participants.

The Call of the Ancestors

In a piece called *The Call of the Ancestors* (Boyce-Tillman 1998) I started to explore the notion of structures with 'windows' in them to contain a diversity of musical styles. My own intention in writing it was to explore a musical construction that could bring together various cultures with integrity. This musical structure was intended to mirror a just society that would reflect a respect for diversity. This, in turn, would influence the lives of the participants and the listeners. My own intention in writing *The Call of the Ancestors* was to explore the meeting of various musical structures that could bring together various cultures with integrity. It was written for the Church Colleges Choirs Festival in March 1998 in Winchester Cathedral, UK. Underpinning it at the Spiritual level was the notion that the call to Wisdom is a universal call but that each culture has to rework it within its forms and structures. At the level of Materials, different performing groups were used, this included improvising groups of various kinds (non-notated traditions), which in this performance were Kenyan drums, rock group and Thai piphat, a Western brass quintet, the moot horn an Anglo-Saxon instrument, a large four-part choir, in this case the combined choirs of the participating colleges. At the Expressive level, the work brings together a number of different texts from differing cultures including King Alfred's (871–99) prose translation of Psalm 45 and the Antiphon to Wisdom by Hildegard of Bingen (1098–1179) (Boyce-Tillman 2001b). By using a text from man (Alfred) and a woman (Hildegard), the male and female lines of an ancestry are reflected. It was choreographed by my colleague, Olu Taiwo who used movements taken from the capoiera tradition. The four dancers represented shapes floating in space and also a combination of the awe and wonder generated by the large space and a childlike playfulness. These reflected the character of the carvings on the moot horn of a bishop and a lion rampant. The form of the piece is that of a responsive psalm. Each verse is sung by the choir, accompanied by brass quintet and responded to by an improvising group. These are held together by the notion of a fractal design, which is a pattern found in the natural world in which each of the parts has the same shape as the whole. The groups were placed around the Cathedral, with the choir and brass group at the east end, the rock group at the back and the drums and piphat in the north and south aisles. The audience was thus enclosed by the music which appeared to "move." The level of Value was reflected in letting the non-notated traditions make their own structures rather than forcing them into the structures of the notated Western classical traditions.

The Healing of the Earth

I followed this with another "windows" piece. This was intended for children. The piece entitled *The Healing of the Earth* (Boyce-Tillman 2001a) has been performed in several situations but I will concentrate here on a performance for the Queen's Jubilee in 2002 with 500 children aged 6–16 in Battersea Technology College, London, UK.

The starting point of the piece was in the areas of Value and Spirituality. It is a piece with an intentionally ethical system based on the valuing of diversity and connecting with the environment. This drew on feminist theoreticians of music especially Rose Rosengard Subotnik (1996) in which she explores how prevailing Western value systems permeate the apparently value free Western classical traditions. It is based on a notion of building a community musically, within a single musical event in which, through participatory performance, professional musicians and children work together with integrity (Sharp 2000). There are few examples in the music making traditions of the West where adults can behave as adults and children as children and they can both be included in a musical event. There are situations, like the cathedral choir, where children have to behave like adults in order to be accepted. Other situations, like nursery classes, ask adults to behave like children to facilitate group music making. In this work, I tried to develop an inclusive structure, in which experienced musicians played quite complex textures, while children had sections which they themselves devised.

The Valuing of the environment is reflected in the titles of the nine movements: Wisdom, Water, Knowledge, Fire, Technology, Earth, Compassion, Air, and Communication. Many of the pieces include theological and musical ideas taken from Hildegard of Bingen, a twelfth century abbess whose theology saw the whole of the cosmos as in interrelationship and flourishing only when its different parts are in right relationship (Boyce-Tillman 2001b). The themes of the songs are ecological but this ecology includes the recycling of ourselves and our experiences alongside care for the environment. It is extended to include personal and community transformation.

This pluralistic Value system is reflected in the range of cultures from which the songs are drawn. These include Native American, Urdu, Israeli, Yoruba, Muslim, and Christian sources. These fit alongside newly composed material in a more Western classical style, in a patchwork style format. Diversity is put together with respect for both the differences and common elements. Again here, music provides an example of how Values might work in the wider society.

The Value systems of the Western classical concert with its separation between the composer, performer and audience are, in this work, balanced by a more democratic approach to creation and performance. There are the devised sections – so the performers have a hand in the compositional process. The players and singers are placed around the audience, who also have to sing. The notion of a musical performance as something packaged by a conductor at one end of a space and then propelled to the other where it is received by an audience, is now replaced by one in which each member of the audience has to construct their own listening experience; this will depend on which group of musicians are near them. So we all collaborate together – performers, composers and audience – to make things happen musically and also ecologically.

In the area of Construction I chose a modular format. Construction in the dominant Western classical tradition had often been managed by notation, tonality and harmony. I had to find a structure that could contain material from a variety of sources – both instrumental and sung material, as well as pieces devised by the children. I therefore developed a structure that retains as far as possible the character of the original culture. So there are a variety of accompaniment textures, such as ostinati, drones, and chords. There are "holes/windows" in the piece for the devised episodes, a technique developed in a piece described above (Boyce-Tillman 1998). The structure is intended to reflect the multicultural nature of our society, including notated and non-notated – literate/orate – elements (Ong 1982). The modular structure enables the piece to be rehearsed in sections and then put together in a final rehearsal. It is the task of the composer/conductor to make the connections work effectively; so the role of director/composer becomes more that of a weaver than a benevolent dictator.

The Materials used are deliberately simple. The accompaniment is provided by a flexible ensemble consisting of a high, low and two middle instruments using whatever players are available. A great deal of the musical Material involves the human voice and the other Materials are left to the choice of the participating schools. In this performance we had a devised piece using steel pans. In a previous performance, there was a section of drumming from the East African tradition.

The valuing of the area of Expression is apparent in the inclusion of sections devised by the children themselves. These improvised sections included movement, dance and drama. The performance included artwork in the form of mobiles and banners with ecological themes, created in association with a local art gallery. This reflects an interdisciplinary view of the arts, balancing the discrete approach to them espoused by the dominant value system. The opening texts are printed in Appendix One.

In the Spirituality of the piece is the notion that through such music making we affect the ecology of the planet. It was, in general, the children who found these ideas easier to accept than the adults, who were already enculturated into a culture of rationality and non-belief in magical systems. However, it was interesting to see how many of the teachers, somewhat cautiously at first, declared their belief in these notions of Spirituality.

I followed up this performance with semi-structured interviews with children, teachers and parents to see how far my ecological intentions particularly, those in the areas of Values and Spirituality, had been realised. Various themes emerged from these.

The valuing of diversity was clearly reflected. In a school in which the head teacher had said that the citizenship agenda could only be delivered through discussion and debate, a 10-year-old boy started his reflections with:

"It was like peace on earth. Everyone did their own thing but it all fitted together."

What was interesting was that although many of the children knew the meaning of the word "unity," they only learned the meaning of diversity through participation in this event – a real reflection of the prevailing value systems.

The piece clearly valued the notion of community above the individualism of the National Curriculum. This was why a number of the head teachers agreed to participate in the project. They commented on the effect the piece had had on children's community building skills. A head teacher in a zone designated as needing special educational resources, commented:

"It improved the children's cooperative skills. I saw them supporting one another and encouraging other schools in their work. This is unusual for our children whose poverty often makes them quite self-centred."

In the area of Expression and emotional literacy there was the development of empathy through music. A 10-year-old girl said that she sings the "setting" of the South African prayer every night. I had told them about the community in Gugulethu South Africa where I had found the prayer. She said:

"I felt close to the people in Africa whose prayer we sang. Now I continue to sing it and think of them."

Teachers often commented on the improvement in their pupils' ability to use music for personal expression. One statement ran:

"It encouraged me to encourage children to make their own music and value their pieces."

Also in the area of Expression is the notion of the development of personal qualities. Parents often concentrated on their children's confidence and self-esteem (bearing in mind many of the schools were in areas regarded as deprived):

"It improved my child's self confidence and assurance. She is always singing the songs around the house."

Bearing in mind the subject of the piece, ecological themes were common and linked with other explorations of this in the school curriculum. An 11-year-old girl in a school that had done a number of recycling projects said:

"It made me think about re-cycling, how it is not just about aluminium cans but also about how our bodies are continually being renewed."

The challenging of the elitist value systems of the Classical tradition was reflected in the notion of inclusivity which appeared in various ways. One teacher who was very afraid of embarking on composing activities said of the final performance:

"I realised that I could not get it wrong."

The importance of the spiritual dimension appeared regularly. A 10-year-old girl commented:

"There was this power there. I don't know what it was. It was simply a power."

I hope to use this research to extend the project and explore musical ecology more fully through performance/composition projects with associated semi-structured interviews, using it also as the basis for a "Music for Peace" project, valuing the interconnections made through music which will be reflected in large and small children's peace choirs.

The Greening Branch

This piece explored how far the structure that shares out function of composing among the performers, to create community, could be used with experienced choirs – to find out how they would respond to being asked to create some episodes. The piece is based on Hildegard's hymn to the Virgin Mary "O viridissima virga" (Boyce-Tillman 2001b) and was written specially for the Church Colleges Choirs' Festival which was held at St Mary's College, Twickenham. (The Church Colleges' Festival involves the church colleges from England coming together to sing once a year. This creates a choir of somewhere between 200 and 250 students.) The piece falls into nine sections based on the nine verses of the hymn. Through it all runs an ostinato taken from the opening of the hymn. This is intended to suggest eternity, against which a number of temporal episodes take place. Four themes were taken from the Hildegard hymn:

- The praise of Wisdom as revealed through the Virgin Mary.
- The nativity (which I extended to include birth in general as well as Jesus' birth).
- The earth (which was a real concern of Hildegard's and is reflected in the imagery of this hymn).
- The poor (drawn from the theme of generosity in the hymn).

I wanted it to be a collaborative piece where everyone had a hand in creating and performing the music. So, some sections are composed by me and some are to be composed by the participating choirs using the texts set out in the score. The singers came to be situated around the audience, who also have to sing. This is to show that we all can collaborate together – performers, composers and audience – to make things happen musically. The piece is ultimately about making connections and minimizing divisions.

The plan of each section of the piece is roughly as follows:

- A verse of the Hildegard hymn
- A response by the choir
- A devised piece by one of the choirs.

The choral sections are often simple chants or rounds. Combined with the ostinato on the orchestra, they create a complex texture.

For this performance I divided up the creative work so that each college has one piece to devise/improvise/compose. A poem was suggested on the themes of the piece and taken from medieval mystics and some musical lines that the orchestra will play. This is an ostinato taken from the opening of the Hildegard hymn which runs through the entire work. Four lines in parallel fifths are suggested in each devised episode. The individual college choirs could use some version of this as the accompaniment to their compositions. The outline of some sections of the work is shown in Appendix 2.

These are some of the issues raised in the semi-structured interviews following the performance. (Some expressions used by the interviewees, such as "sort of" have been edited from the following transcripts for the sake of readability):

- The sense of circularity
  It was nice to see everyone to be in the circle . . . and also because, the sounds coming from different areas in the Church, it made good use of the acoustics . . . Plus, it fits the concept of the piece. It fits a sort of Eastern spirituality and, thinking along those lines, the circle does tie in with that. It was good to have a big massed choir and also a separate own piece . . . I mean, as a whole, you felt more a part of it in the circle; as a section in the blocks, you could hear your own section, but in the circle you could hear everything that was going on.

- Surround sound
  It was different in the surround sound from the sound in *Messiah* [Note from the author: another peace in the same concert], where you were all, in a sense, identified in blocks . . . When we were all up on the stage, all the men were together . . . You've got the different parts all around, so it was like more of a fuller sound.

- Shared responsibility
  Several interviewees said that it was like throwing a ball from one choir to the next or passing a relay baton on, as the authority passed from the main conductor to the conductors of the individual choirs.

I thought, conceptually, it was a good idea. I think the idea is excellent. One of the problems for me with such an idea, though, is when you give responsibility to other people to make inserts, you lose control, and you take that as read when you do it. So, as a piece, I think it was enormously successful, but then if I was going to go one stage further it becomes slightly disjointed. Not so much in terms of the feeling that comes from each of the choir's inputs, but rather in terms of the scale of things. It becomes actually quite gargantuan as a piece.

- Diversity

  I liked this circular idea. It goes through all kinds of different traditions of music at different times. However, I would like to say that there were lots of different types of music, and . . . I think one of the successes was that there was a huge range . . . Each choir played to its strengths . . . It was nice for the students to have a sense of their own part . . . Although you had written the framework into which everything fitted, which was easy to learn because it used the different musical idioms, giving it fluidity . . . then each small episode that the choirs individually produced gave them a sense of ownership of the pieces as well, so there was a clarity which was an experience that was good for the students. And again, each choir could play to its own strengths . . . It was a lovely idea but it did have inherent problems and delays and distances from you as the chief conductor of these choirs.

- Contextualization

  It is fabulous when you try to write something to match the style of what was going on before and after it. Yes, I thought that was fine. And, again, you produce something tailored to what your choir can do, so that obviously pre-supposes that, when you've got different choirs, you're going to have different styles.

- Engagement

  It's not entirely new to me because in Taizé, where people from all over the world gather, they have this style of singing where they have like the grand ostinato and different things happening . . . I go back to this thing of attentiveness – it does refresh your attentiveness because that authority does pass from one to the other. Your whole attentiveness in music has been different.

- Role of the audience-inclusivity

  I thought [the layout] was a good idea. We're back to this circular thing. I think it made it more interesting from the audience's point of view . . . I thought that was a great idea. It had the feeling of more music making for everybody because we all contributed the part that the audience sang, so you weren't just sitting listening to a concert.

- Simplicity
  It was great . . . I thought that . . . the choral composition itself was very attractive and very strong. I loved the idea of the very simple, you know, modal, medieval feel to it, and using forms that could, in themselves, be taken out independently. Our intellectual, musical friends would virtually, I'm sure, tear your music and my music to shreds in terms of "Well, what is this? This is very straightforward and very simple." The thing is, the majority of people, as you demonstrated, could sing that, so you could actually present it to an audience for the first time and engage them in that same concept. That takes some doing, I think.

- Emotional power
  I mean, certainly, emotion before intellect, and that's not disparaging.

- The relationship to the wisdom tradition of theology
  As chaplain I really welcome the resurrection of this whole notion of Wisdom and the Sophia and the feminine qualities that it brings, but they're not necessarily gender-specific Feminine aesthetics can be found in the male gender just as much as in the female gender. I think it brings back to the fore both in the thinking of women and men, the whole nurturing, the nourishing, the birth and the re-birth. All of these sorts of themes, I think they tie in or they clash very much with the technological age that's full of measurement and kind of cold and hygienic in what it represents; so I liked the recovery of the importance, or the earthiness, of who we are and where we came from. So you do look around and the world of music does tend to be populated more by men.

- Spirituality
  I felt it was quite nice – maybe not on the spiritual level, but it was nice, having not rehearsed it as a full choir; it felt just very warm.

  I mean, the whole feeling of the choirs being together, I felt that was a kind of great religious thing anyway. Very spiritual, yes.

In summary, this was not so much an experiment in interculturalism as in democratic, collaborative ways of composing and challenging the individualistic models of the Western world.

Remembering Christ

In this project I explored the use of the combined arts to produce reconciliation including music as one of them. It was an Easter project at Holyrood House – a centre for theology and healing in the North of the UK. The project took place over a week and the central image was created by the participants. They made squares of material to represent people, situations and natural elements to which they were connected in some way. This included negative as well as positive connections – people with whom they had broken or difficult relationships. These were then attached to sashes on a large structure that resembled a traditional maypole with wide sashes hanging from it. We made music and poetry around these ideas. On Maundy Thursday we made the interconnected web; on Good Friday we cut into the web that we had made and the pieces were hidden all over the garden. On Saturday we hunted for them and sewed them back together. On Easter Sunday we used the now restored banner as the centre piece of singing and dancing at sunrise. On Monday we pitched it like a tent with the sashes outstretched and danced in and out.

The overall effect of the week was remarkable with one person speaking to her father for the first time in five years and one person returning to her family after a year of absence. Others just felt profoundly moved by the experience of building community, fracturing it and rebuilding it expressed through the combined arts.

PeaceSong

This was an extension of the Greening Branch project, written for the same festival which took place in Winchester Cathedral in March 2006. In this piece the space was used more dramatically. It also asked the various choirs to create episodes in the piece. They were asked to set prayers from various faith traditions such as:

Five movements entitled:

- If these walls could only speak
- Shalom
- Invocation
- Swords into ploughshares
- Natural connection.

These represent:

- Peace with the past

- Peace with the Spiritual
- Peace with other faith traditions
- Justice-making
- Peace with the earth.

The first movement represented the walls of the cathedral yielding up the sounds that have happened in that place and all the musicians hidden in side chapels were singing pieces like Bruckner's *Locus Iste* and *Praise God, from whom all blessings flow*. These were fragmented as calls across the space.

The second movement was based on choirs moving around the building singing "shalom" on a single note and carrying candles. The building gradually filled with this sound which was an ohm-like sound with "ssh" in it. Over it the instruments explored Hildegard's antiphon "Caritas Abundat" (Boyce-Tillman 2001b):

Strengthening love
Is blooming in everything,
At her most excellent in the deeps
And the rising stars
And the most fascinating heart of all things,
Because she has embraced the Highest Sovereign
In peace.

The third movement included the faith prayers set in the context of the Hindu prayer for peace, sung by choirs and congregation, such as:

The Muslim Prayer for Peace

In the name of Allah, the beneficent, the merciful. Praise be to the Lord of the Universe who has created us and made us into tribes and nations, that we may know each other, not that we may despise each other. If the enemy incline towards peace, do thou also incline towards peace, and trust in God, for the Lord is the one that heareth and knoweth all things. And the servants of God, Most Gracious are those who walk on the Earth in humility, and when we address them, we say "PEACE."

The Native American Prayer for Peace

O Great Spirit of our Ancestors, I raise my pipe to you. To your messengers the four winds, and to Mother Earth who provides for your children. Give us the wisdom to teach our children to love, to respect, and to be kind to each other so that they may grow with peace in mind. Let us learn to share all the good things that you provide for us on this Earth.

(Peace Seeds 1986)

The fourth movement was based on the following song which I had written as part of a Christmas letter:

Can there be peace when the war lords rule?
Can there be love when the fists are clenched?
Can there be hope as the coffins fill?
Listen, struggle, understand.

Chorus

We are committed to work for peace;
We are committed to work with love;
We are committed to work with hope,
Reconciling, mediating, understanding.

Can there be joy while the tears pour down?
Can we be gentle when crude violence reigns?
Can there be patience when the pain spears bite?
Listen, struggle, understand.

Chorus

Can there be justice for the poor and weak?
Can there be caring for our rich dark earth?
Can there be sharing of the planet's wealth?
Listen, struggle, understand.

Chorus

In this movement a Nigerian drumming group run by a research student at the University moved from the back of the cathedral to the front. The final movement included the arrival of the children singing "Hevenu Shalom Aleichem." It leads to the "Song of the Earth" sung by everyone.

The Materials used were quite large musical forces: a brass quintet, flute and saxophone, a choir of about 250 students and 100 school children. Significantly, it made use of a very large, old and beautiful building with amazing acoustics, which was explored in the piece. The choirs were either moving or positioned around it, enveloping the audience with the sound and including them in some movements. The Expression involved a variety of moods and valued the compositional skills of the performers. The Construction was modular and wove together a variety of Materials including some created by the performers into a sort of musical tapestry. In this way it resembled women's art like patchwork and appliqué, organising materials from a variety of sources into new patterns. The Value system reflects a variety of areas where peacemaking is desirable as well as adopting a more democratic way of producing a performance.

Conclusion

In these performance pieces I have tried to put into practice some of the principles of the subjugated ways of knowing set out in my previous chapter:

- Using more circular structures and layout
- Simplifying the Materials used
- Revaluing Expressive elements
- Revisiting structures that separate functions like composing, performing and listening and value unity above diversity
- Embracing a Value system that supports nurture
- Revisiting the racism and sexism of the classical canon in the area of Values
- The inclusion of deliberately Spiritual elements from the Wisdom tradition.

So, notions of peacemaking with value systems that have been devalued by Western culture are embedded in these pieces at every level. Heidi Westerlund, in her critique of Western music education, sets out her philosophy of music education:

> My intention was also to show that music could be a genuine way to *create* situations, to *construct* social relations in situations, to *communicate* in a holistic way that combines body and ethics, individual and community.
>
> (Westerlund 2002: 144)

This is what I have attempted to do in these pieces. The values of the constructional systems of the Western classical tradition are revisited and reworked. The notion of the possibility of multiple metanarratives in the area of spirituality is in the texts chosen and the subject matter addressed (Boyce-Tillman 2001). Peace with various cultures is addressed in the use of a variety of Materials of various origins and the use of 'windows' in the piece to allow them to create in their own traditions. Justice-making is implicit in these decisions. These pieces present a challenge for the students involved that perhaps will enable them to explore new possibilities themselves that may set up a counter culture to the prevailing one of individualistic and nationalist war-making.

Appendix 1

The Healing of the Earth Opening

Introduction

The Song of the Earth: Song

CHORUS (including the audience):
Sing us our own song the song of the earth,
The song of creation, the song of our birth,
That exists in belonging to you and to me,
To the stars and the mountains, the sky and the sea.

Hold Fast to the Earth: Song

Hold fast to the earth,
Swim deeply in the sea,
Leap high in the fire,
Float gently on the breeze. (June Boyce-Tillman)

Water Movement

Ocean: Instrumental Piece Based on Hildegard

Rain Song

Avare varsad,
Gebariyo parsad,
Uni, uni rotali
Ne karelanum shak.

Come, come, rain,
We will give you sweets,
Hot, hot chapatis
And vegetable feasts. (Trad. Gujerati collected from Habib Latif)

The Fountain: Instrumental Piece by the Children Based on the Poem

Rippling water
Bubbling up
Rippling water
Crystal clear

Refreshment
Fountain playing
Splashing freely
Purifying

Crystal clear
Rippling water
Bubbling up
Rippling water (June Boyce-Tillman)

Appendix 2

Some Sections from *The Greening Branch*

SECTION ONE: *Solo:* Hildegard
1. O praise a branch of great greenness,
Mary, you answer some of the changing, uncertain questions
The saints have been asking.
Choir: Come, Spirit, circle us, Keep love within, evil outside.

Devised piece 1: Wisdom

I heard God speaking to my soul:
I have loved you
With an everlasting love
Before the world was born
I have called you into the dance of life
Let me put a spring into your step
So that you may be led
Into joy beyond all knowing. (based on Mechtild of Magdeburg)
All including audience:
May Wisdom guide us into all truth, Hear our prayer.
Make ev'ry birth a Wisdom birth, Hear our prayer.
Nourish the poor, defend the weak, Hear our prayer.
And fill the springs that nourish the earth, Hear our prayer.

Devised piece 6: The Needy

To the God of my ancestors, I pray: I am lying down without food;
My belly is empty although others have eaten and are satisfied;
Even if it is a small creature like a rock rat,
Please give it to me;
Then I shall be grateful.
Hear my prayer God of my ancestors. (South African prayer)

References

Boyce-Tillman, J. (1998) *The Call of the Ancestors*, London: The Hildegard Press.

Boyce-Tillman, June (2000a) *Constructing Musical Healing: The Wounds that Sing*, London: Jessica Kingsley.

Boyce-Tillman, J. (2000b) *The Creative Spirit – Harmonious Living with Hildegard of Bingen*, Norwich: Canterbury Press.

Boyce-Tillman, June (2001a) *The Healing of the Earth*, London: The Hildegard Press.

Boyce-Tillman, J. (2001b) "Sounding the Sacred: Music as Sacred Site," in K. Ralls-MacLeod and G. Harvey (eds) *Indigenous Religious Musics*, Farnborough: Scolar.

Boyce-Tillman, June (2003) *The Greening Branch*, London: The Hildegard Press.

Ong, W. (1982) *Orality and Literacy: The Technologizing of the Word*, London and New York: Methuen.

Peace Seeds (1986) Taken from *Peace Seeds*, 12 prayers for peace prayed in Assisi, Italy, http://www.peaceabbey.org

Sharp, I. (2000) *Classical Music's Evocation of Childhood: Studies in the History and Interpretation of Music*, Vol. 78, New York: The Edwin Mellen Press.

Shepherd, John and Wicke, Peter (1997) *Music and Cultural Theory*, Cambridge: Polity Press.

Subotnik, R.R. (1996) *Deconstructive Variations: Music and Reason in Western Society*, Minneapolis: University of Minnesota Press.

Westerlund, H. (2002) *Bridging Experience, Action, and Culture in Music Education*, Studia Musica 16, Helsinki: Sibelius Academy.

Interviews:

    with students and staff at Chichester University College, March 2003;

    with staff and students at St Mary's College, Twickenham, March 2003;

    with Professor Grenville Hancox, Canterbury Christchurch University College, March 2003;

    with staff at Newman College, Birmingham, March 2003;

    with students at Canterbury Christchurch University College, March 2003.

Index